THE INFANIB

A Reliable Method for the Neuromotor Assessment of Infants

Patricia H. Ellison, M.D.

Therapy Skill Builders *®

a division of
The Psychological Corporation

3830 E. Bellevue / P.O. Box 42050
Tucson, Arizona 85733
1-800-763-2306

The Learning Curve Design is a registered trademark of The Psychological Corporation.

Printed and published by

Therapy
Skill Builders [logo] ®
a division of
The Psychological Corporation
3830 E. Bellevue / P.O. Box 42050
Tucson, Arizona 85733
1-800-763-2306

ISBN 0761642668   Catalog No. 4266

10 9 8 7 6 5 4 3
Printed in the United States of America

For information about our audio and/or video products, write us at: Therapy Skill Builders, a division of The Psychological Corporation, P.O. Box 42050, Tucson, AZ 85733.

Acknowledgments

The photographs in the book were taken and printed by Mark Christensen, a project that required patience and understanding. My appreciation for these is unending.

Assistance in focusing and expanding the original ideas for this book were greatly assisted by the following:

Dr. Bonnie Camp, former director of the JFK Center for Developmental Disabilities in Denver;

Shirley Cliff, physical therapist at Zia Therapy Center, Alamogordo, New Mexico;

and Dr. Martha Piper, Professor and Dean, Faculty of Rehabilitation Medicine, University of Alberta, Edmonton.

About the Author

Patricia Ellison was born in Madison, Wisconsin, in 1934. She received the B.A. degree (with distinction) from Cornell University in 1956, and the M.A. degree from Teachers College, Columbia University in 1961. She attended the University of Pittsburgh School of Medicine from 1966-1970, graduating with honors.

Dr. Ellison has five years of residency training: two in pediatrics at the Children's Hospital of Pittsburgh and three in neurology, including one year in a pediatric neurology fellowship, at Albany Medical College. She is board certified in both pediatrics and neurology with special competence in child neurology.

She was an assistant professor of pediatrics and neurology at Albany Medical College from 1975 to 1979, and then an associate professor in pediatrics and neurology and Director of Neonatal Neurology at the Medical College of Wisconsin in Milwaukee from 1979 to 1983. An NIH (National Institutes of Health) Senior Research Fellow in the Department of Psychology at the University of Denver from 1983 to 1985 and a Research Professor there until May 1991, Dr. Ellison then joined the faculty of the University of Colorado School of Medicine as an adjunct professor. In addition, she has her own private practice, Neurology in Colorado, which opened March 1, 1989.

Dr. Ellison's research has focused on children from the neonatal intensive care unit. She has collaborated in four longitudinal studies about these children in Albany, New York; in Milwaukee, Wisconsin; in Copenhagen, Denmark, and in Dublin, Ireland. Her many papers are about these works as well as about other aspects of neonatal and pediatric neurology. She is particularly interested in the neurological evaluation of prematurely born and full-term newborns, infants, and preschool and early school-age children.

Contents

3

The Progression of Different Types of Abnormalities

4

Some Typical Infants

5

Helpful Hints in Other Important Diagnoses

6

What to Say When

7

The Construction of the *Infanib*

Introduction

At no time in life is the neuromotor examination more useful than infancy. First, the evaluation in infancy is highly reliable, particularly when it includes adequate evaluation of tone and posture. The evaluation in infancy is strongly related to function, motor more so than mental. Finally, the neuromotor evaluation in infancy is strongly associated with the neuromotor evaluation in pre-school and early childhood years. It is also significantly, but less strongly, associated with mental function in pre-school and early school years.

The neuromotor examination in infancy can be an important part of the evaluation of special children: those born prematurely, those treated in the neonatal intensive care units, those who develop sickness during infancy, such as meningitis or heart failure, and those who are developing slowly.

The observations and research studies about the infancy neuromotor examination from the last 30 to 40 years provide a wealth of information. Much of the early work was descriptive. Observant clinicians simply noted the changes in the neuromotor examination from small prematures to full-term neonates through infancy (which will be defined here as 18 months corrected gestational age). Concurrently, they noted differences between newborns and infants who were healthy and those who were sick. They also noted differences between infants who developed at a normal rate and infants who were slow in development.

Some clinicians directed their questions at the identification of infants who would benefit from therapies such as occupational and physical therapies. From this, several clinicians developed methods of evaluating the neuromotor condition that they considered useful in separating normal from abnormal. These methods were surprisingly different, although some items appeared in more than one method.

I was initially trained in the typical *American pediatric neurology method*. This evolved in the 1950s and 1960s largely through the writings of Richmond Paine and Thomas Oppé (Paine 1960; Paine and Oppé 1966). Some of the impetus for its evolution came from the planning and the execution of the National Collaborative Perinatal Project, a large multi-center prospective study of more than 50,000 children from 1959 through 1966. The neurological examinations at birth and at four, eight, and twelve months were done in a predetermined manner with the items spelled out and the choices described.

Probably, most of the training in neurological evaluation of newborns and infants given to pediatricians, pediatric neurologists, and developmental pediatricians in the 1960s and 1970s reflected the work of Paine and Oppé. The items included primitive reflexes as well as typical neurological testing items such as cranial nerves and the tapping of reflexes. The scoring sheets that evolved were a step forward in that they required some scoring and they were computer-compatible. The forms required forced choices on many items (for example, "yes, no, abnormal, suspect, or normal").

During my training in pediatric neurology and in my early years as an assistant professor of pediatrics and neurology at a medical school and its affiliated hospitals, I performed neurologic evaluations in the follow-up program for graduates of the neonatal intensive care unit. It was readily apparent that the methods that I had learned in neurologic residency were not satisfactory. I could not identify early spasticity unless it was severe. It was difficult to describe well the progress of change across months. Furthermore, the seasoned developmental pediatrician in the follow-up program insisted that her predictive validity with the *Gesell Screening Inventory* (Knobloch et al. 1966) was better than mine with the neurologic examination. Humiliating as this was for the budding pediatric neurologist, I had to acknowledge that her opinion was correct—until I went to Paris in 1976.

The writings of the neonatal physicians at Port-Royal Hospital in Paris captured my attention because they were based on keen observations, extensive experience with newborns, longitudinal work, EEG, and pathology. You cannot imagine my enthusiasm and excitement when, in 1976, the World Health Organization awarded me a six-week fellowship to study with Claudine Amiel-Tison, Jeanne Claudie Larroche, Nicole Monod, and S. Saint Anne Dargassies.

When I came home, I immediately started applying a limited version of the French method of neuromotor examination. My predictive validity improved, and I knew I was on the right track toward better neurologic evaluation of infants.

The use of the "French angles" (André-Thomas et al. 1960; Amiel-Tison and Grenier 1986)—*scarf sign, heel-to-ear, popliteal angle,* and *leg abduction*—adds important additional information to that of primitive reflexes and the classical pediatric neurologic method. The French angles are the best ways to ascertain early hypertonia in infancy, particularly the items *heel-to-ear* and *popliteal angle.* Early hypertonia tends to be proximal rather than distal—that is, it is generally seen first in the hips and knees, not the feet. There is more variability in the abnormalities in the arms, but the most common pattern is one of early hypotonia as in the *scarf sign* plus *head lag* on pull-to-sit and other head control items.

The items are well-known to clinicians because they are used to estimate the gestational age of newborns. In general, clinicians develop better judgment when they are familiar with items that they use. Since the items change across the months of infancy, each clinician must gain experience in testing normal children in order to gain skills in interpretation of deviation from the norm.

The major problems lie in the reliability of these items. First, there is variation in the force that the examiner applies to the limbs of the infant. Second, there may be variation in the measurement of the angle. In recent years, some examiners have used a large protractor to measure rather than estimate the angle. This should improve the accuracy of measurement, but is not yet in widespread use and, indeed, may never be widely accepted. Thirdly, although the items change at approximately three-month intervals, no neurologic item constitutes an abrupt change for all normal infants at a set time. The very beautiful work of Capute et al. (1984) for primitive reflexes shows that the wide variation in the disappearance of primitive reflexes would also be expected to some degree in the evolution of the French angles. Nevertheless, many clinicians consider these items important additions to the neurologic examination of infants. Personally, they remain my favorites.

I learned about the *Milani-Comparetti and Gidoni method* after moving to Milwaukee in 1979 and participating in a follow-up program in which this method was used. A data bank was already in the computer for almost 1000 infants. Computer work with the Milani-Comparetti and Gidoni method (Milani Comparetti and Gidoni 1967a; Milani Comparetti and Gidoni 1967b) in serial evaluations was the beginning of my explorations into statistics and data analysis.

This method uses some primitive reflexes, some motor developmental items, and a number of items that test the ability of the infant to determine its position in space. There are fewer items in the earlier months and a total of 27 items for the older infant. The correlations among the items on the test are generally high. (This indicates that the entity that is being measured is similar from item to item.) The method is richest in its assessment of the ability of the infant to determine its position in space. Nine items do this specifically: the four parachutes (forwards, sideways, downwards and backwards) and the five tilt-board items (prone, supine, sitting, all-fours, and standing). Other items, such as "righting" items, must test a similar neurologic process. An example is "head in space," in which the infant is held in vertical suspension, then tipped to either side; the clinician notes the ability of the infant to return the head to midline. In unpublished data on the Milani-Comparetti and Gidoni method for the large sample of infants described above, groups of these items were found to sequence in well-defined patterns. For example, infants developed appreciation of position in space before they learned to walk. When some of the Milani-Comparetti and Gidoni items are grouped, as in the work with *The Infanib,* they correlate much less with French angle items (also grouped) than they do with other items from the Milani-Comparetti and Gidoni method. Thus it is likely that the Milani-Comparetti and Gidoni method and the French angles method are evaluating different aspects of neurologic integrity.

It is quite clear the Milani-Comparetti and Gidoni method identifies infants with delay in righting and position in space skills. It is also clear that abnormalities such as spastic tetraparesis would be well identified through the items that test primitive reflexes and developmental progress. Some of the items that test righting and position in space are redundant. That is, there is no evidence that it is important to test these functions in such detail to identify abnormality, to treat the infant, or to predict function later in childhood.

Infants are given an age equivalent in the scoring proposed in the initial articles. We have published the results of using a different scoring method with fewer items that is sufficient to identify neurologic abnormality (Ellison et al. 1983).

A group of American doctors also focused on primitive reflexes (Capute et al. 1978). Their careful work documented the natural progression of selected primitive reflexes and the ages at which they disappeared (Capute et al. 1984). As indicated previously, the ages of disappearance are fairly broad. Even with this variation these are key items in identifying either the persistence or development of extensor tone and posturing. Thus they are key in the identification of spastic tetraparesis. The number of these reflexes is small; they assess the same aspect of neurologic integrity. Use of them is most like the conceptualization of Vojta (Vojta 1981) and, of course, is included in the methods of Milani-Comparetti and Gidoni. Some of them are included in the full assessment recommended by Amiel-Tison and Grenier (Amiel-Tison and Grenier 1986). Primitive reflexes are less likely to identify clearly milder abnormalities.

The last method with which I became acquainted was that of Vojta (Vojta 1981). Eventually, I translated the text from the German to study it. The method is little used in the United States, but is used in some countries in Europe, and it has been taught to a number of clinicians from Third World countries. Both infants and older children are suspended in space—horizontally, upside down, or vertically. Extensor posturing is brought out well by these maneuvers. However, for moderately to severely impaired children with excessive extensor posturing, most experienced clinicians would recognize the nature of the problem without the suspensions in mid-air, particularly for children past infancy. It is also unclear why the examiner would choose this method when children with these handicaps often tolerate such maneuvers poorly.

The method is scored. The number of items, however, is very small and insufficient for describing a wide range of neurologic abnormality/normality, particularly for children with mild impairment.

Why should we continue to examine infants neurologically?

The technological advancements in medicine are awesome and have perhaps diminished the interest and development of skills in clinical examinations.

Technological Advances

Computed tomography and then magnetic resonance imaging of the brain, as well as the widespread use of cerebral ultrasonography for newborns, has yielded more reliable information about intracranial hemorrhage, earlier and better identification of certain brain malformations and hydrocephalus, and identification of delays in myelination. However, these technological advances have still not yielded that ultimate secret: a measure of brain function. Mild cerebral hemorrhage, including intraventricular hemorrhage, mild hydrocephalus, and even certain malformations are not, in general, associated with sufficient cognitive dysfunction to be labeled as mental retardation. Other lesions identified by neuroimaging are strongly associated with dysfunction (for example, major hemorrhage within the brain tissue, major hydrocephalus, and large areas of encephalomalacia or hypodensity within the brain parenchyma). Sometimes the clinician is enlightened by the neuroimaging, but most of the time is not. The studies indicate normal function, yet the child malfunctions.

The methods of modern technology are not a substitute for careful clinical neurologic examination, particularly in infants.

The Difficulty of Setting Good Cut-Points

Frequently physical and occupational therapists do not agree with the physician(s) on the results of the neurologic examination of an infant. This may result from different interpretations of results, even when similar methods of examination have been used. Many of these differences seem to revolve around the interpretations of deviations from the "normal." With almost all methods of neuromotor evaluations, the vast majority of infants are normal. When there are some abnormalities, they vary in number and they vary in intensity. They also vary in importance. For example, a facial nerve palsy is only one abnormality. It may be mild, but still it will matter greatly to parents who hoped for the perfect baby. On the other hand, some mild delay in head control and hypotonia of head and neck will result in several abnormal items on some methods of assessment. But they may never be noticed by the parent and they have little neurologic significance. Significantly, parental reaction has entered into this issue of cut-points—and it is unlikely to go away.

The establishment of good cut-points depends on the purpose of the examination, the judgment of the examiner or the clinician who set the guidelines on the test method, and the use to be made of the results. Often the physician uses the information to "name" a condition, that is to make a diagnosis. On the other hand, the physical or occupational therapist is not allowed to diagnose but hopes to treat deviant infants and return them to normal or near normal. It is at this crossroad that opinions may differ.

Perhaps some of the differences of opinion stem from the convictions of therapists that treatment will help, convictions bolstered by the lack of good studies that indicate which infants to treat. The tendency of the physician to devalue or value less mild departures from the normal in an age of technology may also add to the differences of opinion.

The establishment of good cut-points in this area becomes a fine art.

Developing a Working Knowledge of Abnormality

Clinicians of any discipline who have done hundreds of neuromotor examinations of infants, including infants with abnormalities, usually have pretty definite ideas about normality and abnormality. But for many frontline physicians, whether from pediatrics or family practice, the number of infants with neurological abnormalities seen is small, and it is difficult to build a good working knowledge and ability to interpret such abnormality. It is particularly important for clinicians to use a systematic and reliable approach to the neuromotor examination of infants that can be scored and will provide good guidelines for discussions with parents and recommendations for diagnostic testing and treatment.

1

Which Babies Should We Follow?

There are not enough resources in most facilities to follow up all the infants we would like to evaluate. Most programs must utilize some selection process. What are our choices? There are five helpful approaches to the selection of infants for follow-up.

1. We can assess the severity of certain sicknesses or conditions in the newborn period that are associated with neurological sequelae in some children.

2. We can follow infants in limited gestational age or birth weight categories.

3. We can use reliable assessment methods of neurologic integrity to identify infants who probably do not need to be followed.

4. We can use parental reporting.

5. We can consider the personal and extended support system of the main caregiver(s).

Assessment of Prenatal, Pregnancy, Labor, and Delivery— At-Birth and Neonatal Hospitalization Variables

The severity of certain sicknesses or conditions in the neonatal period and initial hospitalization can be used to select infants for follow-up after hospital discharge. Since suggestions are often made that prenatal, pregnancy, and labor and delivery variables also be used, some important studies will be cited to show the association between a number of these variables and some outcomes that reflect neurologic impairment. In general, it is best to use large samples of children when seeking a perspective on this rather than quoting from personal experience (for example, "Once I saw a child whose mother . . . during the pregnancy") or referring to case reports or papers with a few illustrative children. Actually, the impact of prenatal events on the outcomes of children is relatively modest; obviously, though, a single child could be so affected.

My favorite study for this is the National Collaborative Perinatal Project because the sample size is so large (more than 50,000 children) and because it was conducted at a time when health care was quite good and interventions by physicians were modest (1959-1966).

7

There was no electronic fetal heart monitoring. In comparison to present practices, the rate of Caesarean section was very low. There was little regionalization of newborn or obstetrical care or transport of mothers prior to delivery to special centers in situations with maternal or fetal risk. Respirator use for newborns was, at best, primitive by contemporary standards. Special techniques such as continuous positive airway pressure or the installation of surfactant were not even on the drawing boards.

My own children were born in 1958, 1960, 1962, and 1963. I thought then and think now that we were well attended medically. Childbirth at that time was not approached with forebodings of disaster. Now as a research scientist, I consider it an excellent time to have accumulated all this information about childbirth and the subsequent functions of the children—in order to gain further understanding about how some processes occur. I believe that we are more likely to make discoveries in a time of limited intervention than during a time of frequent intervention in the birthing process, like the present.

A series of papers about the relation of demographic factors, maternal factors, labor and delivery factors, and the development of cerebral palsy were written by Dr. Karen Nelson (a pediatric neurologist), Dr. Sarah Broman (a psychologist), and Dr. Jonas Ellenberg (a biostatistician)—all employed at the National Institutes of Health, using data from the National Collaborative Perinatal Project.

In the paper that examined the relationship between single prenatal variables and cerebral palsy at age seven (Nelson and Ellenberg 1985), the two maternal prenatal variables with the greatest increase of risk for cerebral palsy were maternal mental retardation as estimated by the physician (for babies with birth weights over 2500 grams) and seizures in the mother (for all babies). While these maternal conditions increased the risk of cerebral palsy by 10.3- and 8.6-fold, respectively, in babies with birthweights over 2500 grams, they accounted for very small amounts of the variance in predicting cerebral palsy. That is, they increased the overall number of cases of cerebral palsy very modestly. Furthermore, many scientists would question the reliability of physician estimation as a measure of maternal intelligence. Nor were data analyses published that examined the relation of maternal retardation to other variables (education, income, psychiatric hospitalizations, etc).

So we might want to question what this variable represented. Maternal epilepsy has also been a complex issue. In the prenatal period, considering the reason for the maternal seizure disorder might be of most interest in relation to the development of cerebral palsy in the child.

Conditions during the pregnancy that increased the risk of cerebral palsy more than 5-fold were: recurrent, tonic-clonic seizures (7.2), incompetent cervix (5.9), thyroid and estrogen use (8.0), and severe late proteinuria (5.1).

The impact of maternal seizures during pregnancy could involve variables such as medications used for seizure control, the number and duration of seizures during the pregnancy, and again, underlying conditions that caused the seizures. In pediatric neurology in general, this issue has been focused more on dysmorphic features and mental retardation in the children than on cerebral palsy. Incompetent cervix has been associated with premature delivery, which has a high association with cerebral palsy. The reasons for increased cerebral palsy in mothers with thyroid and estrogen use are less clear to this observer, although the condition may have been related to medical practices either no longer observed now or more finely tuned now. As an isolated variable, severe late proteinuria is more complex and could have been associated with maternal toxemia, some kidney conditions, or perhaps even some more severe cases of maternal diabetes.

Many maternal variables were available for analysis in this study. Only those mentioned above had any importance, and even that importance was small. In conclusion, prenatal (*before* the pregnancy) and maternal conditions (*during* the pregnancy) had little impact on the development of cerebral palsy.

Perhaps more surprising to me as a researcher, who has been intensely interested in these different time subdivisions as used in the data analysis of Nelson and Ellenberg (prenatal, during the pregnancy, labor and delivery, at birth, and neonatal), are the few variables from labor and delivery that were associated with the development of cerebral palsy. For children with birth weights over 2500 grams, placenta previa increased risk of cerebral palsy 6.2-fold, and face, brow, or transverse presentations increased the risk of cerebral palsy 5.3-fold. For all birth weights, maternal hemorrhagic shock was also important (5.0-fold increase). In another analysis of the same data, the presence of polyhydramnios was significant. For babies with birth weights less than 2500 grams, breech delivery, chorionitis, and prolonged rupture of membranes over 24 hours were important.

The problems with placenta previa have decreased significantly with the use of ultrasonography during pregnancy because the location of the placenta is very reliable with this technology. Abnormal presentations are also better identified and Caesarean section used for intervention. Maternal shock remains a major problem for the fetus—and abruptio placentae continues to be a key cause of neurologic handicap. For the premature babies in the study, chorionitis and prolonged rupture of membranes were probably associated with neonatal infections. There has been an increased use of Caesarean sections for delivery of fetuses in breech position for the prematures as well as the full-term, although the obstetrical recommendations for the use of Caesarean section remain under discussion. Polyhydramnios is usually associated with congenital abnormalities. If hypotonia is considered as a form of cerebral palsy, then I would expect an increase in cerebral palsy if the mother had polyhydramnios. It is less clear why spastic cerebral palsy would increase much with polyhydramnios.

An important outcome in assessing the labor and delivery variables in the National Collaborative Perinatal Project is *early death,* defined as death within the first year of life in some of the data analyses. It is highly probable that a number of the babies who died would have had cerebral palsy if they had survived. The use of early death as an outcome should add considerable information about problem areas in labor and delivery.

The conditions associated with early death in the babies with birth weight under 2500 grams were: placenta previa, abruptio placentae, breech presentation, face-brow presentation, cord prolapse, oxytocin augmentation, meconium, chorionitis, prolonged rupture of membranes, short cord, polyhydramnios, and uterine dysfunction. Early death for babies over 2500 grams was associated with: abruptio placentae, breech delivery, face-brow presentation, cord prolapse, meconium, polyhydramnios and lowest fetal heart rate <100 beats per minute during labor and delivery. The variables cord prolapse, oxytocin augmentations, meconium, uterine dysfunction, abruptio placentae, and lowest fetal heart rate <100 beats per minute *are all* markers for perinatal asphyxia. In summary, most of the babies with these conditions during labor and delivery died because of conditions related to asphyxia. Many of them would have developed cerebral palsy.

Serious controversy revolves around the key issue of the relation between fetal asphyxia and the development of cerebral palsy in the data from the National Collaborative Perinatal Project. This fire has been further fanned by the controversies about medical malpractice cases involving children with handicaps. We must not lose sight of the important goals of providing good prenatal, labor and delivery, and neonatal care for all mothers and children. We must continue to seek knowledge about ways to decrease handicaps and improve function. The National Collaborative Perinatal Project provided considerable data about problem areas that need improvement.

At birthing, a lot more information can be obtained about the baby. It should not seem too surprising that our ability to predict outcome improves with this additional information. For example, birth weight becomes a powerful predictor. Smaller babies tend to have more cerebral palsy. The National Collaborative Perinatal Project data about prematures are really old. This was before the use of continuous positive airway pressure (CPAP), before the use of Caesarean section for birthing of many prematures, before the regionalizations of care for high-risk babies. For many preterm babies immediate resuscitation, warmth, oxygen, and glucose were not readily available. Even on ambulance trips in the early 1970s, little had been done for many small prematures prior to the arrival of the transport team. These data about prematures are not very useful now. It is not particularly helpful to know that inadequate care of premature babies yields excessive death and a high rate of handicaps.

The data about babies with birthweights over 2500 grams are important. A delay in crying after birth of ≥5 minutes increased the risk of cerebral palsy 10.8-fold. A delay in breathing after birth of ≥3 minutes increased the risk of cerebral palsy 12.5-fold, and an Apgar score of 0-3 at 5 minutes increased the risk of cerebral palsy 20-fold. If the Apgar score was 0-3 at 10 minutes the risk of death or cerebral palsy increased 50-fold.

These variables are more powerful than those from the prenatal, pregnancy, or labor and delivery periods in predicting cerebral palsy. They indicate babies with prolonged depression after birth that could result from drugs given to the mother during labor and delivery. They could be the result of asphyxia, that is some decrease in oxygen and/ or blood flow during labor and delivery. In the infant, this is called hypoxic-ischemic encephalopathy. Some have argued that they could reflect an already impaired baby, that is, one with abnormalities that occurred earlier in the pregnancy who could not withstand the process of labor and delivery. They could also reflect inadequate attempts at resuscitation. And they could reflect inadequate oxygenation and/or blood flow after delivery.

The addition of information from the neonatal hospitalization adds even more to the prediction. Again it is not very useful to consider the premature from this early time. For the baby with birth weight over 2500 grams, there were two big predictors—a 63.3-fold increase in cerebral palsy if neonatal seizures developed; and a 99-fold increase when the doctors thought there was brain abnormality. Other major predictors were: respiratory distress syndrome (49.3-fold increase), and ≥3 days in the incubator (22.4). Predictors that increased the risk of cerebral palsy less than 20 but more than 5-fold were: diminished cry (12.9-fold), suspect septicemia (10.1-fold), any respiratory problems (7.7-fold), lowest hematocrit under 40% (6.2-fold), and any suspect infection (5.7-fold). Some of these babies were probably infected since suspect septicemia or any suspect infections and use of antibiotics were all associated with increased cerebral palsy. Some may have been infants of diabetic mothers with respiratory problems, and some were anemic. But a significant number of them should again reflect asphyxia with the subsequent respiratory distress characteristic of such babies. It is important to consider again that use of the respirator *was not* central in the treatment of newborns at that time. Severely asphyxiated babies often require assistance with ventilation until their brain stem begins to function well. Poor ventilation and inadequate oxygenation would contribute to further brain damage and death.

Major noncentral nervous system malformations and microcephaly, both of which develop in utero from a variety of causes, were also associated with the development of cerebral palsy.

Thus, prematurity and its associated problems were the best predictors of cerebral palsy; asphyxia was significantly associated with cerebral palsy; and, to lesser extents, congenital malformations, infection, and poor intrauterine head growth were associated with the development of cerebral palsy. Neither the data analyses nor the limited technologies of the time permit us to trace these pathways as well as we would like.

Fetal Heart Monitoring

Fetal heart monitoring was not a part of the National Collaborative Perinatal Project. Since its introduction in the 1960s, it has brought hope that an already compromised fetus could be detected as well as a fetus in the process of deterioration, particularly during labor and delivery. In certain situations this technology has been fairly reliable—for example, in the recognition of a dying fetus who previously might have been stillborn. It has been less reliable in the detection of fetuses with hypoxia-ischemia of the central nervous system and secondarily decreased regulation of heart rate (Ellison et al. 1989)

Most of the papers written about fetal heart monitoring used outcome variables such as still birth or Apgar scores, which are "at birth" measures. Some have included neonatal seizures, which is a measure from the neonatal hospitalization. In our work, we were very fortunate to be able to describe the relation between a number of labor and delivery variables—fetal heart monitoring patterns and the neonatal neurologic examination at 0-48 hours and 72 hours to one week. Those newborns who were examined were those with whom there was any suspicion of a neurologic problem. The pediatrician who did the evaluations was readily available, very eager to do the evaluations, and friendly with nurses, house staff, and attending physicians, so it is very likely that most newborns who "turned a hair" were so examined. Two fetal heart-rate patterns as assessed by electronic fetal heart monitoring were significantly related to the neurologic examinations: late decelerations to the first examination at 0-48 hours and late decelerations and marked bradycardia to the second examination at 72 hours to 1 week. Many more abnormal fetal heart rate patterns were described than babies who had abnormal neurologic examinations. The neonatal neurologic examination should be a better predictor to later neurologic problems than Apgar scores.

More Recent Longitudinal Studies

There are many longitudinal studies of infants and children from more recent times. It will be impossible to cite more than a few. Instead, some key points will be emphasized. In most data sets from research about children once treated in the neonatal intensive care units there are thousands of data points. One of the tough problems in this work is finding good methods with which to examine and analyze the data carefully, organizing the data, and presenting the results in ways that do not misrepresent the data. In a study of 102 four-year-olds with birthweights ≤1500 grams, 139 children with birthweights 1501-2300 grams, and 92 children who had birthweights ≥2500 grams and who were healthy as newborns, all cared for in the neonatal care unit and nurseries of Rigshospitalet, Copenhagen, and born between October 1980 and March 1982, outcomes were generally described in terms of the relation between two variables—the three birth weight groupings and the subscales on the intelligence test (see figure 1.1) (Bloch et al. 1990). The control group of normal birthweight children scored well on the *McCarthy Scale of Children's Abilities* (McCarthy 1972). Their mean score was set at zero and the scores of the other two groups shown as standard deviations below that.

The groupings rank as was hypothesized: normal birthweight children highest, children with birthweights ≤1500 grams lowest, all significantly different statistically. This type of analysis identifies the presence of significant differences, but it does not provide any information beyond the relation to birth weight as an explanation for the differences.

Multivariate analyses permit description of the relations among many variables. In contrast to the two variables examined in figure 1.1 (birthweight and intelligence) with general cognitive index and

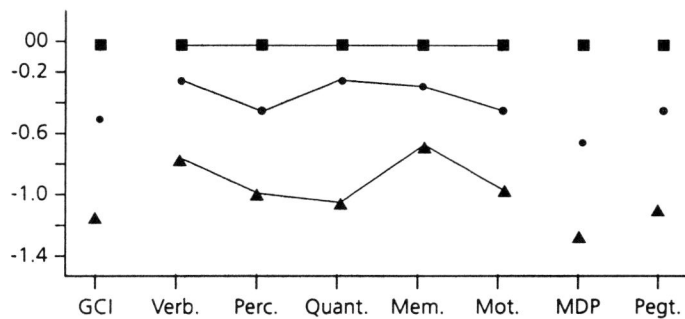

Standard-deviation score

Figure 1.1. Mean standard-deviation scores for 92 NBW children (■—■), 135 LBW children (●—●) and 87 VLBW children (▲—▲). The handicapped children excluded. *The McCarthy Scales of Children's Abilities:* general cognitive index (GCI), verbal (Verb.), perceptual-performance (Perc.), quantitative (Quant.), memory (Mem.), and motor (Mot.). For comparison, motor developmental phase score (MDP) and pegs/min (Pegt., logarithmic transformation). All differences between NBW and LBW and between LBW and VLBW are statistically significant (*p* = <0.05). For the VLBW group, the mean standard deviation score in all test areas was about -1 (i.e., the average VLBW child performed at the 15th percentile of the NBW distribution). *Danish Medical Bulletin*

subscales, in multivariate analyses, one could use birthweights, gestational age, use of respirator, the development of a pneumothorax, the development of intraventricular hemorrhage, and intelligence. Each of these variables could be composed of other variables. Large numbers of variables can be examined in hopes of expanding our knowledge about the relations between earlier conditions and later outcomes. These many variables are organized mathematically through the data analyses (not simply through a belief that they ought to belong together). A much more comprehensive description of our approach to this type of data analyses is published elsewhere (Ellison and Foster 1992).

Manifest and Latent Variables

Variables that can be observed and measured directly, such as birthweight, are called "manifest" variables. With a statistical procedure called "factor analysis," manifest variables can be grouped and pruned to form variables called "latent" variables. One cannot actually measure a latent variable, but it gives a better approximation of a condition, assuming that one uses good manifest variables in the first place. Use of latent variables also reduces the error term, which decreases the reliability of much clinical work.

An easy way to describe the relations among many variables at three ages is shown in table 1.1. These data are about a very large sample of children (*n* = 999) born in southeastern Wisconsin from 1975 to 1978, and treated in the regional neonatal intensive care units in Milwaukee. Table 1.1 shows the Pearson Product Moment correlations between 41 latent variables: the first 10 from the neonatal hospitalization; latent variables 11-24 from the evaluation with the Milani-Comparetti and Gidoni method and the Denver Developmental Screening Test at age 6 months; and latent variables 25-41 from the evaluation with the same assessment methods at age 16 months.

There is a large and statistically significant relation between certain neonatal conditions and neurologic and developmental outcomes at both 6 and 15 months. See, for example, the strong association between asphyxia, intraventricular hemorrhage/hydrocephalus and meningitis, and neuromotor assessment in infancy. Respiratory distress syndrome, patent ductus arteriosus, apnea/anemia, and chronic pulmonary disease had smaller but statistically significant associations with neurologic integrity in infancy.

Table 1.1 Correlations between latent variables formed from neonatal, 6 months and 15 month data

Column key (number = variable):
1 PRM (prematurity) · 2 UBM (urban minority) · 3 ASP (asphyxia) · 4 RDS (respiratory distress syndrome) · 5 IVH · 6 PDA · 7 AP/ANM (apnea/anemia) · 8 MNG (meningitis) · 9 CPD (chronic pulmonary disease) · 10 SMG (small for gestational age) · 11 CORAGE (corrected age at 6 months testing) · 12 NASAWA (early attention) · 13 SPONEX (early exploring) · 14 VARES P (visual responsiveness) · 15 HEADCO (upper body control) · 16 REFRES P (early reflexes) · 17 ERLOCO (early locomotion) · 18 TRUEREC (righting) · 19 BALSIT (sitting responses) · 20 ERSTAN (early standing) · 21 SPONSIT (attempts sitting) · 22 PUREX (purposeful exploration) · 23 EARVERB (early verbal) · 24 FIGMOCO (sit/stand/grasp) · 25 COREAG (corrected age at 15 months testing) · 26 TILT (tilt responses) · 27 REFLEX P (primitive reflexes) · 28 GENTON (head and hands) · 29 EARLVES (early vestibular) · 30 LATEVES (late vestibular) · 31 LEGS (feet, stand, cruise) · 32 VISMOT (visual motor) · 33 SIT (assumes sit) · 34 STANDS (stands alone) · 35 WALKS (walks alone) · 36 EARLCO (early communication) · 37 EARTALK (early talking) · 38 RECPTLA (receptive language) · 39 COORD (advanced leg/arm) · 40 LATEVIS (late visual motor) · 41 LATETAL (advanced language)

Variable	#	1	2	3	4	5	6	7	8	9	10	11	12	13	14	15	16	17	18	19	20	21	22	23	24	25	26	27	28	29	30	31	32	33	34	35	36	37	38	39	40	41
PRM	1	100																																								
UBM	2	16	100																																							
ASP	3	-26	4	100																																						
RDS	4	21	-16	14	100																																					
IVH	5	15	1	12	21	100																																				
PDA	6	33	3	12	31	14	100																																			
AP/ANM	7	3	5	20	5	17	7	100																																		
MNG	8	24	-8	23	72	30	37	9	100																																	
CPD	9	45	9	1	13	14	18	17	16	100																																
SMG	10	19	14	-1	-7	7	2	5	1	8	100																															
CORAGE	11	1	-10	2	0	1	-4	3	1	5	-6	100																														
NASAWA	12	0	1	24	4	13	5	7	6	2	0	1	100																													
SPONEX	13	0	1	27	10	18	9	13	14	9	1	3	55	100																												
VARES P	14	3	1	27	15	22	10	14	18	6	4	6	47	70	100																											
HEADCO	15	0	-1	19	7	28	6	11	14	6	1	4	38	58	58	100																										
REFRES P	16	1	-3	31	13	29	7	14	19	7	0	6	43	69	64	65	100																									
ERLOCO	17	4	-3	26	13	24	15	17	22	11	3	6	28	47	54	56	64	100																								
TRUEREC	18	6	-12	27	16	26	16	14	24	12	3	13	29	48	51	57	65	65	100																							
BALSIT	19	7	-15	17	16	20	11	13	21	13	5	14	19	36	43	43	51	54	64	100																						
ERSTAN	20	4	-12	19	12	18	10	14	18	12	4	12	22	36	37	43	49	53	59	61	100																					
SPONSIT	21	14	-8	21	21	19	18	13	27	15	11	19	20	34	38	40	46	55	59	57	53	100																				
PUREX	22	15	-4	21	17	21	16	11	22	15	10	27	20	40	51	39	41	49	49	57	48	51	100																			
EARVERB	23	6	-6	1	0	3	6	6	8	3	6	21	9	14	18	13	23	13	19	25	21	21	26	100																		
FIGMOCO	24	4	-19	6	13	0	5	6	10	9	5	38	3	4	8	8	8	17	7	24	21	21	27	18	100																	
COREAG	25	-3	-7	2	-3	0	0	2	0	9	-1	8	-1	-1	-1	-1	2	2	2	7	3	4	-1	-5	0	100																
TILT	26	-5	-4	18	-1	15	-3	12	-2	9	-2	39	39	56	32	36	53	36	30	23	24	20	14	7	3	-3	100															
REFLEX P	27	-4	-6	25	5	21	-2	13	5	12	-2	53	53	66	56	50	66	41	40	29	28	26	28	8	5	3	54	100														
GENTON	28	3	-3	24	12	18	6	16	16	9	-3	46	46	57	56	44	65	44	42	35	30	29	32	10	5	-3	45	75	100													
EARLVES	29	3	-5	28	12	21	8	17	20	15	3	50	50	57	57	63	72	58	57	42	38	41	40	11	8	-1	47	73	82	100												
LATEVES	30	-8	-8	27	14	30	4	19	20	13	-2	40	55	59	60	61	70	61	60	51	44	44	45	12	9	1	43	63	68	82	100											
LEGS	31	5	-7	22	17	44	10	17	24	13	-2	55	55	60	62	62	69	60	58	49	51	44	42	12	8	2	38	61	67	79	84	100										
VISMOT	32	2	-2	30	12	29	15	16	13	13	-2	39	52	56	67	62	57	48	49	35	33	40	42	10	4	3	36	66	62	70	65	66	100									
SIT	33	8	-6	26	19	36	11	14	28	10	0	54	54	55	55	49	57	55	55	35	32	48	34	13	6	0	36	59	62	74	73	66	57	100								
STANDS	34	9	-6	21	9	27	11	17	23	16	-1	39	46	58	58	51	53	58	55	33	48	42	35	14	0	0	39	55	68	73	71	57	59	54	100							
WALKS	35	12	-8	21	9	27	18	17	17	15	7	25	35	42	45	43	42	51	54	50	51	45	37	11	7	9	30	46	57	51	54	54	50	46	88	100						
EARLCO	36	7	4	22	10	30	13	17	16	9	-1	39	32	39	50	44	45	45	49	42	34	37	31	15	10	-1	21	39	38	49	51	50	47	42	38	53	100					
EARTALK	37	4	-5	27	16	24	15	12	22	11	0	25	17	27	44	38	34	25	20	34	32	35	37	12	9	0	39	34	36	45	46	43	37	41	44	38	47	100				
RECPTLA	38	10	-4	24	15	20	12	16	12	15	6	17	27	38	31	34	31	30	28	40	36	42	45	10	10	-3	25	25	30	36	45	41	36	41	53	55	46	47	100			
COORD	39	15	3	11	10	21	6	13	16	4	-1	16	26	26	34	31	31	36	39	21	20	35	37	12	8	-1	26	25	36	36	39	41	36	36	48	55	39	35	43	100		
LATEVIS	40	4	5	10	10	9	9	16	13	2	0	9	9	11	20	18	18	21	21	20	20	21	24	12	5	2	13	18	28	36	23	20	21	21	24	23	20	25	35	23	100	
LATETAL	41	8	16	20	4	9	11	12	9	9	6	-3	10	11	14	13	13	16	20	22	15	26	23	13	6	-3	12	11	16	18	20	16	22	23	25	25	26	38	34	25	22	100

N.B. Decimal points (.00) have been omitted for correlations

Prematurity had some relationships that were important, especially to the more complex skills in each age grouping (sitting spontaneously and purposeful exploration at 6 months; walking alone and leg-arm coordination at 15 months). Urban minority mothers were associated with early motor development at 6 months and lesser language development at 15 months. "Small for gestational age" had very small associations with the outcomes.

In looking at a correlation matrix, one should square the correlation, multiply it by 100, and obtain the percent variance accounted for. That is often humbling, especially if the researcher or clinician once thought that "a" was usually associated with "b." For example, the largest correlation between neonatal conditions and the outcomes at 15 months—that between intraventricular hemorrhage and "legs"— $r = .44$. Squared $.44 = .1936 \times 100 = 19.3\%$, the largest percent variance accounted for. In summary, *most* of the delay in development and abnormality on the neurological evaluation is *not explained*.

Another use of the correlations is to see how much of the variance can be accounted for by all the variances that precede it in the table. This is shown in table 1.2. It may be more satisfying. For example, 79% of the variance can be accounted for "time of walking alone," but most of that comes from the latent variables in the six-month assessment. That is, an infant who sails through the evaluation at age six months will walk alone at the normal age. Use of the six-month evaluation certainly permits us to be smarter as clinicians. If the infant had one or more of these neonatal conditions and was delayed or abnormal at six months, then the infant was very likely to be delayed in walking, that is, not walking alone at the 15-month evaluation.

Table 1.2. r²—squared multiple correlations for variables in table 1.1.

VN	1	2	3	4	5	6	7	8	9	10	11	12	13	14	15	16	17	18	19	20	21	22	23	24	25	26	27	28	29	30	31	32	33	34	35	36	37	38	39	40	41
%	0	0	7	8	2	11	0	7	20	5	0	7	34	51	42	61	48	55	45	44	47	49	14	23	0	41	58	62	81	74	77	64	64	61	79	44	35	44	33	16	26

VN = variable number
% = percent variance accounted for by all preceding varariables

It is also interesting to look at the relations among variables *within* each time period. The relations among variables in the neonatal period range from very small (see $r = .01$ between "small for gestational age" and "meningitis") to quite large (see $r = .45$ between "prematurity" and "chronic pulmonary disease"). A surprisingly large association in this data set is that between respiratory distress syndrome and meningitis ($r = .72$). In all of our longitudinal data acts (Wisconsin, Dublin, and Copenhagen), there are many statistically significant correlations between variables in the neonatal portion of the data. *In summary, sick newborns, especially prematures, are highly likely to have more than one abnormal condition or sickness.* There are also large associations between latent variables of neurologic and developmental integrity within the 6- and at 15-month ages. These variables have what is known as a strong positive manifold—*if the infant is normal on one variable, it is likely to be normal on another. If the infant is abnormal on one variable, it is likely to abnormal on another.* There is also a strong association between the assessment variables at 6 months and those at 15 months.

The Wisconsin data are from a time when regionalization of neonatal intensive care was well-organized in the state, and a lot of community education had been done. Respiratory support was given by neonatologists who were experienced with use of ventilators and continuous positive airway pressure. There was still considerable transport for sick neonates; the movement toward maternal transport was not yet extensive. The outcome of prematures has improved with the widespread use of maternal transport. This may result from more expertise in labor and delivery, better resuscitation and stabilization after birth, and immediate attention to body temperature, blood sugar, oxygenation and acid/base status with assisted ventilation when needed, and support of blood pressure.

In another paper, we compared the Wisconsin (see table 1.3) and Danish-born (see table 1.4) prematures (Ellison et al. 1991). These cohorts were from two time periods, 1975-76 (Wisconsin) and 1980-82 (Denmark), from very different countries (the Wisconsin cohort was more heterogeneous in income, education, and race), and from pre- and post-maternal transport. Most of the Danish prematures were born in Rigshospitalet, Copenhagen.

For the comparisons, we used latent path structural analysis to form models that contained the latent variables of parental education, asphyxia, respirator use, pneumothorax, germinal layer hemorrhage, patent ductus arteriosus, and apnea/anemia from the neonatal period. The children in both countries were evaluated at age four years with the *McCarthy Scale of Children's Abilities* and the *Vineland Scales*. Separate models were formed for each country.

Table 1.3. Wisconsin latent path structural analysis model

The relation between each pair is indicated by the path coefficient (coefficients of less than 12 were suppressed during analysis, the coefficients among the McCarthy scales were forced to zero). The total variances accounted for by the preceding conditions are indicated in parentheses.

Perinatal Conditions
```
Parental education
  0   Caesarean section
  0   0   Gestational age (0%)
  0   0  -22  Asphyxia (5%)
  0   0   0   55  Respirator (30%)
  0   0   35  51   0   Pneumothorax (31%)
  0   14 -13   0   34   0   Germinal layer hemorrhage (15%)
 20   0  -31   0   25   0  -19   Patent ductus arteriosus (20%)
  0   0  -62   0   0    0   14  25   Apnea/anemia (58%)
```

Adapted McCarthy Scales Scores
```
 36   0  -16   0   14   0   0   0   0   Verbal (17%)
 35   0   0  -12   0   0   0   0  -17   -   Perceptual (17%)
 34   0   0  -14   0   0   0   0   0    -   -   Quantitative (14%)
 20   0   0   0   0    0   0   0   0    -   -   -   Memory (4%)
  0   0   13   0  -19  -14   0   0   0   -   -   -   -   Motor (9%)
  0   0   0   0   0   -20   0   0   0   0  21   0   0  44   Vineland Score (39%)
```

In these models the numbers are path coefficients, not Pearson Product Moment coefficients as in the previous tables. This is an important distinction. Path coefficients reflect the *unique* relation among variables. Correlation coefficients may include contributions from other variables (the concept of *shared* variance). For example, the surprisingly large *correlation* coefficient between meningitis and respiratory distress syndrome in the Wisconsin cohort might reflect hand-washing techniques or frequent blood drawing or some other aspect of being premature and very sick. If that .72 was a *path* coefficient, we would have to consider that there was a very special association between meningitis and respiratory distress syndrome.

Probably the most interesting comparisons between these two cohorts of prematurely born children are those for the effects of parental education, gestational age, and the sicknesses of prematurity. Parental education has the largest effect in the Wisconsin study. That should not be surprising. First of all, parental IQ, especially maternal IQ, was the best predictor of intelligence at age seven years in the National Collaborative Perinatal Project. Secondly, correlations and path coefficients are larger when the variance is larger. There is much more heterogeneity (larger variance) in parental education in the southeastern Wisconsin region that includes the city of Milwaukee than there is in Denmark generally or in Copenhagen. Parental education is not quite the same as parental intelligence, but the correlations between the two tend to be large. Parental education also has a strong association with outcome for the Danish four-year-olds, especially for verbal and quantitative scores.

Table 1.4. Copenhagen latent path structural analysis model

Perinatal Conditions

```
Parental education
15   Caesarean section
 0    0   Gestational age (0%)
 0    0  -29   Asphyxia (8%)
 0    0  -44   33   Respirator (39%)
 0    0    0    0   59   Pneumothorax (35%)
 0    0  -32    0   39    0   Germinal layer hemorrhage (39%)
 0    0    0    0   31    0   27   Patent ductus arteriosus (27%)
 0    0  -72    0   16  -17    0    0   Apnea/anemia (61%)
```

Adapted McCarthy Scales Scores

```
30    0   26    0    0    0    0    0    0   Verbal (16%)
19    0   29    0    0  -26    0    0    0    -   Perceptual (23%)
25    0   24    0    0  -16    0    0    0    -    -   Quantitative (17%)
19  -14   22    0    0    0    0    0    0    -    -    -   Memory (10%)
17    0    0    0    0  -26    0    0    0    -    -    -    -   Motor (10%)
 0    0    0    0    0    0  -14    0    0    0   24    0    0   31   Vineland Score (30%)
```

Gestational age had a major effect on the outcome of the Danish children and a much lesser effect on the outcome of the Wisconsin children. It should be noted that this is not a comparison between prematurely born and full-term children—it is only between prematures. In the Wisconsin sample, some of the larger/older prematurely born children had cognitive dysfunction. In the Danish sample smallness tended to be associated with more cognitive dysfunction. The Wisconsin children tended to be sicker; they spent an average of 33 days in the neonatal unit in contrast to 21 days for the Danish children (mean birth weights were 1594 grams and 1603 grams, respectively).

The effect of neonatal sicknesses was shown best in the Danish cohort in the relation between pneumothorax and some cognitive subscales (perceptual, quantitative and motor). The relations between sickness and a four-year function were more widespread in the Wisconsin children, with significant relations for asphyxia, use of respirator, pneumothorax, and apnea/anemia. We think that the frequency of pneumothorax in the Danish sample was related to aggressive use of the respirator.

Birth Size, Gestational Age, or Specific Neonatal Conditions or Sicknesses to Identify Neonates At Risk

Birth Size/Gestational Age

Many clinicians talk and perhaps act as though these factors are somehow quite different. Actually, in all of our data sets, they correlated very highly. It made little difference which one we used. Since weighing the baby is more accurate than estimating the gestational age, we recommend that birth weight be used. In most neonatal units, one could probably follow only those prematures with birth weights less than 1250 grams plus those with well-identified problems. This approach may work well even for those babies between 1000 and 1250 grams. Below this birth weight, prediction becomes a little trickier because of an increase in mental retardation that is not necessarily associated with abnormal tone or neonatal sickness.

Neonatal Sicknesses or Conditions

In some neonatal units in this country, especially with the use of surfactant, we are seeing fewer sick prematurely-born babies, probably more like the Copenhagen cohort. The exception is the tendency to treat fairly vigorously very low birth weight prematures, defined here as less than 750 grams.

Specific sicknesses and conditions can be scored sufficiently well at the time of hospital discharge that the majority of infants with neurologic sequelae could be identified.

Maternal Drug Use

In many U.S. hospitals, a large number of the newborns are identified as undergoing withdrawal from maternal drug use/abuse. Some newborns recover quickly, settle down well, and respond appropriately for age before discharge. Others are very difficult to care for: they are irritable, sleep poorly, have gastrointestinal disturbance, and require great patience from the caretaker. Even a highly motivated mother might find such an infant trying. Unfortunately, many of these babies do not have motivated mothers.

Caretaker Chaos vs. Integration

Many sources indicate that the most frequent problems for children who "graduate" from neonatal intensive care units are those of behavior. In addition, many studies through the years have shown that children from better functioning families with more resources tend to function better themselves, even given the same setbacks at the beginning. Some of these children may have started with "better protoplasm." There must also be a benefit to repetitive good quality caretaker-infant interaction, to good preschool and school programs, to access to toys and books, and to family adventures and celebrations. Family is used here in a very broad sense because it is obvious that there are many good ways to raise children.

Neonatal Neurological Examination

The largest amount of neurologic abnormality that will ever be seen in children who are cared for in neonatal intensive care will be seen during their stay in the unit. As long as we have been able to follow them (through age seven years) there has been a decrease in the frequency and severity of neurologic abnormality. The decrease in neurologic abnormality is greatest in the early weeks and months and levels out by ages four to seven years. Particularly for most prematures, that is a progression from hypotonia to normal tone. Those who progress to spasticity rarely have a time when they appear normal in tone— usually because they keep their head lag and often their arm and even truncal hypotonia. Thus we can make the following statement: Prematurely born infants who recover normal tone by 40 weeks from gestation tend to remain normal in tone. Perhaps we should call this the *Concept of Clearing.* It assumes that a reliable assessment was done by a competent evaluator (not the brief evaluation performed by many physicians at the time of hospital discharge). **If the infant passes at 40 weeks from conception, he/she probably does not need to be seen again.** Unfortunately, most prematures who are doing well leave the hospital before they are 40 weeks old. Often the ones who stay past that are abnormal in tone. On the other hand, some full-term infants with hypotonia may have a transitional phase when their tone is near normal in the early months as they progress to spasticity. The examiner needs to be cautious in that 0-4 month period. (A neurologic examination form for newborns and infants is included in Appendix A.)

A Comprehensive Scoring System

We provide a scoring system for prematures and full-term babies to be used at the time of discharge from the hospital (table 1.5). This was formed from the results of four longitudinal studies, two about babies born in 1975-1978 (region of Albany, New York, and region of Milwaukee, Wisconsin); one from 1980-82 (region of Copenhagen, Denmark); and one from 1981-82 (region of Dublin, Ireland) as well as a review of many other studies. This concept is also based on knowledge that prediction is higher when more variables are used *if we select the right variables.* This is a *weighted* method of scoring. I have argued elsewhere that the items on the neurologic evaluation ought to be given equal weights. I would argue just as fervently that this type of scoring ought to be weighted *unequally.* Not only do some variables count more but both the *severity* and the *duration* of their presence is important. There are different combinations that could yield abnormal scores. Clearly this is not just a method of following all newborns with intraventricular hemorrhage or asphyxia.

Table 1.5. Scoring at Hospital Discharge (Newborn)

Infant Name_____ Date_____

	Max. Score	1	2	4	6	8	10	Points
Gestational Age	10	≥37	33-36	31-32	29-30	27-28	≤26 weeks	
Birth Weight	10	≥2001 grams	1501-2000	1251-1500	1001-1250	751-1000	≤750 grams	
SGA	10	Subtract: Score for GAE—Score for BW; Score for all Positive Numbers = 0; Score for -2 = 5; Score for -4 = 10						
Lowest Blood Serum	10	Full Term 20-30 = 5; <20 = 10; Prematures 15-20 = 5; <15 = 10						
Lowest Blood Serum	5	Score only if obtained >2 hours from lowest Full Term <30 = 5, Premature <20 = 5						
Highest Bilirubin	10	5-10	11-15	16-20	21-25	26-30	>30	
		Multiply score for BW X score for bilirubin. Any score over 10 = 10						
2nd Highest Bilirubin	5	Score only if obtained >6 hours from Highest Subtract: Highest Bilirubin - 2nd Highest. Any difference ≤4 = 5						
Pneumothorax	15	Present—no chest tube = 5		Chest Tube Up To 3 days = 10		Chest Tube of Bi-lateral >3 days = 15		
Use of Respirator	15	Points			1	2	3	
		First 3 days Pip			1 day Pip >19	2 days Pip >19	3 days Pip >19	
		First 3 days Rate			1 day Rate >30	2 days Rate >30	3 days Rate >30	
		Days on Respirator			5	10	15	
		Days FO_2 over 60%			5	10	15	
		Home on Oxygen			/////	/////	Yes	
Apnea/Anemia	15	# of Hb <6.5			/////	1X	2X	
		# of HB 6.5-10			1X	2X	3X	
		Clinical Apnea			mild	moderate	Home on monitor or severe	
		Theophylline/Caffeine			1 week	2 weeks	3 weeks	
		For APNEA: CPAP or Ventilatory Support			5 days	10 days	15 days	
Asphyxia	15	Apgar at 1 minute			4-6	0-3	/////	
		Apgar at 5 minutes			/////	4-6	0-3	
		Apgar at 10 minutes			/////	4-6	0-3 (4 points)	
		Resuscitation			Bagging	Intubation	NaHCO$_3$	
		Clinical Rating			Mild	Moderate	Severe	
Early Crisis in 1st 12 hours	15	Dopamine or similar drug			not used	not used	yes	
		Priscoline			not used	not used	yes	
		Volume expand			none	1X	2X	
		Base deficit			–0-9	–10-15	– >15	
		Clinical Shock			Mild	Moderate	Severe	
Late Crisis after 3 days	15	Heart rate			80-100	40-79	<40	
		Respiratory rate			16-20	10-15	<10	
		Ventilation			Bagging	CPAP	Respirator	
		NaHCO$_3$			not used	1X	2X	
		Calcium			not used	1X	2X	
Seizures	20	Points				5	10	
		# of drugs				1	2	
		EEG or Clinical days of seizure				2 days	>2 days	
Meningitis	20	Points				10	20	
						Abnormal CSF Agent not identified	Agent Identified	
Neuroimaging	20	Points				5	10	
		Full Term	Gross Malformation			Moderate	Severe	
			Hypodensity of parenchyma			Moderate	Severe	
			Ventricular enlargement			Moderate	Severe	
			Inadequate Myelin			Moderate	Severe	
			Hemorrhage			Moderate	Severe	
		Preterm	Hemorrhage			Expands Ventricles	Parenchymal	
			Periventricular Leukomalacia			Moderate	Severe	
			Ventricular Enlargement			Moderate	Severe	
Neurological Examination	20	Preterm at ≥37 weeks at time of exam				Severe Abnormality = 20		
						Moderate Abnormality = 15		
						Mild Abnormality = 10		
		Full Term				Severe Abnormality > 1 week = 20		
						Severe Abnormality ≤1 week or Moderate Abnormality >1 week = 15		
						Moderate Abnormality ≤1 week or Mild Abnormality >1 week = 10		

Cut Points   >50 = High Risk   31-50 = Moderate Risk   21-30 = Mild Risk   Total Score _____

Parent Reporting After Hospital Discharge

This should be reserved for situations in which resources are very limited because we cannot train parents to evaluate tone, and we cannot ask the parent if the baby was sick (*any* baby in the newborn intensive care unit seems to be defined as sick by parents). We can ask for specific steps in development. The infant has to be a certain age before we can get a very good estimate, probably at least six months. This approach has been shown to be quite satisfactory in a study in which the parents filled out forms at home when the baby was 28 weeks and then examined at 40 weeks (Knobloch et al. 1979).

Summary

In most situations, it is unrealistic to follow all children who were treated in the neonatal intensive care unit in a special follow-up program. Many of us have participated in such programs in the past and examined a great many normal infants. Surely any follow-up program ought to be open to parents who express concerns about the development of their infant even if that infant was not on the follow-up "list." The program also ought to be open to physician or therapist referral. Specifically the follow-up program should be identified by parents, therapists, and physicians as the regional resource for assessment.

It is also unrealistic to rely on the local doctor as the screening clinician. In spite of our years of teaching, skills vary tremendously in physician assessment of neurologic integrity and development in infancy.

An excellent plan for a follow-up program could utilize three methods for identification of infants: the comprehensive scoring on hospital discharge, a statement at discharge to the child's physician that this infant had or had not been identified as needing follow-up (if so, then a commitment from that physician and the family to see that the infant is examined if concerns arise), and a parent questionnaire at age 28 weeks for parents whose infants were not followed—as a safety check.

Follow-up After Infancy

Many follow-up programs end in infancy. If the program evaluates infants at 10 months or more, the children with abnormal tone and posture (that is, those who will later be labelled as having cerebral palsy) and those with moderate to severe mental retardation should be identified. Our data indicate that at six months of age abnormal tone and posture is well identified but the assessment of intelligence is less accurate.

At age 15 months, a lot of the abnormal tone—especially hypotonia but even some mild spasticity—will disappear. Our data show that those infants with transient neurologic abnormality at ages 6 to 15 months are more likely to have school problems—in cognition, behavior, motor, or speech. About 20 percent of the infants from the newborn intensive care unit will be so identified, which is still a great many children to follow post infancy. More work needs to be done to narrow the number of children identified as "at risk" out of the group with transient neurologic abnormalities.

Even at 15 months, some children with mild mental retardation will not be identified. The language items required to "pass" at 15 months are few. As with other early testing situations, the children who are *above* average for age are at extremely low risk for later identification of language delay unless there is an intervening factor such as chronic ear infections. We may also be led astray because the language reported by parents is sufficient to pass the developmental testing. To this observer, it seems more likely that a parent will over-report language skills than that a parent will over-report sitting, standing, or walking. I think that is because language is less well anchored. On testing, standards require that *no body cues* be given for receptive language. Yet the parent may give many such signals or few—we simply don't know. In short, we may not gain an accurate assessment of language by parent report. For expressive language, the repetitive use of a somewhat recognizable sound is accepted to pass—and very few such sounds are required. Furthermore, it is really difficult to test or ask the parent to test whether a sound such as "ma" is used for only one classification ("the mother"), all mothering women for that child (mother, grandmother, older sister), or all parenting adults (mother and father). Studies have shown that mild mental retardation will be identified in an additional small number of children when language is more readily tested—age two or more (Aylward et al. 1987).

A language questionnaire to the parents between ages two to three may resolve some of these problems. Indeed, it would also identify a group at risk for "learning disabilities" because learning skills are so tied to language development.

Why Do We Follow Up?

If a center could decide why follow-up is being done, perhaps it would be easier to decide *who* to follow, *when* to see them, and *what* to evaluate. Computers are clogged with data from follow-up with little valuable output. Communities vary—some programs might be more useful in some places than in others. Some programs might be more acceptable in some communities than in others. Ask again: **Why are you doing this?** Time and resources for children are dear. If we would serve them well, we must choose wisely.

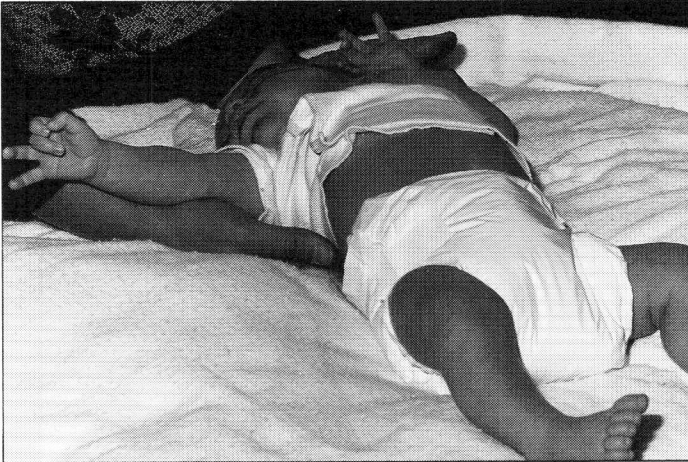
Figure 2.1. Hands open/closed, normal infant.

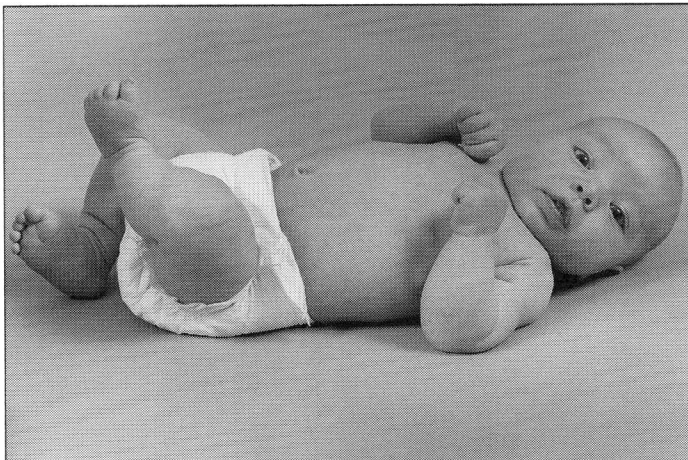
Figure 2.2. Hands open/closed, neuromotor abnormalities at 2 months.

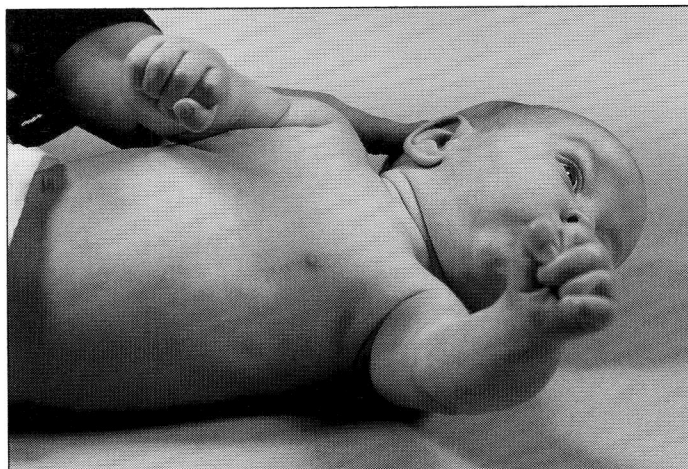
Figure 2.3. Hands open/closed, neuromotor abnormalities at 3.5 months.

2

The Infanib

The 20 items in the *Infanib* are first described in text to help the examiner understand how to perform that item or how to obtain the necessary information about that item. This is followed by a picture of a normal infant, then one or more pictures of a transiently abnormal or abnormal infant demonstrating that item. Additional photographs of normal and abnormal infants as they progress in their first year are shown in chapter 4. For an example of the *Infanib* score sheet, see Appendix B.

1. Hands Open/Closed

As you perform the other items, note the position of the infant's hands. At birth, most newborns hold their hands closed some or all of the time. However, clenching of the hand or "fisting" is not normal at any time. By age two months and until age three months, some normal infants will still close their hands, particularly with stimulation. By age three months, the hands should be held open. In the *Infanib,* this item is scored as abnormal only for excessive closing of the hands or for clenching of the hands—as indicators of excessive extensor tone. Of course, a very loose open-hand position may also be abnormal—an indicator of decreased body tone. But this will be well identified in other terms.

In figure 2.1, a normal infant of age one month holds his hands open even when the examiner induced stress and tried to increase tone with the asymmetric tonic neck reflex. In figure 2.2, the 2-month-old infant with transient neuromotor abnormalities holds his hands clenched without stimulation. In figure 2.3, the abnormal infant, at age 3.5 months, clenches his fists with self-induced stimulation, such as being placed on a firm surface, or with examiner-induced stimulation. In this infant, the clenching occurred with all items during neurologic evaluation.

2. Scarf Sign

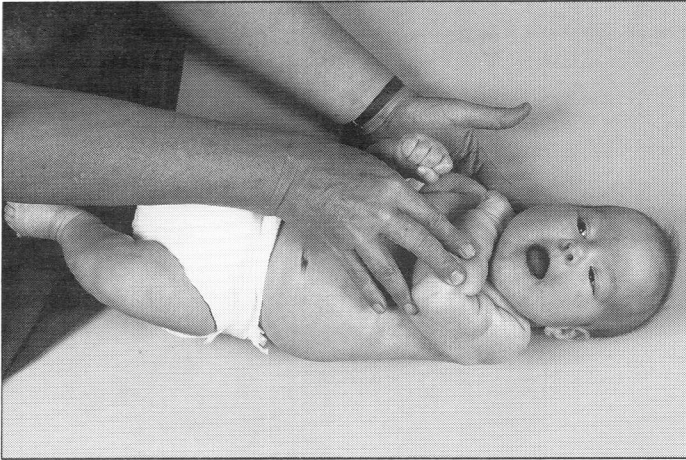

Figure 2.4a. Normal scarf sign, 0-3 months.

The scarf sign changes occur in the quarters of the first year, progressing from lesser flexibility to greater flexibility. This is the opposite of the changes made from extreme prematurity to full term—then the flexibility progresses from greater flexibility to lesser flexibility. Many clinicians are familiar with the use of the scarf sign for assessments of gestational age prior to the normal 40 weeks of gestation (full term). The examiner holds the arm near the elbow and moves it across the chest as far as it will move easily, without using force. The angle is measured between an imaginary line dropped from the armpit and the upper arm (with the armpit as the fulcrum). The normal progression is shown in figures 2.4a through 2.4d.

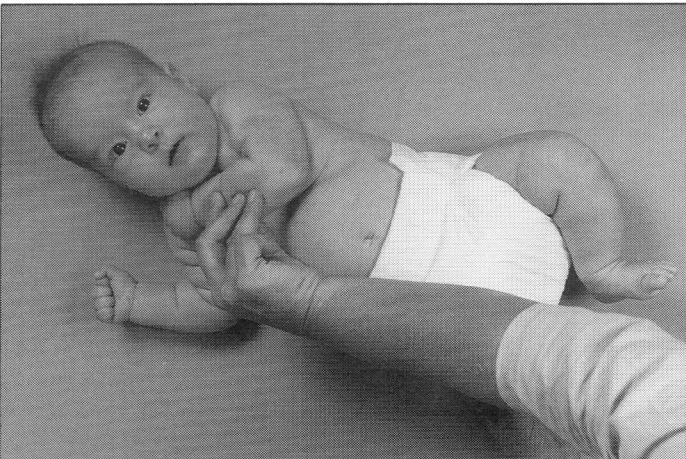

Figure 2.4b. Normal scarf sign, 4-6 months.

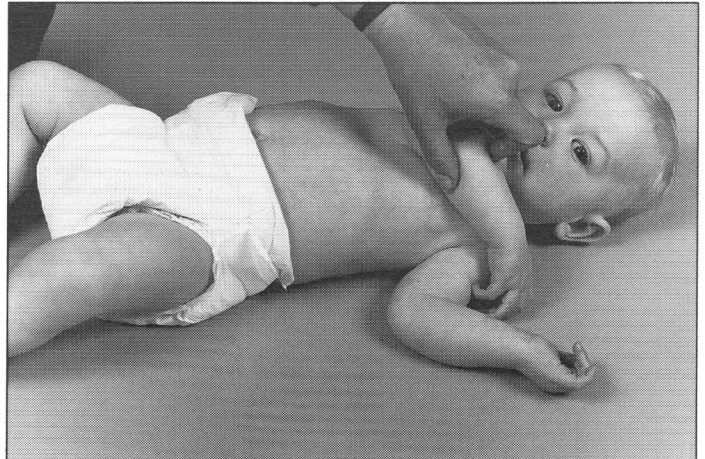

Figure 2.4c. Normal scarf sign, 7-9 months.

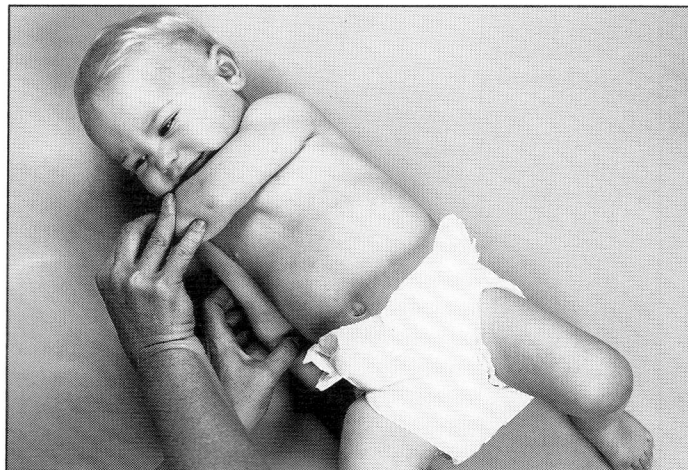

Figure 2.4d. Normal scarf sign, 10-12 months.

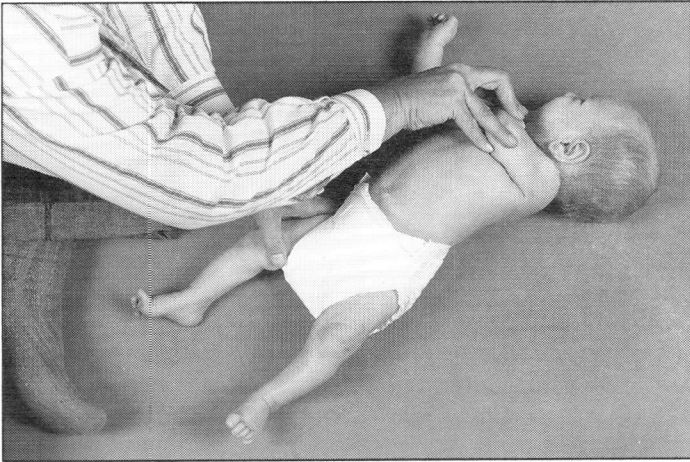

Figure 2.5a. Abnormal scarf sign, 0-3 months.

Early hypotonia is frequently seen in infants who were born prematurely and who were sick. The arm is more easily moved than it should be—for age. Early hypertonia is uncommon, although it is seen in some infants with severe brain damage. However, the scarf sign is less helpful in identifying early hypertonia than items such as those in Factor 1. Some infants progress from hypotonia to hypertonia. This is seen well in figures 2.5a through 2.5d. This infant was neurologically abnormal from the neonatal period on, first with a marked hypotonia, then with a gradual progression to spastic tetraparesis/dyskinesia. His scarf sign showed excessive extension through the early months (0 to 3). At each subsequent evaluation, the arm extended less easily and was clearly hypertonic at 7 to 9 months and 10 to 12 months.

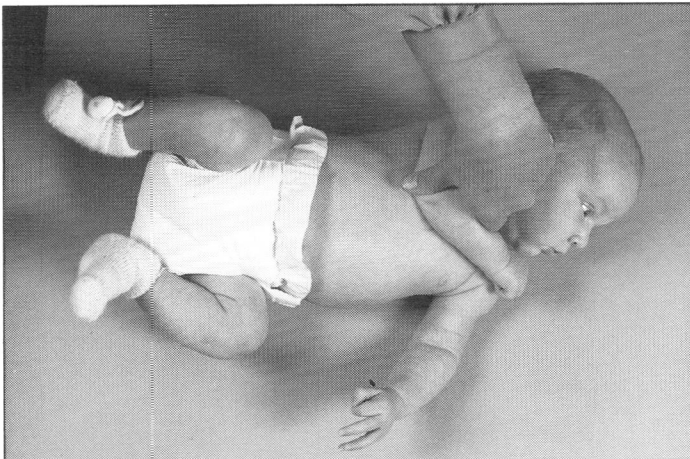

Figure 2.5b. Abnormal scarf sign, 4-6 months.

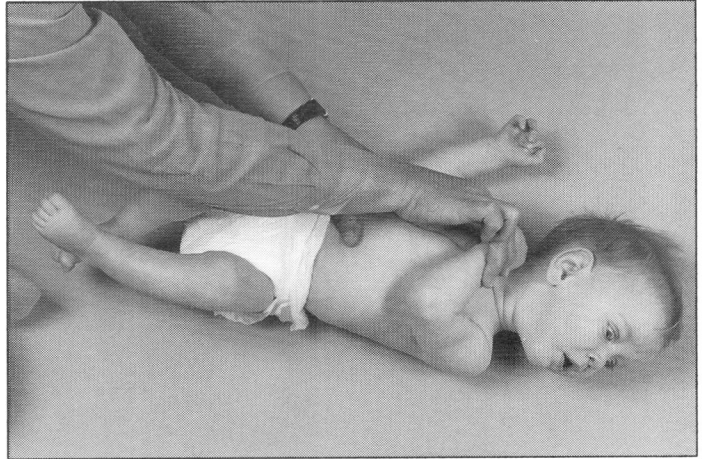

Figure 2.5c. Abnormal scarf sign, 7-9 months.

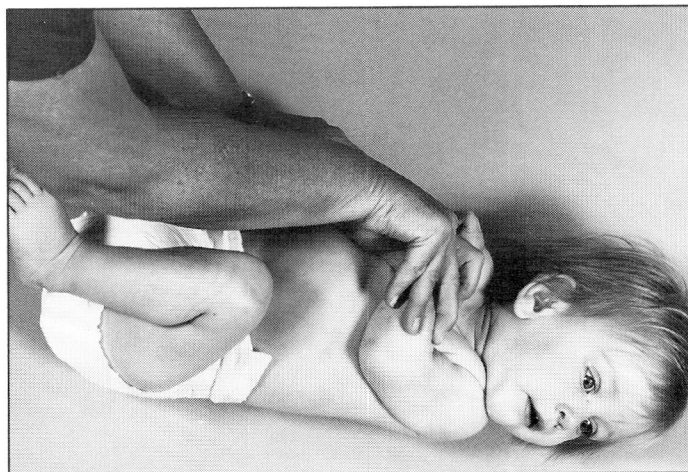

Figure 2.5d. Abnormal scarf sign, 10-12 months.

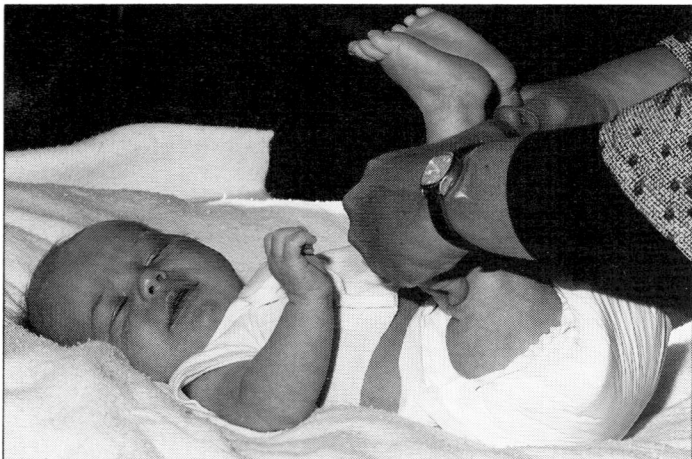

Figure 2.6a. Normal heel-to-ear, 0-3 months.

3. Heel-to-Ear

This is a measure of the flexibility of the hips, not a measure of the flexibility of the lower spine. The examiner grasps the legs around the knees so that the legs are extended. The buttocks are kept on or close to the examining table as much as possible. The angle is formed by the extended legs, the fulcrum of the hip, and the trunk. As with the scarf sign, the resistance to movement decreases during the first year of life. In figures 2.6a through 2.6d, the progression is shown for the normal infant in the quarters of the first year.

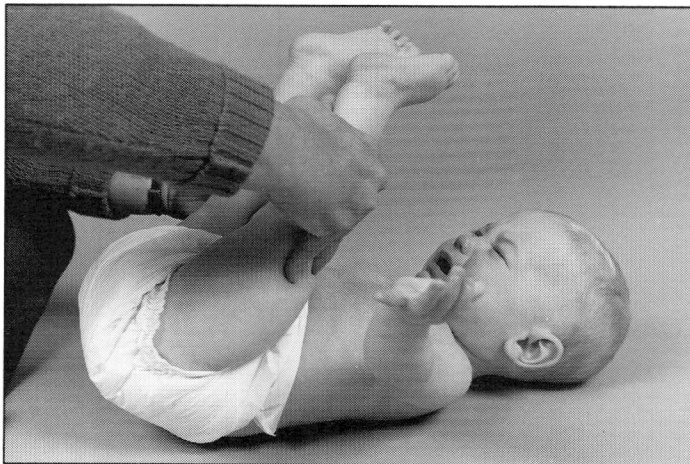

Figure 2.6c. Normal heel-to-ear, 7-9 months.

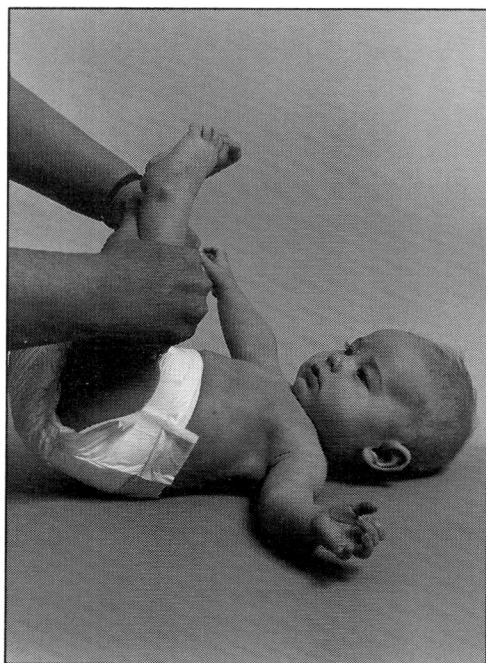

Figure 2.6b. Normal heel-to-ear, 4-6 months.

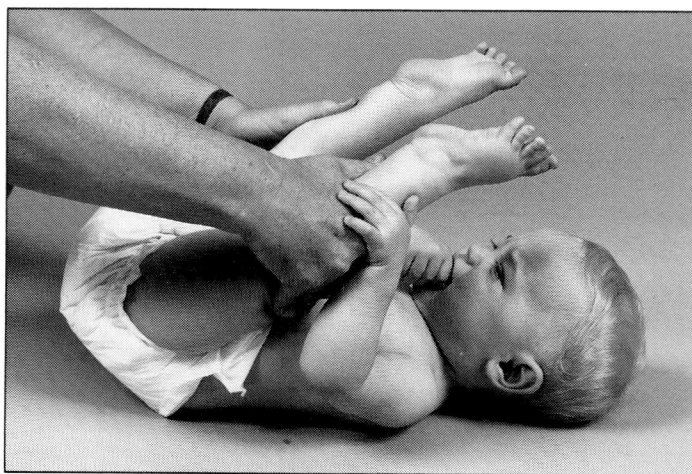

Figure 2.6d. Normal heel-to-ear, 10-12 months.

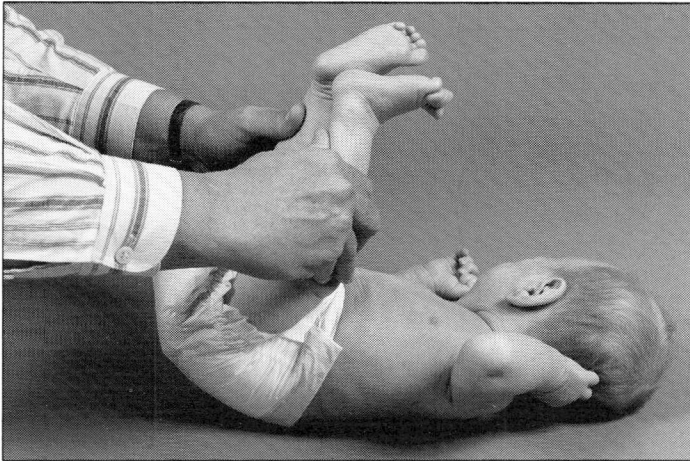
Figure 2.7a. Abnormal heel-to-ear, 0-3 months.

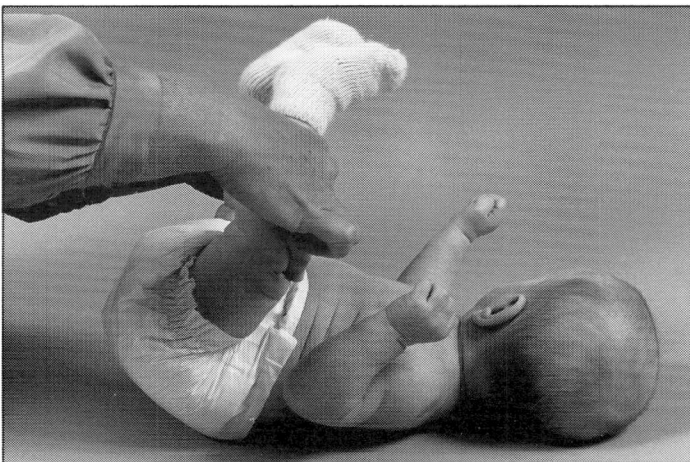
Figure 2.7b. Abnormal heel-to-ear, 4-6 months.

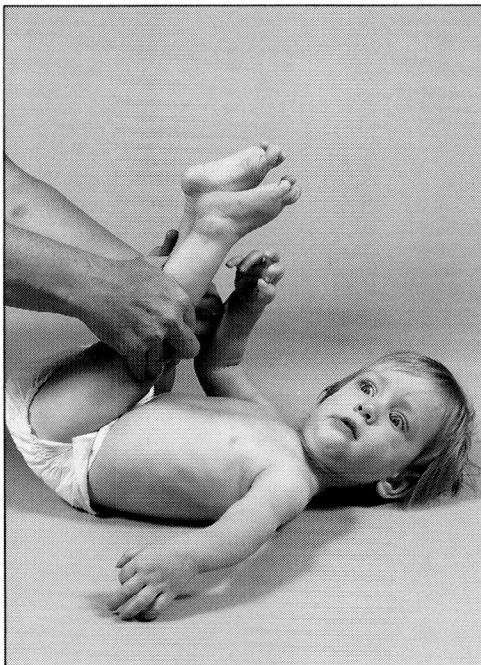
Figure 2.7d. Abnormal heel-to-ear, 10-12 months.

This is an excellent indicator of hypertonia. If you understand and use this item and the popliteal angle (item number 4), you will usually be the first examiner to describe the onset of spasticity, whether spastic diplegia (manifested most strongly in both legs) or spastic tetraparesis/dyskinesia. Many examiners have been trained to look for extension of the feet or tightness with dorsiflexion, but that usually appears later.

An infant with abnormality shows increasing evidence of spasticity, particularly in the 7-to-9-month and 10-to-12-month evaluations. Failure to progress normally will also be reflected in development items such as "plays" with feet, from the *Gesell Screening Inventory* at age 28 weeks. An infant who has decreased flexibility at the hip will have difficulty reaching and playing with his feet and will be delayed in this milestone. In figures 2.7a through 2.7d, the progression is shown for the infant with abnormality in the quarters of the first year.

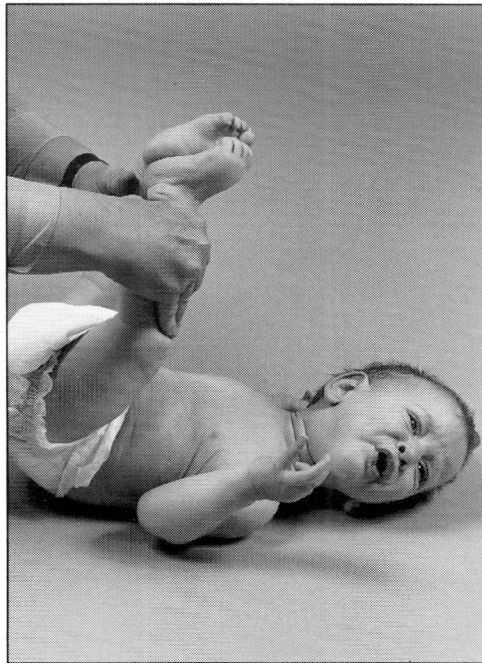
Figure 2.7c. Abnormal heel-to-ear, 7-9 months.

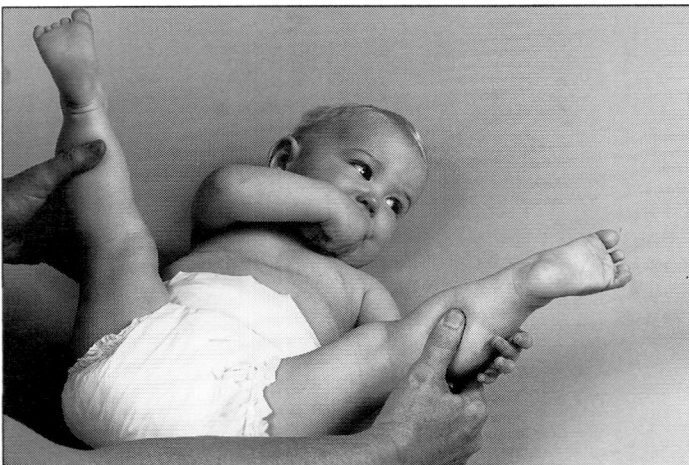

Figure 2.8a. Abnormal popliteal angle, 0-3 months.

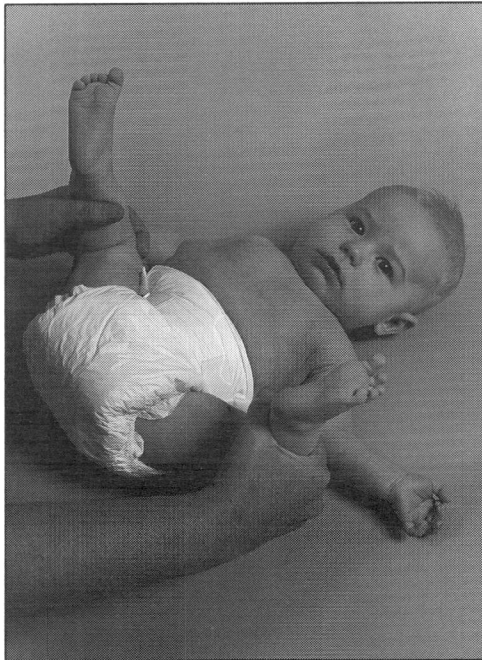

Figure 2.8b. Normal popliteal angle, 4-6 months.

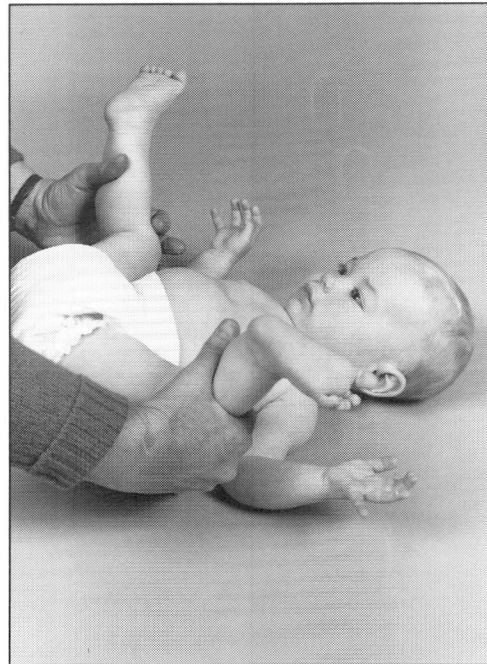

Figure 2.8d. Normal popliteal angle, 10-12 months.

4. Popliteal Angle

Different examiners have different "favorite" items. The popliteal angle has long been one of my favorites. It was the first indicator that I learned for easily recognizing spasticity, and it still works well. As with other French angles, its natural progression during the first year is further opening of the angle, that is, improved flexibility.

Grasp the legs near the knees and flex the legs at the hips. The legs are somewhat abducted, going out to either side of the infant, not against the infant's body. The buttocks remain near the table. The angle is measured between the lower leg and the upper leg, with the back of the knee joint as the fulcrum. In figures 2.8a through 2.8d, the normal progression is shown for the quarters of the first year.

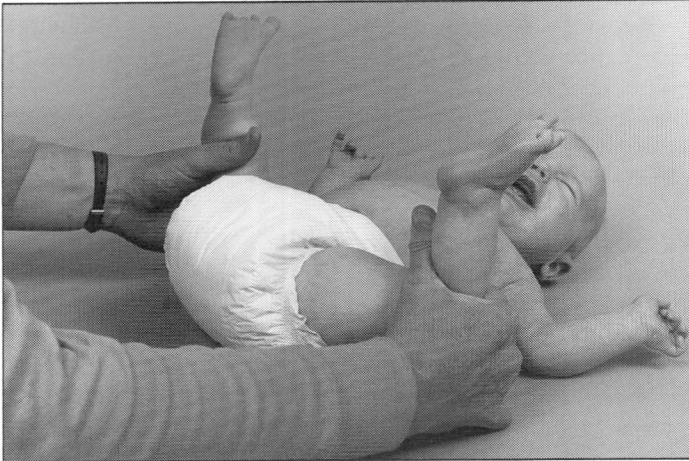

Figure 2.8c. Normal popliteal angle, 7-9 months.

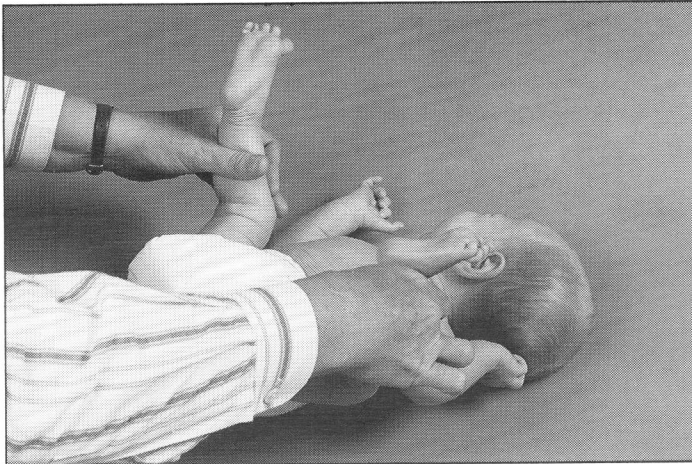
Figure 2.9a. Abnormal popliteal angle, 0-3 months.

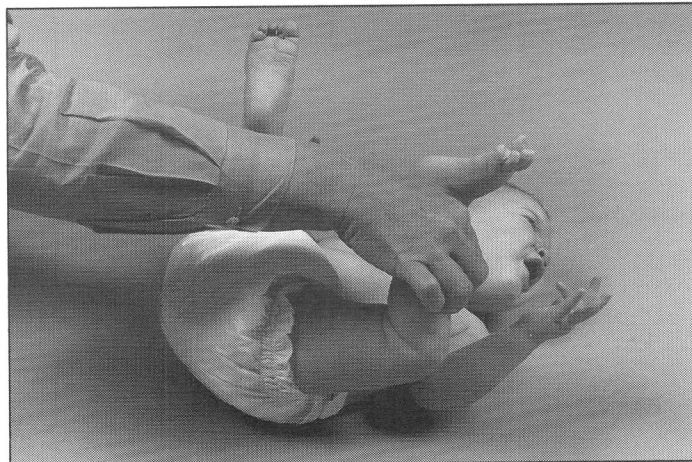
Figure 2.9c. Abnormal popliteal angle, 7-9 months.

In figures 2.9a through 2.9d, the progression is shown for an abnormal infant. His increase in tone (spasticity) is larger in the heel-to-ear maneuver than on the popliteal angle. On the other hand, the popliteal angle is a better indicator of the mild spasticity in our prematurely born infant, than the heel-to-ear.

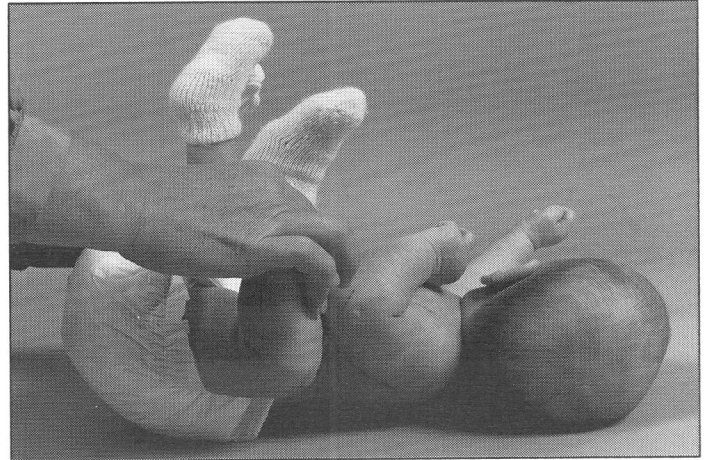
Figure 2.9b. Abnormal popliteal angle, 4-6 months.

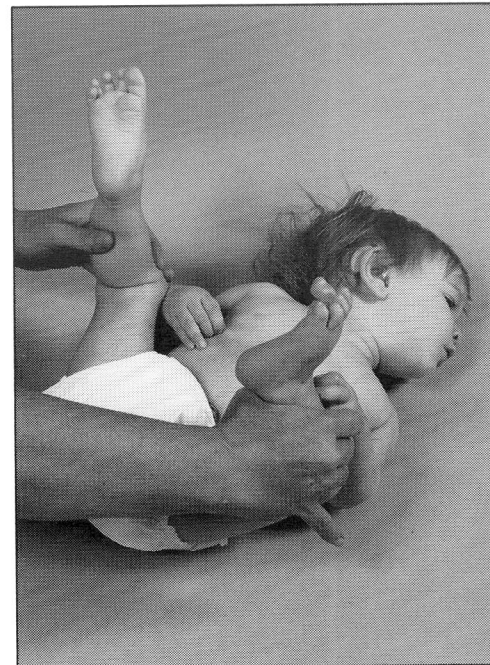
Figure 2.9d. Abnormal popliteal angle, 9-12 months.

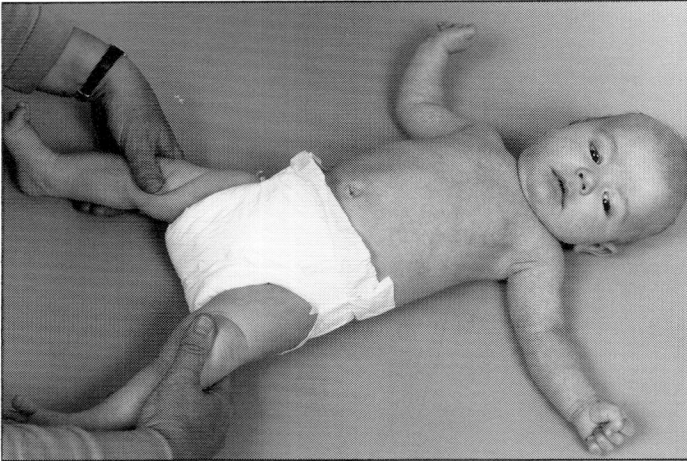

Figure 2.10a. Normal leg abduction, 0-3 months.

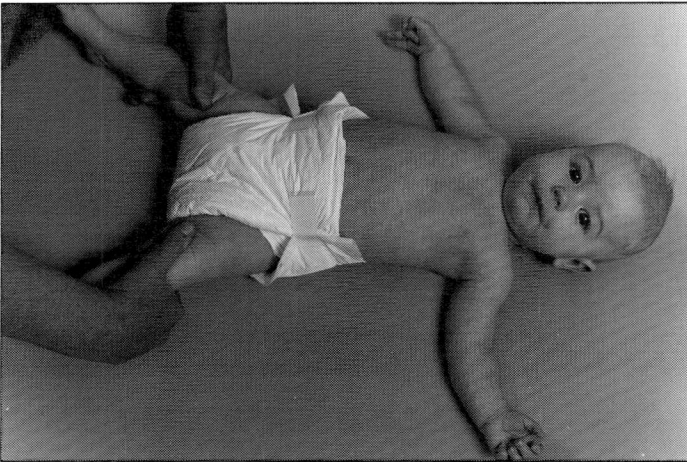

Figure 2.10b. Normal leg abduction, 4.6 months.

5. Leg Abduction

The examiner holds the leg at the knee and proceeds to abduct the leg. The angle is formed between the legs, with the crotch as the fulcrum. As with the other French angles, in normal infants the flexibility increases with age. This progression is shown well with the normal infant (figures 2.10a through 2.10d).

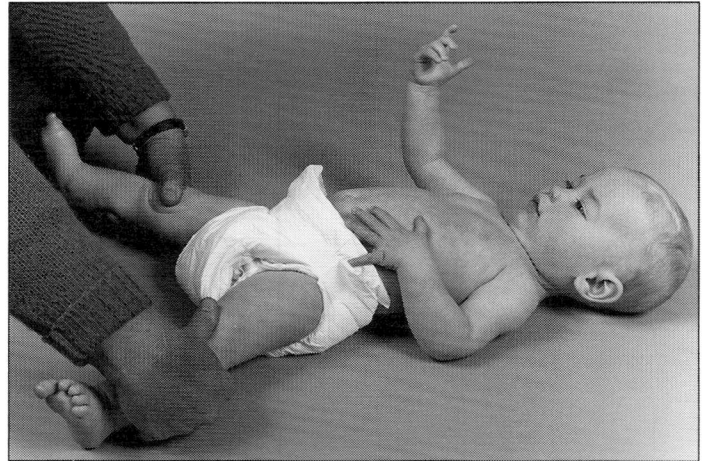

Figure 2.10c. Normal leg abduction, 7-9 months.

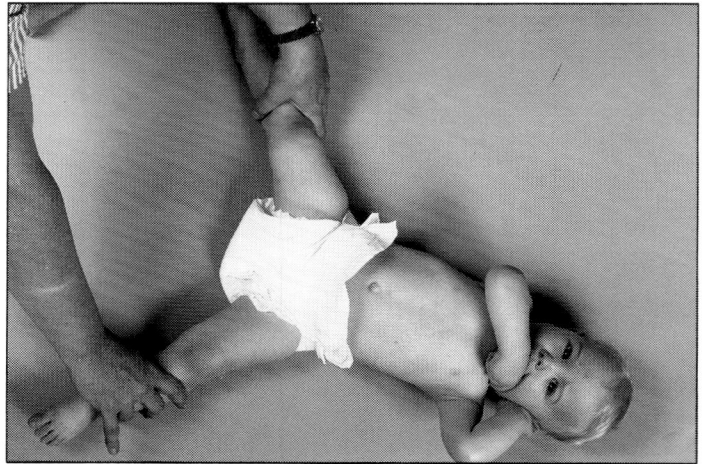

Figure 2.10d. Normal leg abduction, 10-12 months.

His progression is in striking contrast to the abnormal infant, who demonstrates little change in the first year (see figures 2.11a through 2.11d).

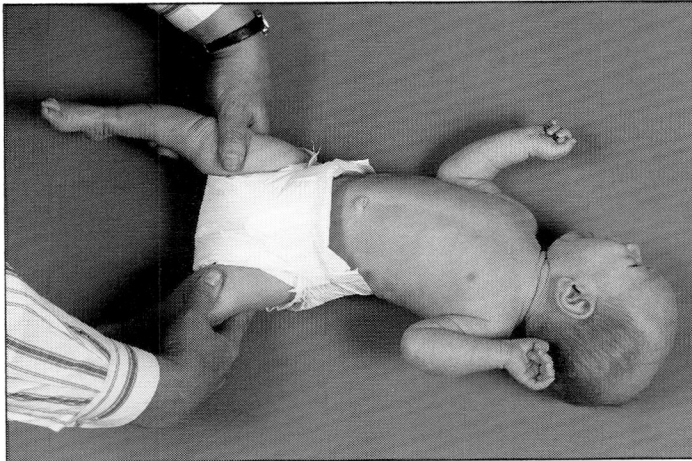

Figure 2.11a. Abnormal leg abduction, 0-3 months.

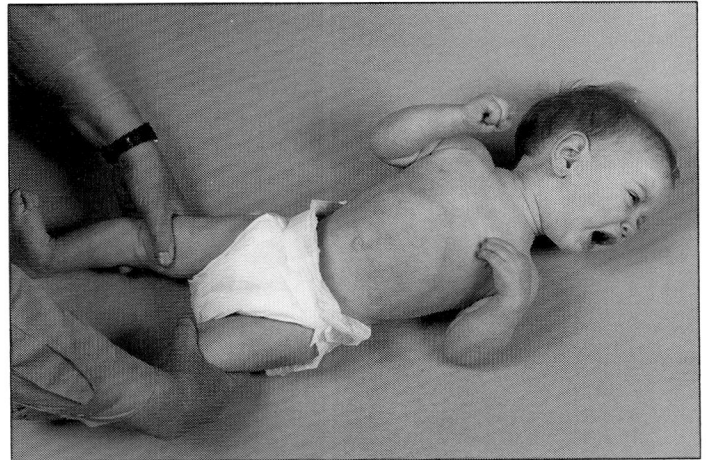

Figure 2.11b. Abnormal leg abduction, 4-6 months.

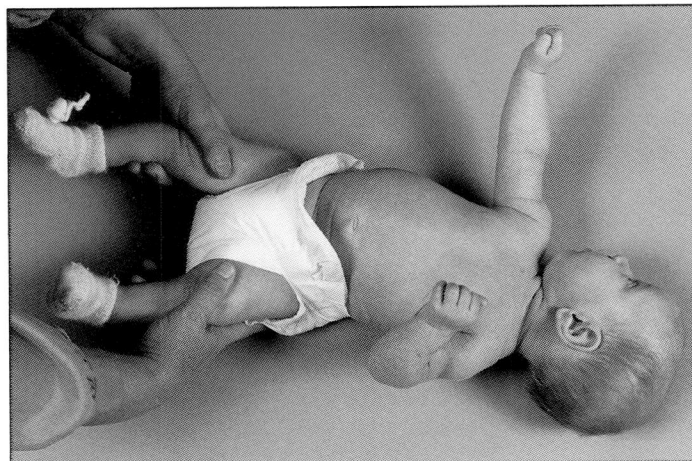

Figure 2.11c. Abnormal leg abduction, 7-9 months.

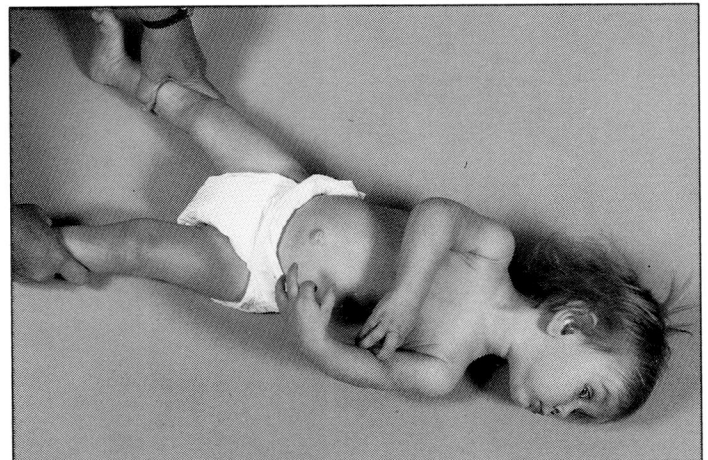

Figure 2.11d. Abnormal leg abduction, 10-12 months.

Again this infant showed abnormality more in the hips than in the knees or feet. Our prematurely born infant had less evidence of increased tone by leg abduction. Leg abduction is less sensitive than heel-to-ear or popliteal angle as an early indicator of hypertonia. It indicates hypotonia well, but so did many other items.

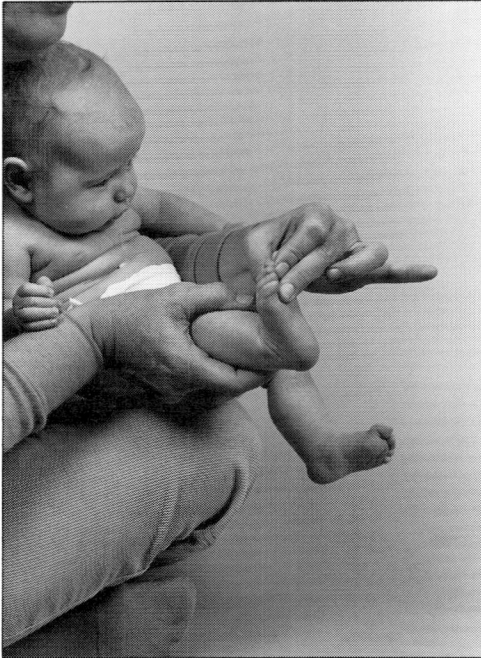

Figure 2.12a. Normal dorsiflexion of the foot at age 2 months.

Figure 2.12b. Abnormal dorsiflexion of the foot at age 4 months.

6. Dorsiflexion of the Foot

The examiner flexes the foot, pushing it against the leg until resistance is met. These photographs show the infant on the examiner's lap. Usually the infant is on the mother's lap or on the examining table and the examiner is pushing the foot up (not pulling). The angle is formed between the lower leg and the foot with the ankle as fulcrum. The flexibility decreases with age, in contrast to the French angles described above.

In figure 2.12a, the normal infant at age two months easily dorsiflexes the foot. The examiner exerts more pressure on the foot of our infant with neurological abnormality (figure 2.12b) at age four months. However, the degree of dorsiflexion is still less than normal for age.

A few infants with severe neurological damage and hypertonia show extended feet in the neonatal evaluation and keep that extension in infancy. More frequently, the feet are hypotonic in very young infants with abnormalities and become more hypertonic during infancy, but later than the heel-to-ear, popliteal angle, and leg abduction. Infants who develop hypertonia of the feet will walk on their toes or stand on their toes, if they walk or stand at all. Therapy is then directed toward repetitive flexion of the ankle in order to permit a standing position.

The examiner will not want to confuse those infants who *choose* to toe walk with those who *must* toe walk. This can be observed by placing the infant in a standing position and observing whether the infant drops the heel spontaneously as well as by the examiner dorsiflexing the foot. A tiny number of infants who choose to toe walk may continue to do that for years. In some senses, they are like women who wear very high heels all the time: the foot is simply maintained in an extended position for hours. Both these infants and the women who love high heels can drop their heels to the floor.

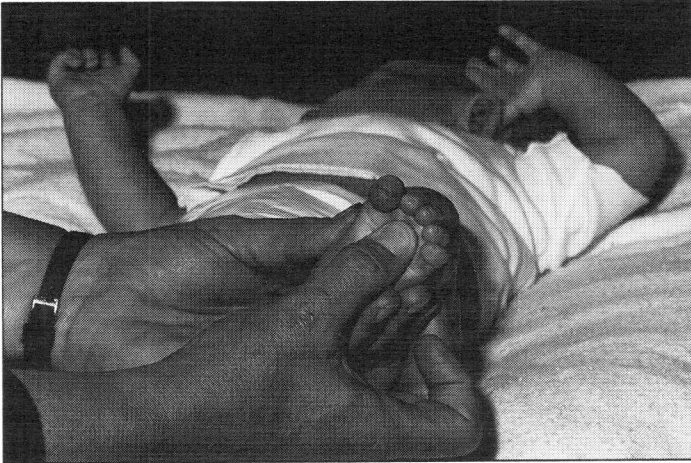

Figure 2.13a. Normal foot grasp at age 1 month.

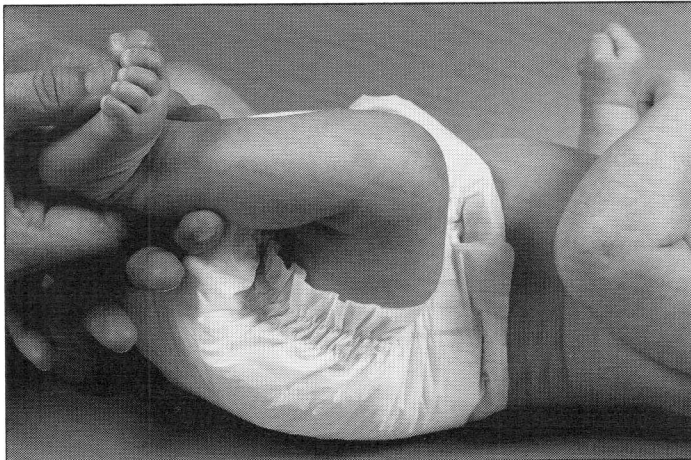

Figure 2.13b. Abnormal foot grasp at age 3 months.

7. The Foot Grasp

The examiner uses his/her thumb or finger to exert pressure on the infant's footpad, then observes the extent to which the toes curl downward.

Foot grasp is one of several reflexes that are present in the neonate, then disappear in infancy—classified as primitive reflexes. These reflexes are abnormal when they are *exaggerated* during the time in which it is normal for the reflex to be present. They are also abnormal when present *after* the expected time of disappearance. Careful studies of normal infants have shown variability in the ages at which the primitive reflexes disappear. The scoring of the *Infanib* is such that infants with a mild delay in the loss of only one or two primitive reflexes would not be described as "abnormal."

In figure 2.13a, the normal one-month-old infant has an easily obtained but not exaggerated foot grasp. In figure 2.13b, an infant with neurological abnormality has an exaggerated foot grasp in early infancy.

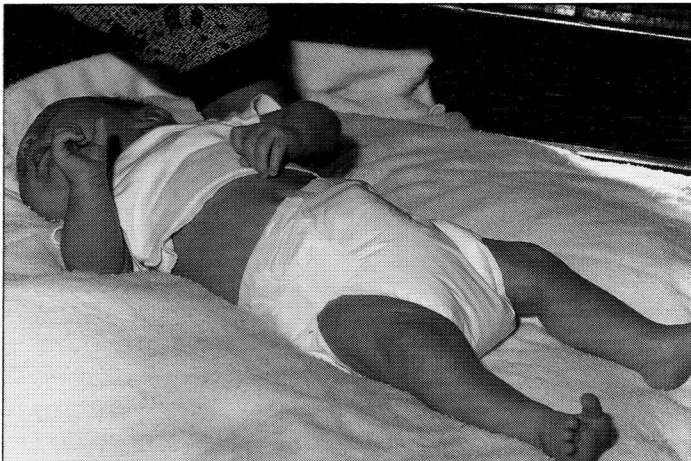

Figure 2.14a. Normal tonic labyrinthine supine at age 1 month.

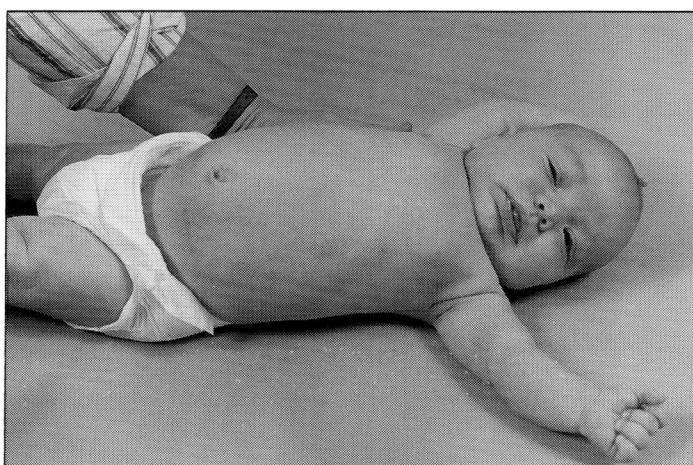

Figure 2.14b. Abnormal tonic labyrinthine supine at age 1 month.

8. Tonic Labyrinthine Supine

The examiner places one hand underneath the infant and between the shoulder blades and rubs the infant's skin. The classical response is one of extension of either or both arms and legs. However, some infants will respond with flexion which we also consider an abnormal response.

In figure 2.14a, a one-month-old normal infant shows little response to this maneuver. In figure 2.14b, the infant with transient abnormality, who also has clenched fists and hypertension of head and neck, immediately extends both arms and legs. The same infant at age two months (figure 2.14c) flexes both arms and legs, which we also scored as abnormal. This infant developed a very pronounced asymmetric tonic neck reflex that became spontaneous whenever he was placed on a firm surface or tried to roll. This item is another primitive reflex. It is also abnormal when exaggerated during the time it is expected to be present and abnormal when it is expected to have disappeared.

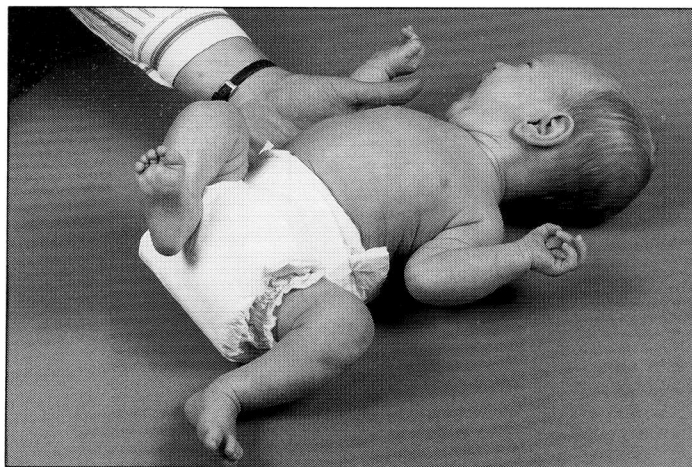

Figure 2.14c. Abnormal tonic labyrinthine supine at age 2 months.

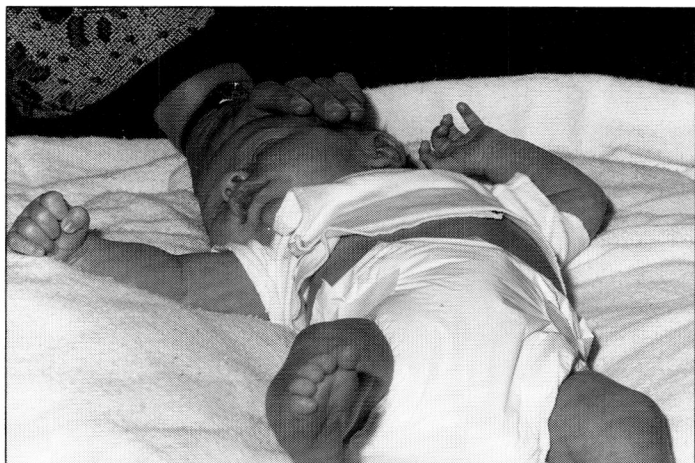

Figure 2.15a. Normal asymmetric tonic neck reflex at age 1 month.

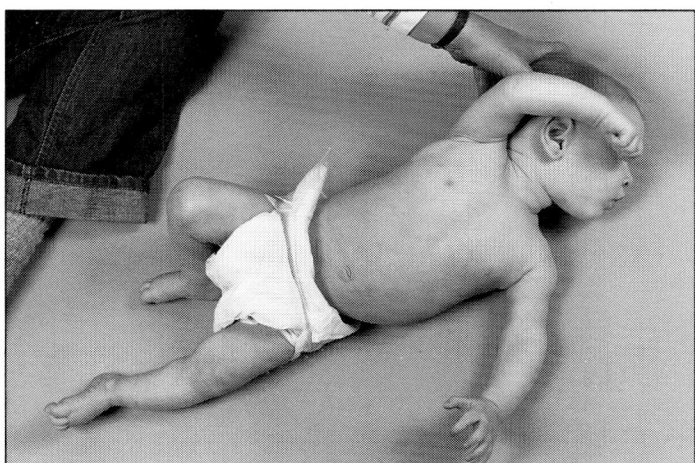

Figure 2.15b. Abnormal asymmetric tonic neck reflex at age 5 months.

9. Asymmetric Tonic Neck Reflex

To elicit the posture, the examiner grasps the infant's head with one hand and turns the head to one side and watches for asymmetric tonic neck posture. This has also been described as a "fencing position," with extension of the arm toward which the head has been turned, then flexion of the arm behind the head. The leg also extends on the side toward which the head has been turned.

In figure 2.15a, a normal one-month-old infant assumes the posture when his head is turned; then he overcomes the posture. In figure 2.15b, the posture is readily elicited from an infant with neurological abnormality. By age five months, it had become exaggerated and persistent. This persistent asymmetric tonic reflex interferes with the development of skills such as rolling over. Every time he initiates a roll, his arm extends and prevents him from proceeding.

In the young infant, exaggeration is manifested by failure to break out of the position after the examiner has provided the stimulation (turning of the head). In the older infant, exaggeration may be represented by spontaneous assumption of the asymmetric tonic neck posture when the infant is placed on a firm surface. This is probably one reason why many infants with abnormal tone and posture that is eventually labeled as cerebral palsy are so uncomfortable and irritable when placed on firm surfaces.

Many normal infants make little or no response to the head stimulation. That is normal. Others will assume some or all of the posture initially and then move their arms and legs out of the posture. That is also normal.

10. Pull-to-Sitting

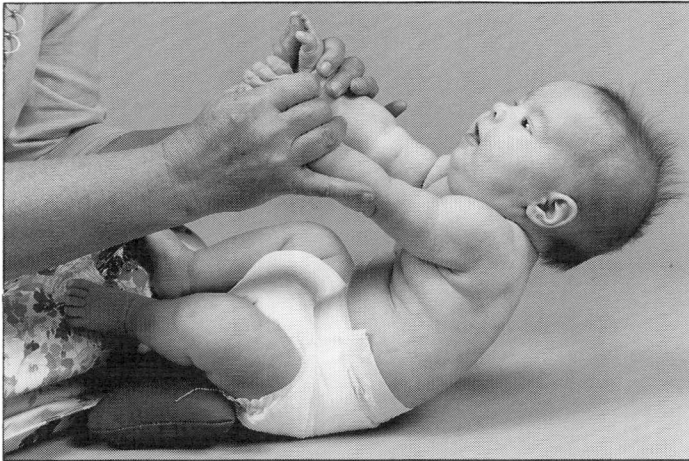

Figure 2.16a. Normal pull-to-sitting at age 2 months.

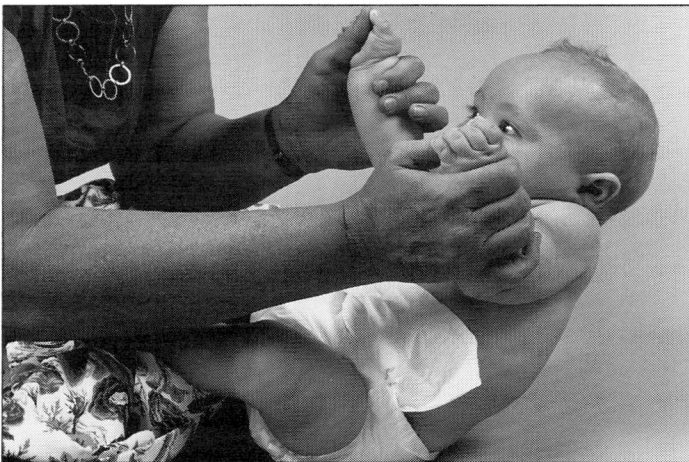

Figure 2.16b. Abnormal pull-to-sitting at age 2 months (note excess head control).

For infants with some upper body tone and head control, the maneuver is readily performed by grasping the infant's hands and pulling the infant to a sitting position. For infants with very poor tone and poor head control, a sitting position may not be reached unless the examiner provides more support, such as grasping the upper arm. However, it is not necessary to reach a sitting position if it is already obvious that the infant has markedly decreased tone and delayed development of head control. *When there is a discrepancy between the head position and the arm position on the figure on the scoring sheet, the head position is used for the scoring.*

In figure 2.16a, the normal two-month-old has good head control but does not really "help" much. In contrast, the transiently abnormal infant (figure 2.16b) has too much head control for age, flexes his body a little. An infant with abnormality at age seven months has a major problem with head control and truncal hypotonia as well as having the exaggerated asymmetric tonic neck reflex described previously (figure 2.16c).

Many infants who were treated in the neonatal intensive care units have delay in head control and hypotonia of the neck and upper trunk. A much smaller number of infants have hypertonia of head and neck as in figure 2.16b. Poor head control for many months is common in most infants with abnormalities.

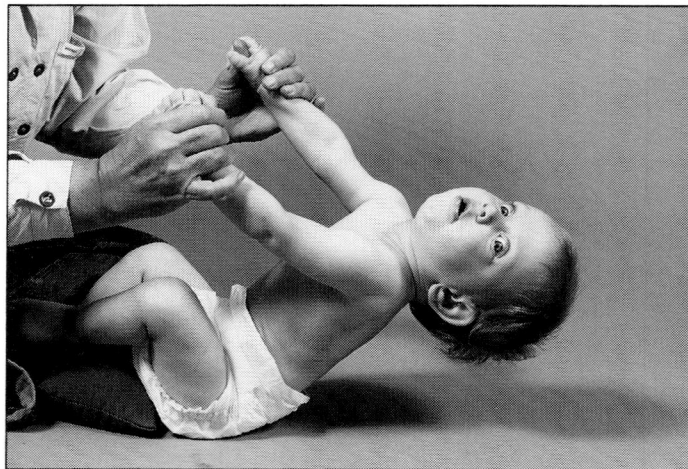

Figure 2.16c. Abnormal pull-to-sitting at age 7 months.

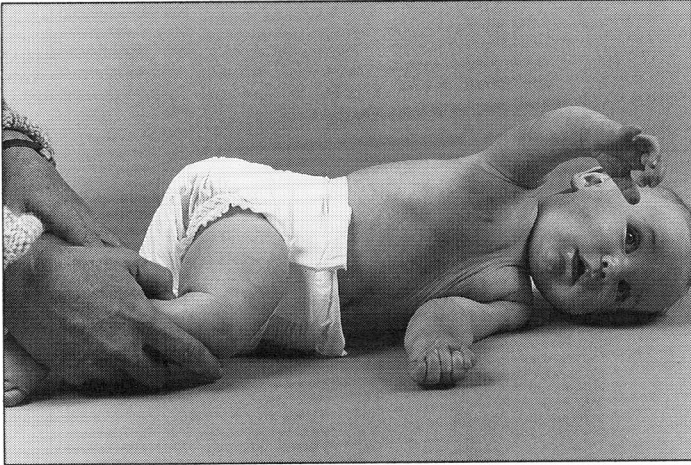
Figure 2.17a. Normal body derotative at age 4 months.

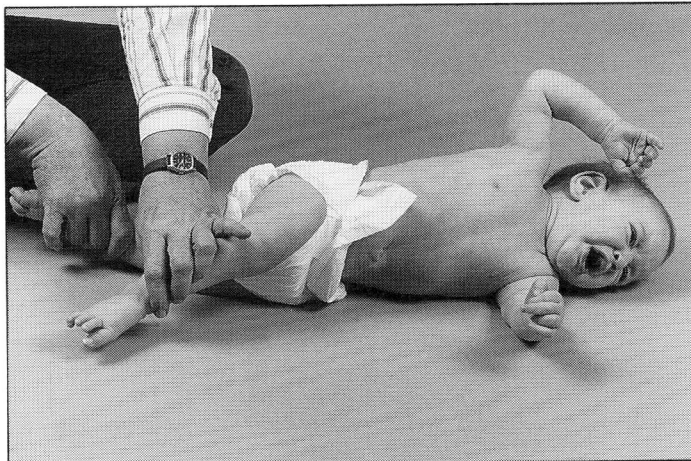
Figure 2.17b. Abnormal body derotative at age 4 months (note asymmetric tonic neck posture).

11. Body Derotative

In this maneuver, the examiner initiates rolling over for the infant. For some older infants, the examiner may not get a chance to do this—the infant rolls over and crawls or stands up. This task is a test of the examiner's alertness and ability to keep the child from falling off the table. Other infants may be able to roll from back to front, but they do not choose to do so. For that reason, the infant is given credit for the skill if the caretaker reports presence of the skill. The examiner takes hold of the lower legs and turns one leg over the other to initiate rolling over.

In figure 2.17a, a normal infant at age four months extends the upper arm in anticipation and readily rolls over. In figure 2.17b, an infant with abnormal asymmetric tonic neck posture simply gets stuck. He flexes or extends the downside arm and essentially prevents himself from rolling.

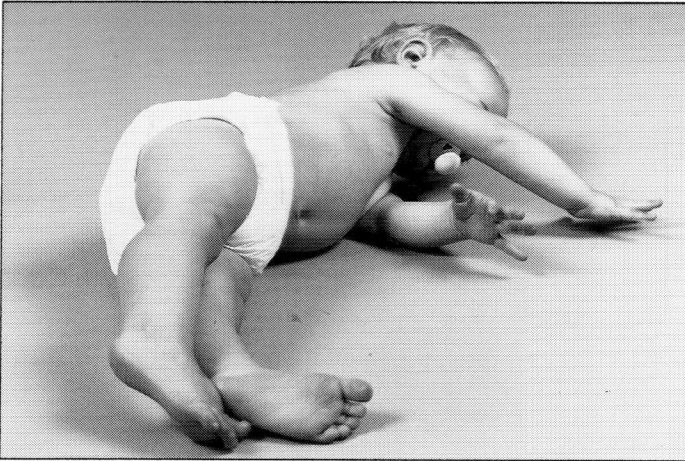

Figure 2.18a. Normal body rotative.

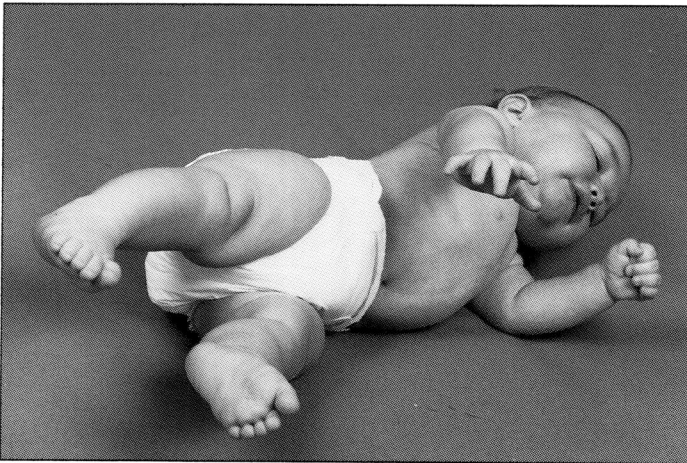

Figure 2.18b. Abnormal body rotative (infant with transient abnormality).

12. Body Rotative

This is simply spontaneous rolling over from back to front followed by a pull to standing position. An infant does not always pull-to-stand after rolling over. Again the examiner may ask the caretaker if this is achieved at home in order to give a passing score. For an active infant, this may be demonstrated spontaneously more than once in the course of the evaluation.

In figure 2.18a, the normal infant easily rolls over and positions himself for his next venture. This contrasts to the more awkward rolling of the infant with transient neuromotor abnormalities (who had fisting and exaggerated primitive reflexes in early infancy) in figure 2.18b. He rolls more slowly and rolls his body as a unit, in a logrolling style. However, this did not interfere with his developing skills in walking by the age of 13 months. On the other hand, our most abnormal infant could not roll at all at ages 10 to 12 months; he assumed an asymmetric tonic neck reflex each time he tried.

Rolling over from supine to prone followed by pull-to-stand requires loss of any asymmetric tonic neck reflex, intact vestibular function and maturation, and sufficient truncal tone and leg tone to support the body.

13. All-Fours

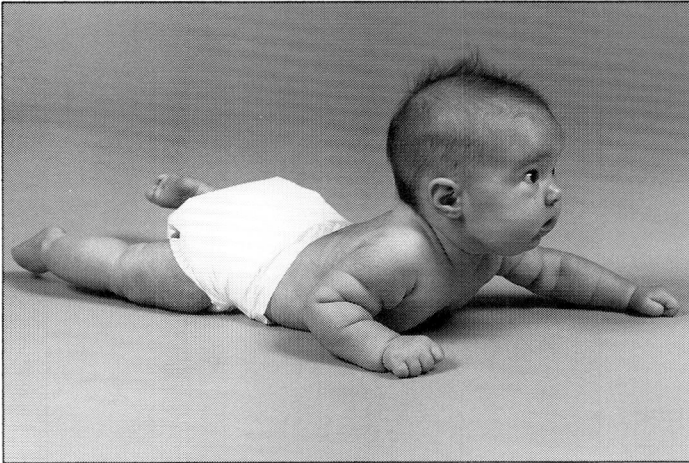

Figure 2.19a. Normal all-fours at age 2 months.

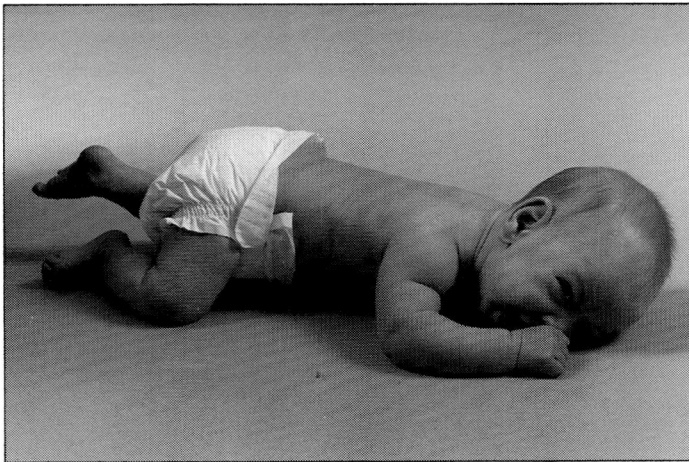

Figure 2.19b. Abnormal all-fours at age 4 months.

The examiner turns the infant over into a prone position. Observation is then made of the position of the head, arms, and legs. In early infancy, the key position is that of the head, which should be used for scoring if there are discrepancies in the maturation of head, arm, and leg use. This is an excellent item for the examiner to use to provide encouragement for very young infants who do not yet appreciate that the world is theirs once they master prone position.

In figure 2.19a, one of our normal infants, now at two months, easily holds her head up 90°, resting on one forearm and extending the other arm. On the other hand, our infant with abnormality (figure 2.19b) does not hold his head up at all at age four months, although he was reported to do so briefly at home.

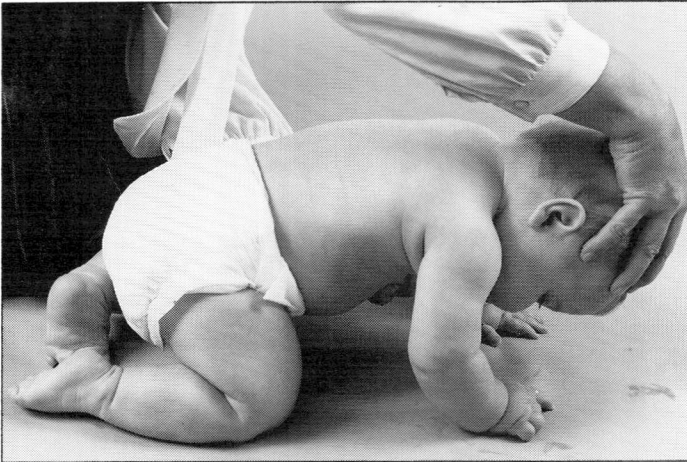
Figure 2.20a. Normal tonic labyrinthine prone.

Figure 2.20b. Abnormal tonic labyrinthine prone.

14. Tonic Labyrinthine Prone

Place the infant in a prone position again. If he/she is able to support himself/herself with arms extended and knees somewhat, place your hand under the abdomen to assist in maintaining that position. If the infant simply lies on the surface, your hand under the abdomen will be necessary to lift the infant enough that the knees can be flexed under the body. Then the examiner takes the other hand and flexes the infant's head. Look for shoulder retraction and flexion of arms, hips, or legs under the abdomen. The examiner looks for exaggeration under age nine months or presence of the reflex after age nine months. The normal response is shown in figure 2.20a. The infant with abnormality has an exaggerated response at age seven months (figure 2.20b).

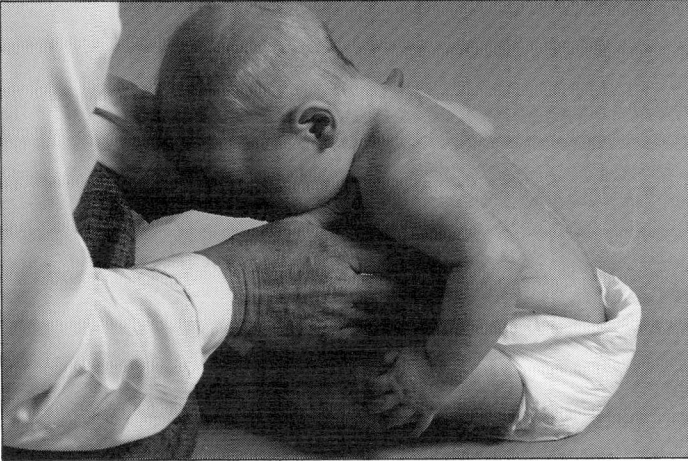

Figure 2.21a. Normal sitting at age 4 months.

15. Sitting

The examiner places the infant in sitting position and holds the infant there unless he/she can maintain a sitting position well independently. Observe the point on the back at which bending occurs. Initially the infant will bend at L3 (see figure 2.21a). With maturation in truncal tone, the infant will then bend from L5.

A few infants will progress too well in sitting, much as in pull-to-sit, and hyperextend the head and neck and/or the back. This is demonstrated well by a four-month-old infant with transient abnormality in figure 2.21b. The more common abnormality is delay in sitting associated with truncal hypotonia. In figure 2.21c, an infant with abnormality bends at several thoracic levels, showing truncal hypotonia.

Some infants with severe spasticity cannot be placed into sitting position at all because of extensor posturing, or they can only be placed in a sitting position by flexing the hips and the knees. These infants would be scored with the most abnormal score (1 point).

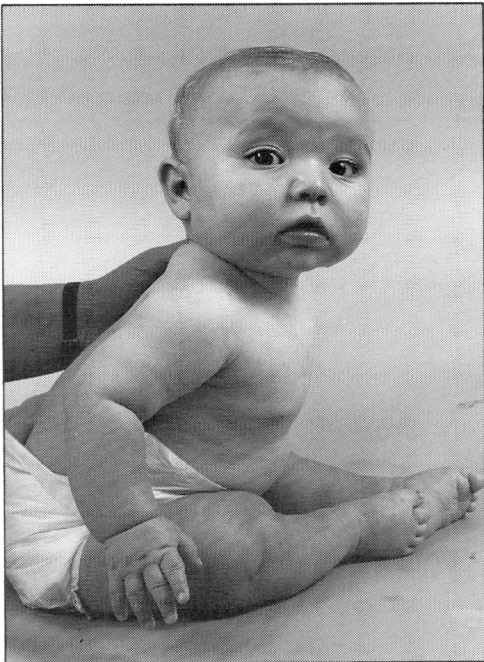

Figure 2.21b. Abnormal sitting. Note that the infant sits "too well" at age 4 months.

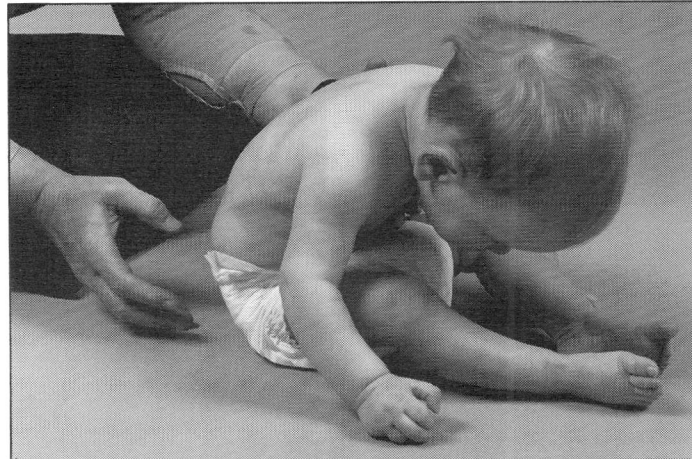

Figure 2.21c. Sitting, infant with abnormality bends at several thoracic levels, age 6 months.

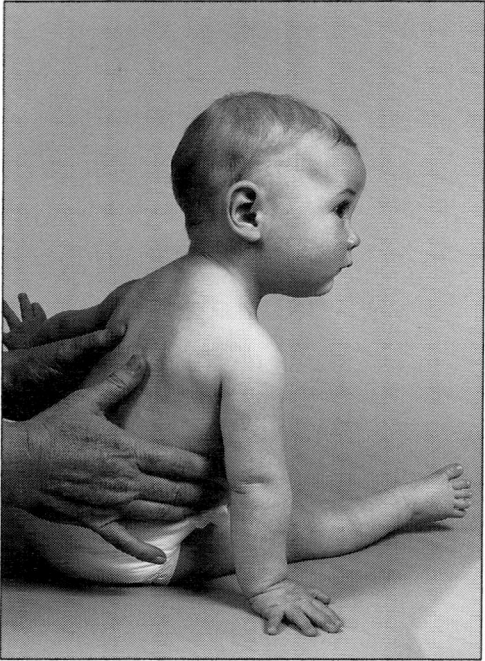

Figure 2.22a. Normal sideways parachute, age 8 months.

16. Sideways Parachute

The examiner places the infant in a sitting position, usually positioned behind the infant, with the examiner's hands on the lateral lower trunk. Then the examiner tips the infant off balance just a bit, first on one side, then on the other, and observes the infant's arm and hand on the side tipped to. The infant should extend the arm and use the hand for balance.

In figure 2.22a, this is readily done by our normal infant at age eight months. In figure 2.22b, it is not done at all by an infant at the same age with abnormality; his arm just falls to one side and is not used for balancing or bracing. Our prematurely born infant also fails to develop a sideways parachute on time (figure 2.22c).

This is an excellent item for assessment of hemiparesis. The infant thrusts the arm less well on the hemiparetic side. Forward parachute is another item that is useful in discerning hemiparesis.

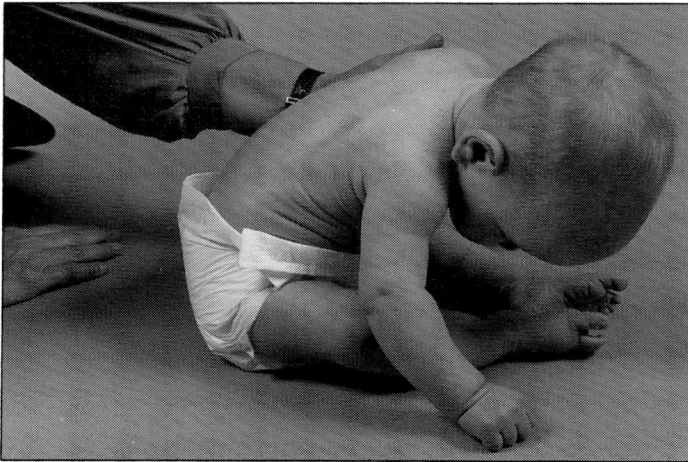

Figure 2.22b. Abnormal sideways parachute, age 8 months.

Figure 2.22c. Sideways parachute, prematurely born infant with transient abnormalities, about age 8 months.

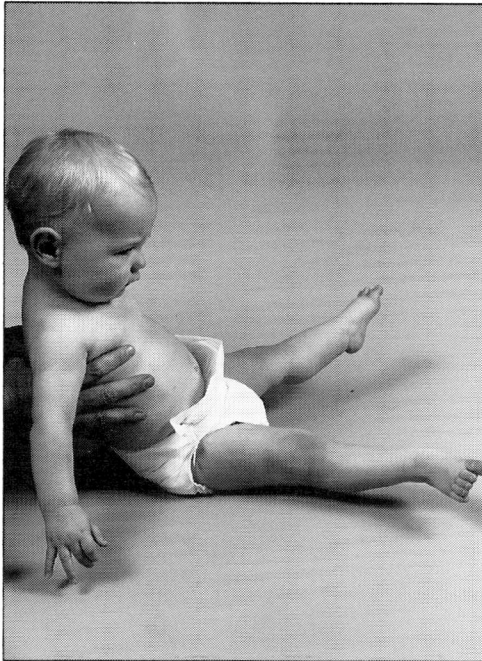

Figure 2.23a. Backwards parachute, normal infant at 9 months.

17. Backwards Parachute

The examiner holds the infant at the trunk. Although the photographs show this being done from the back, it is better done from the side. If done from the front, the infant may grasp the examiner's arms rather than extending them backwards for balance. The infant is tipped backwards. A normal infant may readily turn a little to one side or the other. This is not a good item for hemiparesis since the turning to one side or differential use of these arms may have nothing to do with hemiparesis.

In figure 2.23a, the normal infant at age nine months readily responds by extending both arms behind him. The infant with abnormality, also age nine months, in figure 2.23b really makes no response. He has truncal hypotonia and just lies back on the examiner's hands.

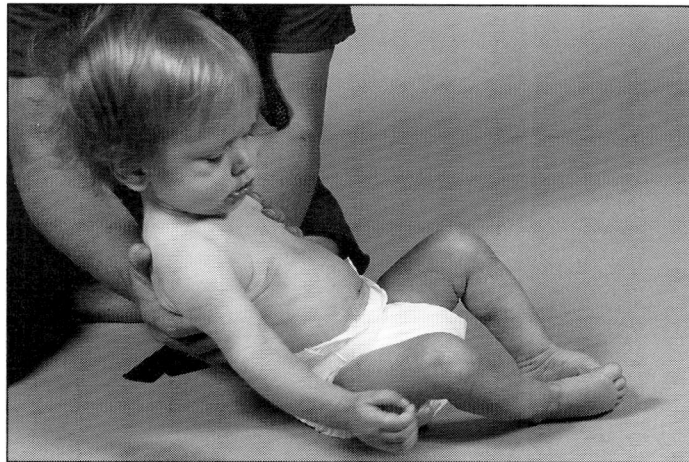

Figure 2.23b. Backwards parachute, infant with abnormalities at almost 1 year of age.

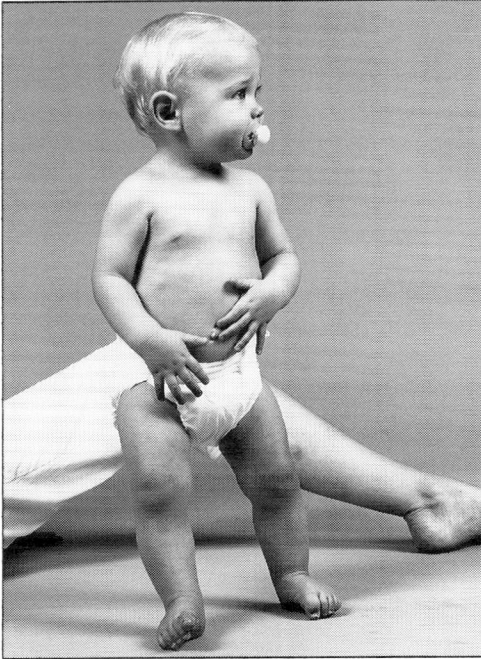

Figure 2.24a. Standing, normal infant at age 10 months.

18. Standing

The examiner holds the infant under the arms, with legs in standing position. Sometimes older infants will need to be faced away from the examiner, facing toward the mothers. The examiner especially observes the feet and legs.

In figure 2.24a, a normal infant was right at home at age 10 months (and very casual) on his feet. The prematurely born infant in figure 2.24b could not muster a standing position. Her legs simply crumpled beneath her well into late infancy. Our infant with abnormality could support his legs but had difficulty maintaining his upper body (figure 2.24c).

Some infants stand too well, too early. This can be a manifestation of increased tone in the legs and feet. Observing the legs for breaking at the knees is very helpful for both increased extensor tone and for spasticity, especially before age five months.

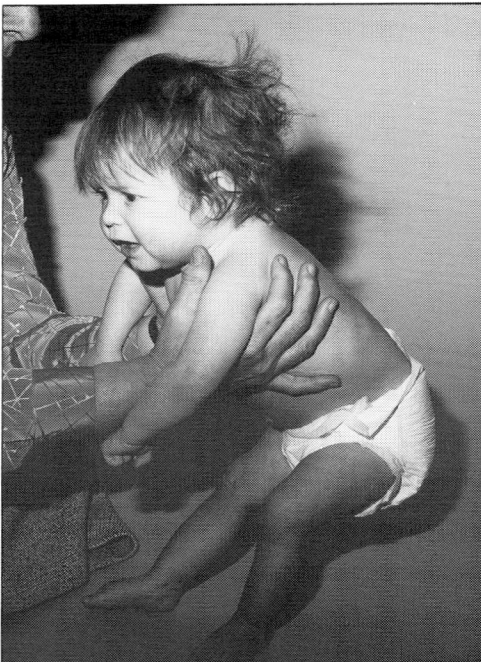

Figure 2.24c. Standing, infant with abnormality.

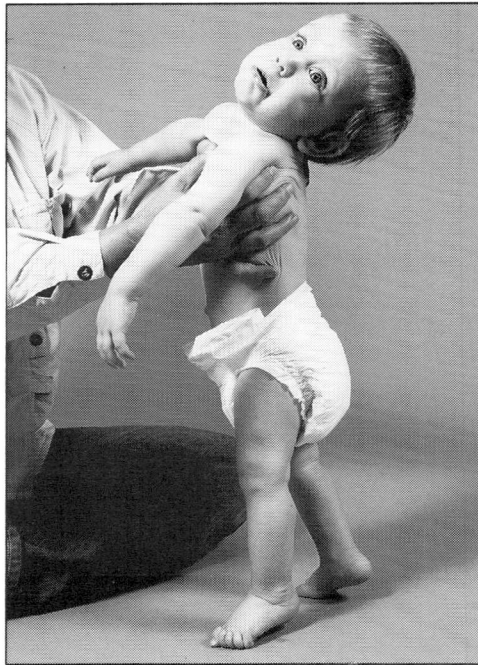

Figure 2.24b. Standing, prematurely born infant with transient abnormality at age 10 months.

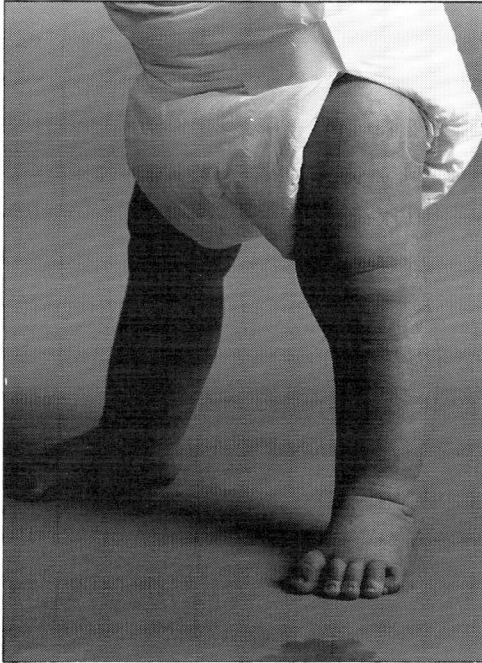

Figure 2.25a. Positive support reaction, normal infant.

19. Positive Support Reaction

This is a double-check for toe walking and for increased tone in the ankle joint. The examiner observes the infant's feet as the infant is placed in standing position. Many infants will stand on their toes initially. Most soon drop to a position with feet flat on the floor. The infant with abnormality does not drop the feet flat.

In figure 2.25a, our normal infant has assumed a position with the feet flat. Note the curled toes and feet positions with elevated heels in an infant with abnormality (figure 2.25b).

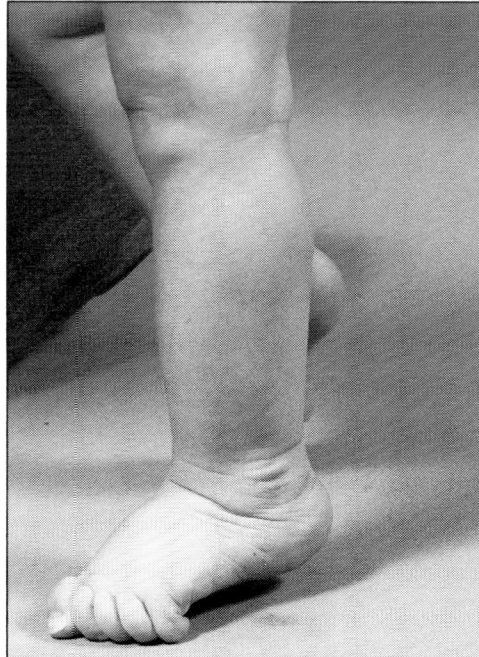

Figure 2.25b. Positive support reaction, infant with abnormality.

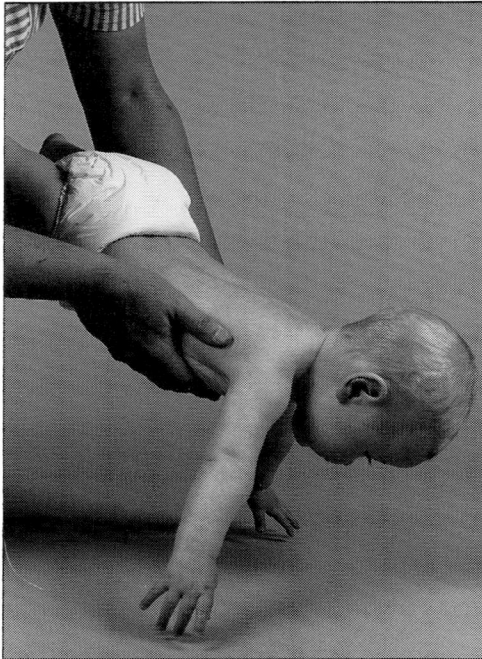

Figure 2.26a. Forward parachute, normal infant at age 7 months.

20. Forward Parachute

The examiner places one hand on each side of the infant's trunk to provide good support and then thrusts the infant toward a surface, head first. A normal infant extends both arms in anticipation, toward the surface. We tend to interpret this as a protective or supportive maneuver. A small number of normal infants who are tossed around by family members in play (*not* in abuse), may appear quite unconcerned and may not extend their arms even though they are neurologically normal in every other respect.

In figure 2.26a, a normal infant, age seven months, readily thrusts his arms and hands forward. In figure 2.26b, an infant with persistent asymmetric tonic neck reflex makes no effort to extend toward the surface. Although his arms are in an extended position that is probably secondary to the thrusting motion of the examiner. The infant's arms have fallen that way.

Figure 2.26b. Forward parachute, infant with abnormalities

3

The Progression of Different Types of Abnormalities

Abnormalities of tone and posture in infants have been classified somewhat differently by various clinicians. The more severe abnormalities of tone and posture, particularly those with significant spasticity, have often been grouped under the umbrella term "cerebral palsy." Cerebral palsy is a nonprogressive chronic disability characterized by aberrant control of movement and posture appearing in early life (Nelson and Ellenberg 1979). There can be different causes of cerebral palsy. Abnormalities of tone and posture that are frequently associated with abnormal movement can be well-described in infancy. Many infants will outgrow these abnormalities. Therefore the term cerebral palsy might better be used for those abnormalities that tend to persist. "Motor dysfunctions of infancy" might be a better umbrella term for all motor abnormalities of infancy, those that remain as well as those that eventually disappear, such as mild to moderate hypotonias or mild spasticities.

Types of Motor Dysfunction of Infancy

There are four basic types of motor dysfunction of infancy: *spastic tetraparesis-dyskinesia, spastic hemiparesis, spastic diplegia,* and *hypotonia.* The description of abnormalities in quality of movement may vary from examiner to examiner.

Spastic tetraparesis-dyskinesia involves all four limbs, which is different from hypotonia. The infant may have hypotonia of the arms and spasticity of the legs. Or the infant may have a dyskinetic quality of arm movement and spasticity in the legs. Or, there can be spasticity throughout, often with greater involvement of the arms (the classic description of double hemiplegia). Clearly different combinations of abnormalities are possible.

Spastic hemiparesis is a one-sided involvement in which there is generally greater abnormality of the arm than the leg.

Spastic diplegia is bilateral involvement of the legs. While this is classically described as the chief abnormality found in prematurely-born children and an abnormality confined to the legs, infants who were not prematurely born can have this type of abnormality. Many of these infants and children, whether full-term or prematurely born, have some mild involvement of the arms, often manifested as some delayed or clumsy fine motor control.

Hypotonia is a floppiness frequently associated with delay in acquisition of motor skills. The infant has delay in head control, delay in learning to sit and sits with a rounded back, and delay in pulling to standing, cruising, and walking independently. In the scoring of the *Infanib,* some hypotonic infants will be defined as abnormal and those with lesser amounts of hypotonia will be defined as transiently abnormal. Hypotonia that does not begin to improve, especially that which is not associated with evidence of mental delay (delayed use of eyes—focus and following—and delayed vocalization), is not a part of a defined syndrome such as Down syndrome, or worsens, often requires further diagnostic testing.

Transient Abnormality of Infancy

The category of transient abnormality falls between the normal and the abnormal. Different examiners have described this in different ways, but the concept permeates the work of those who have examined infants serially. Amiel-Tison described early abnormalities in the French angles that disappeared in late infancy (Amiel-Tison and Grenier 1986). Drillien described dystonic abnormalities more than hypotonic abnormalities; some of these persisted beyond the first birthday (Drillien 1972). Ellison et al. described mild delay in the development of fine motor skills and mild hypotonia, both of which tended to disappear (Ellison et al. 1982). The scores on the *Infanib* have been set such that the examiner can be confident that the abnormalities have a very high probability of improving.

Progression Across Time

Spastic tetraparesis-dyskinesia tends to look worse and score worse between ages 6 and 18 months even though it stems from a nonprogressive brain problem. The experienced observer is usually not surprised by this because he/she will already have identified the increasing proximal spasticity at ages 4 to 6 months. However, the less-experienced observer may not be familiar with these patterns of progression and some may be distressed by the evolution of a considerable degree of neuromotor abnormality that tends to remain. In the National Collaborative Perinatal Project, 84 percent of infants ($n = 50$) with a diagnosis of moderate or severe quadriplegia at one year had a diagnosis of cerebral palsy at seven years (Nelson and Ellenberg 1982).

Spastic hemiparesis is somewhat less likely to be outgrown than spastic tetraparesis if it is moderate to severe. If it is mild it is less likely to be outgrown than other types of mild abnormalities. In the National Collaborative Perinatal Project, 52 percent of infants with mild hemiparesis at age one year retained a diagnosis of cerebral palsy at age seven years (Nelson and Ellenberg 1982). Eighty-seven percent of infants with moderate to severe hemiparesis at age one year retained the diagnosis at age seven years. In the National Collaborative Perinatal Project, of all the infants with some type of mild cerebral palsy at age one year, spastic hemiparesis was the least likely to be outgrown.

These infants do not show increasing abnormality on neuromotor evaluation as do those with spastic tetraparesis/dyskinesia. Indeed, worsening hemiparesis may need re-evaluation by the neurologist.

Examiners are often asked about the prognosis for cognitive development in these infants. A neuroimaging study is often helpful in increasing the accuracy of prediction of cognition in hemipareses. If the brain lesion is bilateral, or there are large differences in the size of the ventricles, or there is a porencephalic cyst, the IQ will tend to be lower.

The rate at which *hypotonia* decreases is related to the presence of other development abnormalities. Infants with delayed adaptive and personal skills were more likely to have moderate hypotonia at 30-36 months and all were at least clumsy (Ellison 1984). Infants with normal adaptive and personal skills were at most mildly hypotonic at 24-30 months and 36 percent were normal (see table 3.1).

Table 3.1. Follow-Up at 30-36 Months (Albany)

Abnormality (10 Months Corrected Gestational Age)	Follow-Up
Hypotonia-moderate to marked; normal adaptive and personal-social skills (N = 11)	5 had mild hypotonia 2 were clumsy 4 were normal
Hypotonia-moderate to marked; delayed adaptive and personal-social skills (N = 11)	6 had moderate hypotonia 2 had mild hypotonia 3 were clumsy
Spastic diplegia-mild; (n = 3)	2 had mild diplegia 1 was normal
Spastic diplegia-moderate to marked (n = 17)	1 had spastic tetraparesis 16 had spastic diplegia
Spastic tetraparesis-dyskinesia (n = 27)	3 had spastic diplegia 24 had spastic tetraparesis-dyskinesia
Transient Mild hypotonia (n = 55)	51 were normal 4 had mild hypotonia
Mild fine motor abnormality (n = 73)	41 were normal 32 had fine motor abnormality
Mild popliteal angle limitation (n = 4)	4 were normal

In large samples of infants who were initially treated in the neonatal intensive care units, *transient abnormalities of infancy* are frequent. In a study of 999 such infants, 21 percent had transient abnormalities at 6 months corrected gestational age (Ellison et al. 1982). Seventy-nine percent of these became normal by the age of 15 months. In another longitudinal study of 583 infants, 93 percent of infants with mild hypotonia were normal by ages 24-30 months. If transient neuromotor abnormality of infancy was defined as mild fine motor delays at age 10 months, 44% still had mild fine motor abnormalities at age 24-30 months (Ellison 1984).

Examiners who look carefully often describe abnormality of only one limb in infancy. In the study of 999 infants cited previously, 113 infants were described as having *monoparesis* (Ellison 1984). Ninety-five percent of these infants improved. The remaining six infants had progression to other limbs—one to hemiplegia, two to diplegia, and three to hypotonia—but these abnormalities were eventually outgrown. In the National Collaborative Perinatal Project, all the children with monoparesis in infancy outgrew it by age seven years (Nelson and Ellenberg 1982).

Other Studies about Progression

In the data regarding the 999 infants from the Milwaukee study, evaluations were completed for many abnormal infants at more frequent intervals than planned as part of the follow-up. The physical therapists were at liberty to teach positioning and therapeutic techniques to the caretakers. They requested the return of the infants and their caretakers, often monthly, to review the progress of the infants and the use of the therapies. The neuromotor evaluation was repeated on each visit. The infants were subsequently given diagnostic labels by the pediatric neurologist and the mean score obtained for each item for infants in each diagnostic category for serial evaluations (Ellison et al. 1983). In table 3.2, a normal score here is 5; the most abnormal score is 1.

Table 3.2. The progression of mean scores for items assessed at intervals from 6 months to 17 months of age

Item	Spastic tetraparesis/ dyskinesia	Spastic hemiparesis	Spastic diplegia	Hypotonia	Transient
Body lying supine—head lift	→	↗ 15	→	↗ 9	↗
ATNR	↗17	↗ 7	↗ 7	N	N
Pulled to sitting	→	↗ 11	↗15	↗11	↗
Sitting	→	↗	↗15	↗15	N
Sideways parachute	→	→	↗15	↗15	↗
Backward parachute	11↘	15↘	9↘	↗	N
Head in space	→	↗ 11	↗15	↗ 7	N
Downward parachute	→	↗ 9	↗	↗ 9	↗
Standing	6↘	→	↗	↗	↗
Locomotion	→	→	↗	↗	↗
Foot grasp	6↘	→	→	N	N
Body in sagittal plane	→	↗ 11	↗17	↗ 9	N
Forward parachute	→	↗ 17	↗15	↗11	N
All-fours	6↘	6↘	→	↗17	N
STNR	→	↗ 15	↗15	N	N
Body denotative	→	↗ 9	↗ 7	↗ 7	N
Standing up from supine	11↘	15↘	→	→	↗
Body rotative	11↘	15	11↘	→	N
Tilting prone	→	↗ 9	→	↗ 9	↗
Tilting sitting	7↘	N	11↘	N	N

↗ = age (in months) when mean is 4 points or more
↘ = age (in months) when mean is less than 4 points
N = mean score 4 points or more

This table is not about the *Infanib;* it is about the Milani-Comparetti and Gidoni method of evaluation. However, some items appear in both methods. Furthermore, the items in *The Infanib* that best predict spasticity, according to the study of Stavrakas, are largely the overlapping items (Stavrakas et al. 1991).

Stavrakas studied 243 infants on two occasions, ages 6 and 12 months, with the *Infanib.* Her data (see tables 3.3 and 3.4) were used to obtain mean scores for factor and total scores at both ages for infants described as normal, transiently abnormal, and abnormal.

Table 3.3. Mean scores with standard deviations for the *Infanib* at age 6 months

Factors	I. Spasticity	II. Head and Trunk	III. Vestibular	IV. Legs	V. French Angles	Total
		(Data from Stavrakas et al.)				
Normal (*n* = 5)	18.6 ± 2.8	16.4 ± 0.8	7.2 ± 2.0	15.6 ± 2.7	17.6 ± 2.9	75.4 ± 1.5
Transiently Abnormal (*n* = 60)	18.1 ± 2.2	14.7 ± 3.2	4.5 ± 3.0	13.1 ± 2.8	14.4 ± 2.9	64.8 ± 5.2
Abnormal (*n* = 17)	12.8 ± 3.8	8.7 ± 2.5	3.9 ± 3.2	11.1 ± 3.8	10.0 ± 2.9	46.6 ± 6.0

Table 3.4. Mean scores with standard deviations for the *Infanib* at age 12 months

Factors	I. Spasticity	II. Head and Trunk	III. Vestibular	IV. Legs	V. French Angles	Total
		(Data from Stavrakas et al.)				
Normal (*n* = 47)	19.9 ± 0.7	19.4 ± 1.3	19.3 ± 1.5	18.7 ± 1.7	18.4 ± 2.6	95.7 ± 5.0
Transiently Abnormal (*n* = 15)	18.9 ± 2.3	14.3 ± 2.7	15.1 ± 2.6	14.7 ± 3.2	14.5 ± 3.5	77.4 ± 3.8
Abnormal (*n* = 20)	15.5 ± 4.3	9.8 ± 2.8	7.4 ± 4.1	10.5 ± 2.9	9.8 ± 4.6	52.9 ± 11.1

In this sample, 66.7 percent (*n* = 44) of the transiently abnormal infants had become normal by age 12 months; 11.8 percent (*n* = 2) of the abnormal infants became normal; 70.6 percent (*n* = 12) of the abnormal infants remained abnormal. Six infants who were transiently abnormal became abnormal, and two infants who were normal became abnormal. I have no clinical data about these infants and thus cannot relate this to clinical events such as the onset of or worsening of seizures.

In the predictive validity calculations of Stavrakas et al., Factor II, head and trunk, was the best predictor of cerebral palsy, and Factor I, spasticity, the next best. Factor III, vestibular, would not be expected to be predictive since only one item is scored at age six months.

At age six months, the scores of infants with abnormality separate well from those of transiently abnormal and normal infants with the exception of Factor IV, legs. Total scores distinguish well between the three groups—normal, transiently abnormal, and abnormal. In this sample there are few normal infants (*n* = 5) at six months, so we need to be careful about drawing conclusions about the distinctions between normal and transiently abnormal infants.

However, the numbers of infants in each group are more evenly distributed at age 12 months. The normal infants are clearly separated from the transiently abnormal. The standard deviations are reasonable except for Factor V, French angles, which has the largest standard deviations. The transiently abnormal infants are described by

Factors II–V and the total scores are well separated from those of normal infants. The abnormal infants are described by all the factors and the total scores.

Summary of Anticipated Change

These guidelines have changed little since I first described them (Ellison 1984):

1. Young hypotonic infants (0 to 3 months) may become spastic.

2. Older hypotonic infants (6 to 12 months) tend to become less hypotonic.

3. Monoparesis generally is not static:
   a. It usually disappears.
   b. It occasionally progresses to hemiplegia or diplegia but that also tends to be transient.

4. Infants with early spasticity tend to get worse, those with tetraplegia more so and those with diplegia less so.

5. Delayed head control, hypotonia of arms (scarf sign), and limited popliteal angle, as a configuration, are excellent early indicators of cerebral palsy.

6. Use of the reflex hammer is less reliable than evaluation of tone and posture in describing neuromotor abnormalities in infants.

7. Examination of flexibility at the knees is very helpful—the popliteal angle will identify both proximal and distal spasticity. Examination of flexibility at the hips is also helpful—the heel-to-ear angle will identify proximal spasticity. Early spasticity is usually proximal.

Early Neuromotor Abnormality as a Marker of Brain Injury

It should surprise few clinicians who examine infants serially that early neuromotor abnormality of a moderate to severe degree is associated with a significant increase in mental retardation in preschool and early school years. In most infancy follow-up programs, both developmental and neuromotor evaluations are done. In the sets of data we have examined the correlations are high between developmental and neuromotor evaluations in infancy. This means that infants who have neuromotor abnormalities tend to have evidence of cognitive deficit as well. Similarly infants who are normal in one tend to be normal in the other. Now these correlations are not $r = 1.0$, which would mean that these abnormalities are always found together. Indeed, few clinical items have correlations of 1.0. Thus the skillful examiner is always looking for the exceptions: abnormality in one area without abnormality in the other area. Two frequent exceptions are the following: (1) the cognitively normal, alert, hypotonic infant who has delay in acquisition of motor skills, and (2) the black infants who often have neuromotor precocity but who have delay in the acquisition of language skills. These exceptions probably do not reflect brain injury. We do not know the pathophysiology of the benign hypotonias of infancy in infants born at term. We have no evidence that language delay in black infants results from brain injury—rather it is probably cultural. The low-birth-weight prematurely born infants have been carefully excluded from these exceptions—because the hypotonia so common in prematurely born infants, often associated with a little spasticity in the legs, and persisting to at least 6 and perhaps to as much as 15 months, corrected gestational age, is a marker of brain injury.

The later markers for brain injury are delay in language acquisition and delay in acquisition of visual-motor skills as evaluated through "draw a design," "draw a child," and tasks such as the grooved pegboard and the maze. Obviously, these latter skills cannot be tested until preschool years.

The data from the large National Collaborative Perinatal Project give information about this process of "outgrowing" brain injury (Nelson and Ellenberg 1982). Surely it is just as logical to speak of "healing" the brain as of "outgrowing" evidence of brain injury. At age one year, the children were classified in three categories: normal, suspect cerebral palsy, and cerebral palsy. Mental retardation at seven years occurred in 22.3 percent of the children who had cerebral palsy at one year but who outgrew it, 11.3 percent in the group with suspect but outgrown cerebral palsy, and 3.2 percent in the normal group (similar to the frequency usually given for mental retardation in the general population). Hyperactivity at age seven years was 19.1 percent in the definite cerebral palsy at one year but outgrown, 19.6 percent in the suspect cerebral palsy at age one year but outgrown, and 12.1 percent in the normal group. Immature behavior was 21.4 percent in the cerebral palsy at one year and outgrown group, 17.0 percent in the suspect cerebral palsy and outgrown group, and 12 percent in the normal group. Speech articulation defects and myopias were also higher in frequency in the group with cerebral palsy at one year, outgrown by age seven years.

Drillien et al. studied 261 school age children who were low birth weight babies (Drillien et al. 1980). She compared those who had transient neurologic abnormalities of infancy with those who were normal in neuromotor evaluations in infancy. The group with transient neuromotor abnormalities was significantly lower in a wide range of evaluations, including intelligence testing, reading and spelling achievement, speech, and motor tasks.

In our studies in southeastern Wisconsin, approximately 50 percent of the children cared for in the neonatal intensive care units for five days or more in 1975-76 were evaluated at age four years. About 85 percent of the children evaluated at age four years were evaluated at age six-seven years. This sample included both premature and full-term births. Table 3.5 shows the scores from testing with the *McCarthy Scale of Children's Abilities* at ages four and ages six-seven years in relation to the infancy neurologic evaluations with the Milani-Comparetti and Gidoni method, with the evaluations categorized as abnormal, transiently abnormal, and normal (Ellison et al. 1985). These sample sizes are small when broken into these categories, results that are typical of most longitudinal work. Fortunately, the abnormal outcomes tend to be low in frequency. However, we need to be cautious in drawing conclusions from low frequency outcomes, especially when the attrition is large (as it is in most longitudinal studies in this country). At age four years the frequency of mental retardation was 41.7 percent for children who had an abnormal neuromotor evaluation in infancy; the frequencies for motor index scores more than two standard deviations below the mean is similar (50 percent). The children who were transiently abnormal in infancy had a modest increased frequency in mental retardation (5.7 percent) but a fairly large frequency in motor index scores (17.1 percent), more than two standard deviations below the mean. In addition, the children with transient abnormalities in infancy had a very large percentage of children (40 percent) who scored one to two standard deviations below the mean on the motor index. At six-seven years, those children who returned for evaluation and had had neurological abnormalities in infancy had a frequency of 25 percent mental retardation and 37.5 percent with scores more than two standard deviations below the mean on the motor index. Those children who were transiently abnormal in infancy showed a modestly larger frequency in mental retardation than those who were normal in infancy. However, they continued to show higher frequencies of scores below the mean on the motor index than children who were neurologically normal in infancy. The frequencies of scores below the mean decreased from age four to ages six-seven years for the children who were transiently abnormal in infancy.

Table 3.5. General Cognitive Index and Motor Subtests (McCarthy) for children with normal, transiently abnormal, and abnormal infancy MCG scores

	MCG infancy score		
	Abnormal	**Transiently abnormal**	**Normal**
All 4-year children			
General Cognitive Index			
Retarded (>2 S.D.)	41.7% (5)	5.7% (2)	2.9% (6)
Dull normal (1-2 S.D.)	8.3% (1)	11.4% (4)	5.9% (12)
Normal	50.0% (6)	82.8% (29)	91.0% (90)
Motor Index			
(>2 S.D.)	50.0% (6)	17.1% (6)	4.0% (8)
(1-2 S.D.)	16.7% (2)	40.0% (14)	24.5% (38)
Normal	33.3% (4)	42.9% (15)	70.3% (62)
4-year children seen at 6-7 years			
General Cognitive Index			
Retarded (>2 S.D.)	25.0% (2)	7.1% (2)	4.6% (5)
Dull normal (1-2 S.D.)	0.0% (0)	3.6% (1)	6.5% (7)
Normal	75.0% (6)	89.2% (2)	88.9% (96)
Motor Index			
(>2 S.D.)	25.0% (2)	14.2% (4)	4.6% (5)
(1-2 S.D.)	25.0% (2)	42.9% (12)	27.8% (30)
Normal	50.0% (4)	42.9% (12)	67.6% (73)
6-7 year children			
General Cognitive Index			
Retarded (>2 S.D.)	25.0% (2)	7.1% (2)	5.5% (6)
Dull normal (1-2 S.D.)	25.0% (2)	10.7% (3)	16.7% (18)
Normal	50.0% (4)	80.0% (23)	77.8% (84)
Motor Index			
(>2 S.D.)	37.5% (3)	10.7% (3)	4.6% (5)
(1-2 S.D.)	25.0% (2)	25.0% (7)	14.8% (16)
Normal	37.5% (3)	63.3% (18)	80.6% (87)

All S.D. are below mean

The children were also given scores at age six-seven on the *Achenbach Child Behavior Checklist,* in which parents were asked to describe the behavior (Ellison et al. 1985). For boys, there was an excess of scores in the categories over two standard deviations below the mean and one to two standard deviations below the mean. The children who had an abnormal neuromotor evaluation in infancy had the highest percent of abnormal scores (33.3 percent). Both abnormal and transiently abnormal groups had very high frequencies for less deviant but still abnormal behavior (50 percent and 49.9 percent respectively). They were considered by their parents to be behavior problems at home and at school.

Table 3.6. Boys' Scores from the Achenbach Hyperactivity Scale for three ranges of infancy MCG scores

Achenbach hyperactivity	MCG infancy score		
	Abnormal	Transiently abnormal	Normal
>2 S.D. above mean	33.3% (2)	9.1% (2)	9.1% (5)
1-2 S.D. above mean	50.0% (3)	49.9% (9)	25.0% (14)
Normal	16.7% (11)	50.0% (11)	67.9% (37)
Product moment correlation: $r = .28$, $p = .01$			

Yet another way to relate the infancy neuromotor examination to the six- to seven-year-old evaluations is to list the frequencies of a number of problems in the early school years. Children with abnormal neuromotor evaluations in infancy had a high frequency of three or more problems (50 percent). Children with transiently abnormal evaluations had three or more problems with a frequency of 42.6 percent. Children who were normal neurologically in infancy had a frequency of 11.1 percent for three or more problems. The school problems were cognitive, motor, hyperactivity, and other behavior and learning disabilities. In this sample, the interventions prior to kindergarten were much higher for the children with abnormal neuromotor evaluations in infancy than for the children with transiently abnormal evaluations in infancy (92 percent versus 16 percent respectively).

Table 3.7. Number of problems at 6-7 years and abnormal and transiently abnormal MCG scores in infancy.

MCG score in infancy		0	1	2	3	4	5
Abnormal	n	2	2	0	1	2	1
	%	25.0	25.0	0.0	12.5	25.0	12.5
Transiently abnormal	n	6	7	3	9	2	1
	%	21.4	25.0	10.7	32.0	7.0	3.6
Normal	n	41	33	21	7	5	1
	%	38.0	30.6	19.4	6.5	4.6	0.0

It will take more research to pinpoint more precisely which of the children with transiently abnormal neuromotor evaluations in infancy are most at risk for problems in the early school years. Furthermore, it is important to emphasize that the majority of these children function normally in the school setting. We have neither the resources nor the knowledge at this time to develop special programs for all of these children.

Some Typical Infants

The largest group of infants with neuromotor abnormality comes from those who were prematurely born. And generally, the smaller the infant at birth, the more likely the infant is to have neurological abnormalities. In infancy the most frequent abnormalities involve tone and posture, except for the lowest birthweight children (those with birth weights less than 750-850 grams). Delay in mental development is, in general, more frequent in this group. At school age, the more frequent abnormalities are in the area of cognitive dysfunction, generally described as "learning disabilities," and in behavior.

Obviously, some major changes occur across the years. When does the infant begin to make these transitions? Major decreases in abnormalities of tone and posture can occur throughout infancy.

Transient Neurologic Abnormality of Infancy

1. Kate

An excellent example is Kate, a very low birthweight prematurely born child, with respiratory distress syndrome, prolonged use of the ventilator, and bronchopulmonary dysplasia (or chronic lung disease of prematurity). She was finally discharged from the hospital with her trusty oxygen tank and tubing that trailed her everywhere. She was skinny; she turned blue easily with feeding or crying and later with motor activities. She became ill frequently—and the inevitable viruses settled in her lungs. The doctors pronounced repeatedly that "she probably would not survive long." Nevertheless Kate hung in there, as did her foster mother, who persisted in providing therapy and in positioning her well for environmental stimulation, eye-hand use, then trunk and, finally, leg use.

Kate was initially very hypotonic, with very poor head and neck control, excessive scarf sign for age, and poor trunk control. Please note that Kate is at the upper limit of the age range for each quarter in these photographs.

0-3 Months Corrected Gestational Age

Kate's poor head control and head, neck, and trapezius muscle hypotonia are shown well on the pull-to-sit maneuver (figure 4.1).

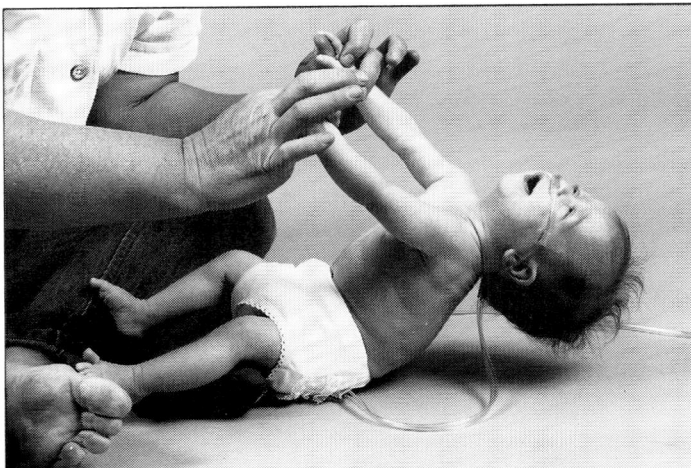

Figure 4.1. Kate performing pull-to-sit, 0-3 months.

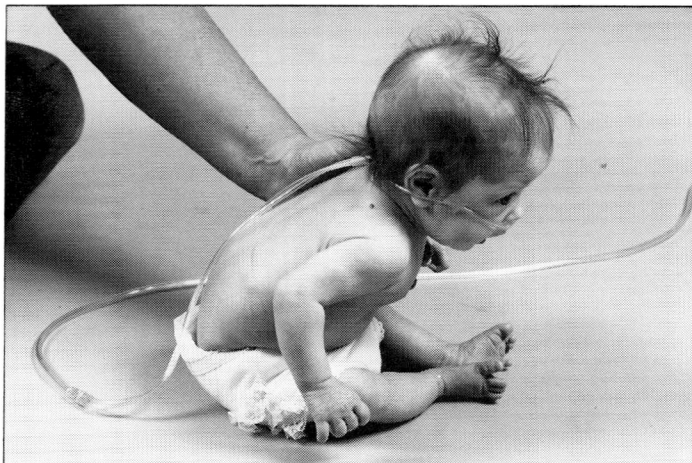

Figure 4.2. Kate placed in a sitting position, age 0-3 months.

Kate's buttocks slide readily along the surface on this maneuver. Thus it was easier to place an object below her buttocks in order to assess pull-to-sit. When placed in sitting position, she bent forward at several lower thoracic vertebrae as well as at L3 (figure 4.2). Without the support of the examiner she would simply slump forward or fall sideways. Nevertheless, Kate could be positioned in a sitting position so that she could observe the happenings around her, and she could grasp objects close at hand. Here she is placed in the corner of an old-fashioned sofa that permits her buttocks to sink into the cushions a bit (figure 4.3). Her head is positioned with a roll made from a washcloth; her buttocks are well-positioned with a roll made from a towel. Her shoulders are positioned somewhat forward, placing her arms and hands in a position that facilitates her use of them. She even breathes fairly easily.

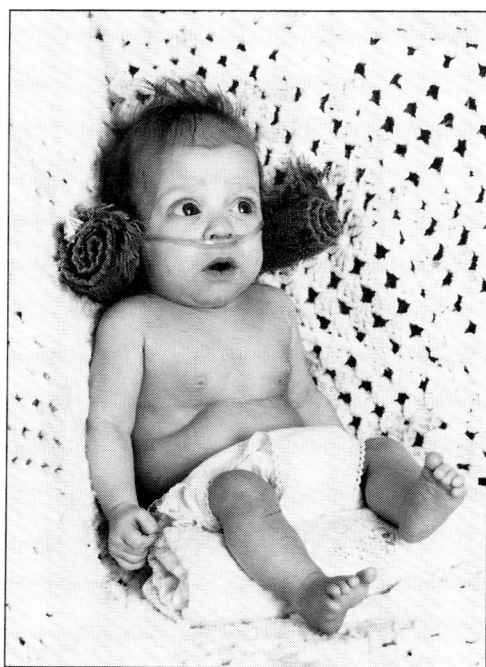

Figure 4.3. Kate positioned with good support, age 0-3 months.

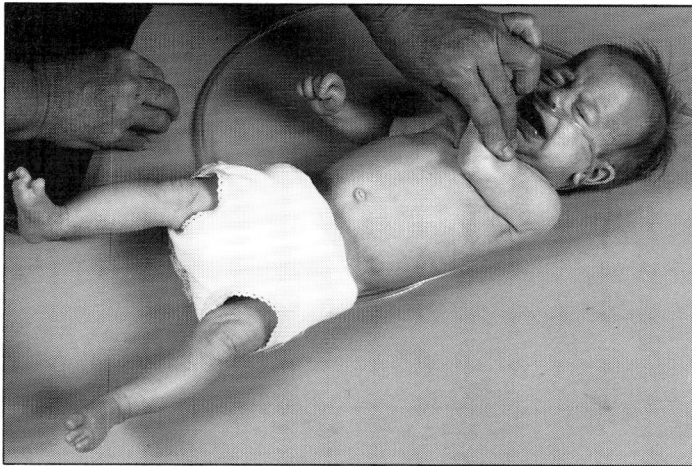

Figure 4.4a. Kate with the scarf sign maneuver, age 0-3 months.

The French angles provide additional information. The scarf sign maneuver (figure 4.4a) demonstrates the hypotonia of the upper arms and trapezius muscles, which one would expect to find after Kate's abnormal pull-to-sit maneuver. The equivalents of the truncal and upper body hypotonia are not found in the hips and knees (figures 4.4a through 4.4d). These are scored as normal for age. However, the examiner should be aware that this tone discrepancy is likely to be more obvious on subsequent examinations with increasing tone (spasticity) in hips and knees.

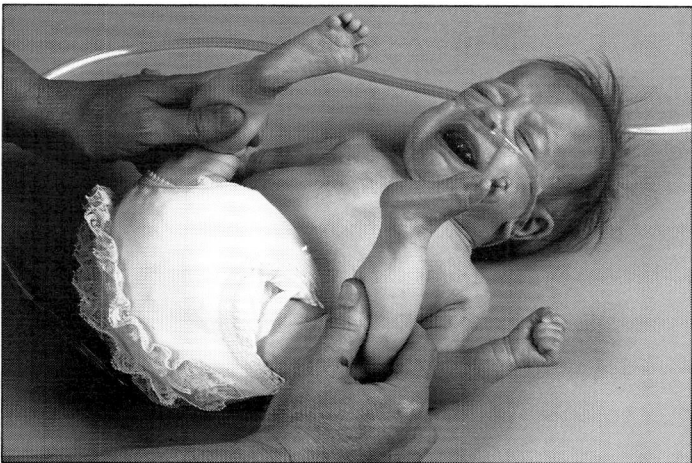

Figure 4.4b. Kate, age 0-3 months, shows normal knee response.

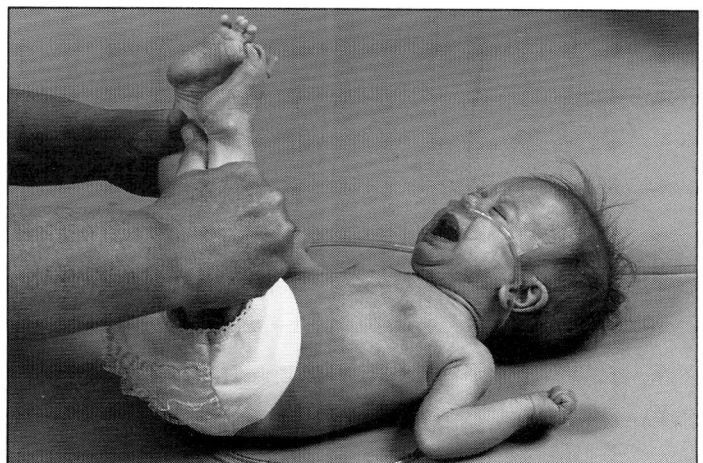

Figure 4.4c. Kate shows normal hip response.

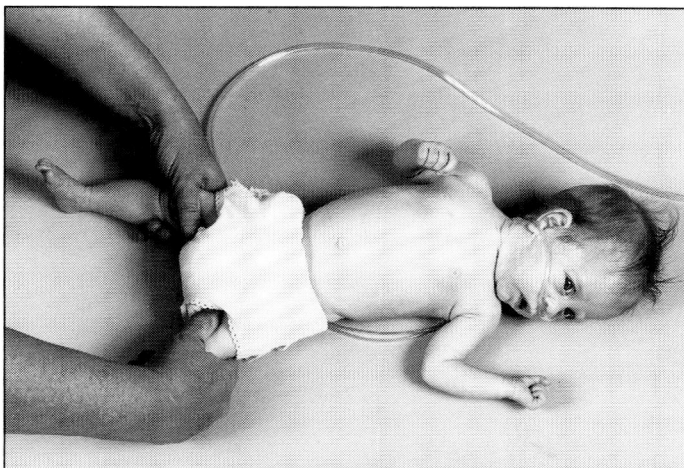

Figure 4.4d. The equivalents of truncal and upper body hypotonia are not found in Kate's hips, age 0-3 months.

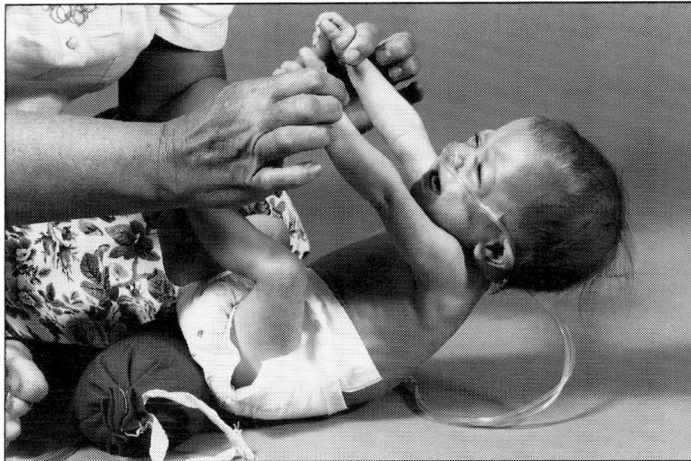

Figure 4.5a. Kate, age 4-6 months, can lift her head and perform pull-to-sit, but her arms remain extended.

4-6 Months Corrected Gestational Age

In the next quarter of infancy, Kate made some improvement in head and neck control. She can lift her head or perform pull-to-sit, but her arms remained extended (figure 4.5a). This is scored for the head position in *The Infanib*. However, she remains very hypotonic in a sitting position (figure 4.5b). Again she would slump forward if not held by the examiner. The bending of the spine is less thoracic and more lumbar.

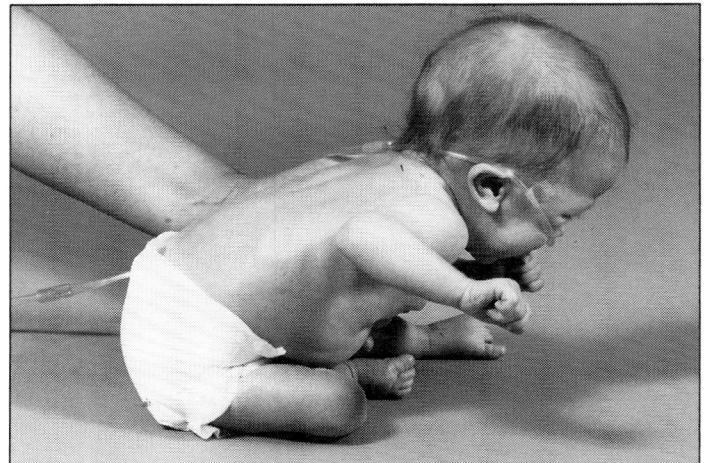

Figure 4.5b. Kate shows signs of hypotonia in a sitting position, age 4-6

The French angles show some increase in excursion on the scarf sign, again in keeping with the extended arms on pull-to-sit. The hips and knees have changed little in three months (figure 4.6). In short, Kate has some mild spasticity in her legs.

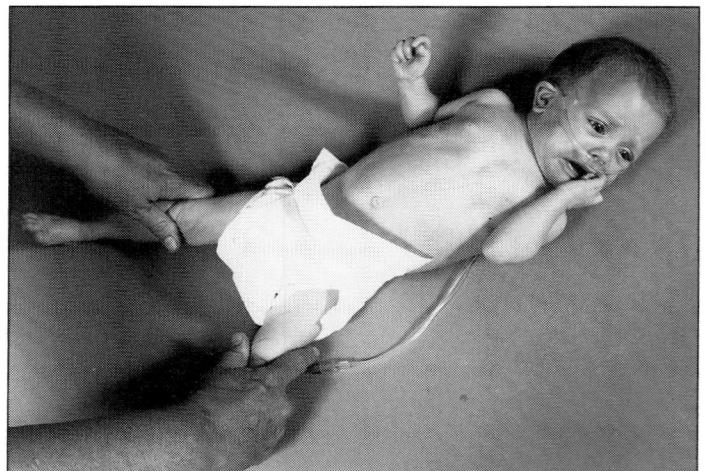

Figure 4.6. Kate, at age 0-3 months, exhibits mild spasticity in her legs.

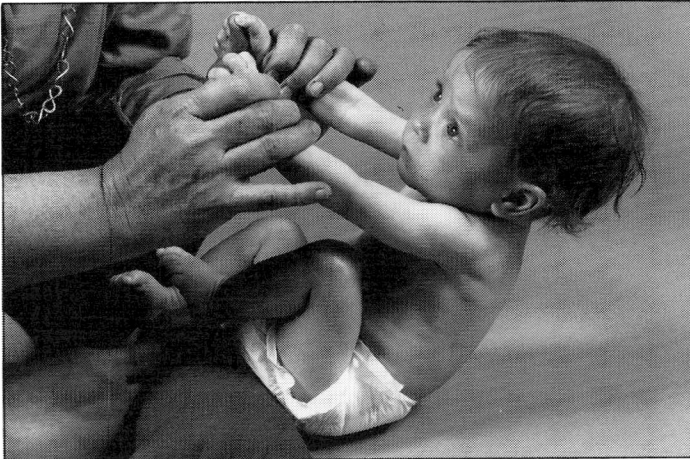

Figure 4.7a. At age 7-9 months, Kate has improved significantly in the pull-to-sit maneuver.

7-9 Months Corrected Gestational Age

Kate now does well on pull-to-sit in terms of head control, but she still provides no assistance with her arms (figure 4.7a). Her trunk control remains minimal, although she is better able to use her arms for support (figure 4.7b). She is also delayed in the acquisition of sideways parachute (figure 4.7c).

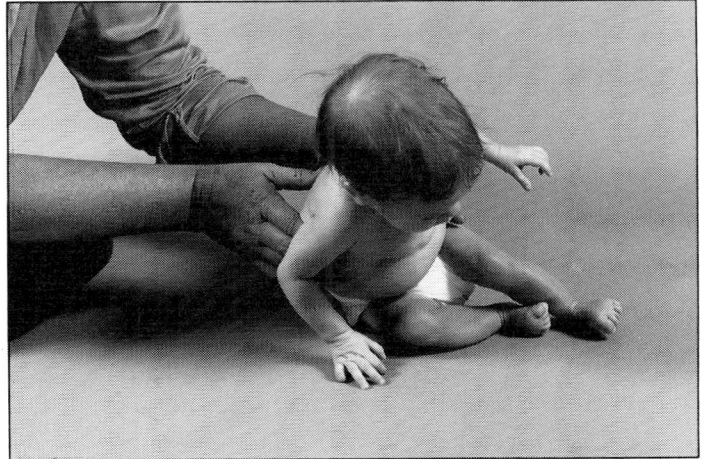

Figure 4.7c. Kate, at age 7-9 months, is delayed in acquiring the sideways parachute.

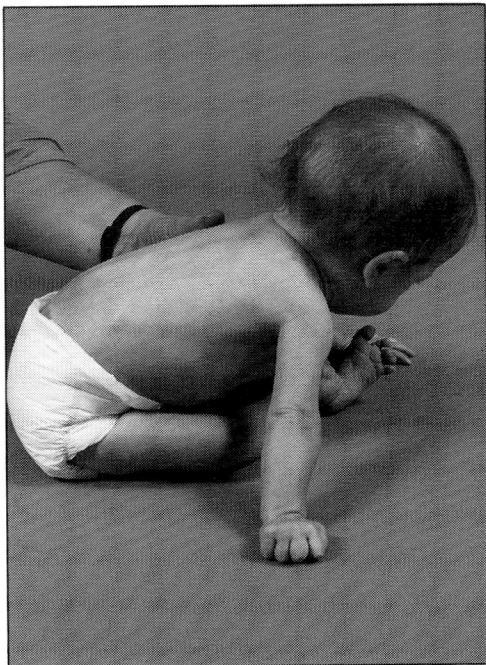

Figure 4.7b. Kate shows poor trunk control at age 7-9 months.

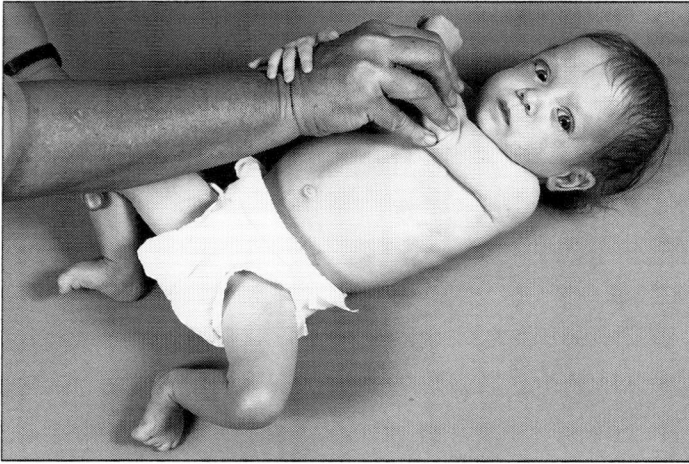
Figure 4.8a. Kate at age 7-9 months, performing the scarf sign.

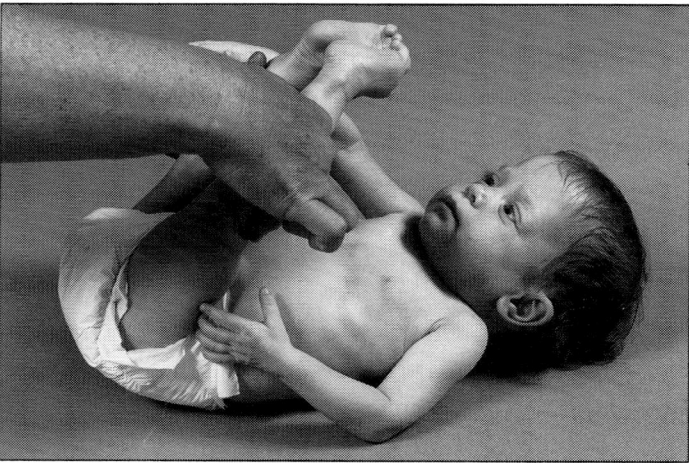
Figure 4.8b. Kate performs heel-to-ear at age 7-9 months.

Kate's French angles, however, show some improvement in the hips and knees. She is finally beginning to loosen up (figures 4.8a-4.8d).

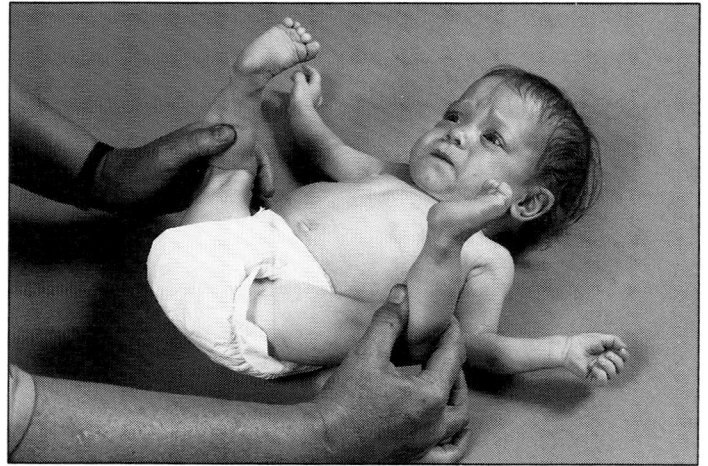
Figure 4.8c. The popliteal angle at age 7-9 months.

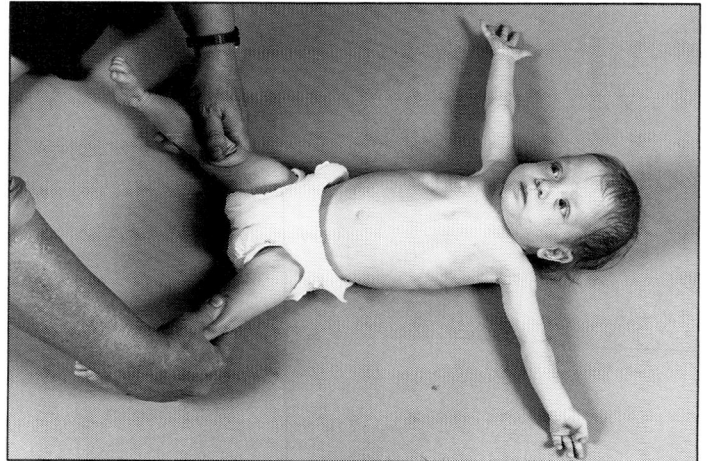
Figure 4.8d. Leg abduction—Kate at age 7-9 months.

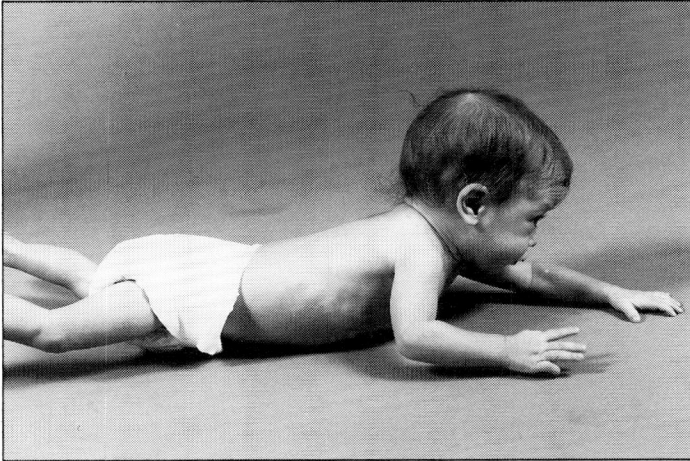

Figure 4.9a. Kate in an all-fours position at 7-9 months.

The improvements in examination of her hips and knees with the French angles are not reflected as well in Kate's use of her legs. When placed in all-fours position, she keeps her abdomen on the floor and extends her legs (figure 4.9a). Any forward movement is achieved largely with the use of arms. In standing position, she again extends her legs, but cannot support herself well, nor can she straighten her trunk (figure 4.9b). Obviously Kate has not yet pulled to stand.

Figure 4.9b. Kate in a standing position, age 7-9 months.

10-12 Months Corrected Gestational Age

Kate has finally mastered a sitting position (figure 4.10a). She is very uncomfortable on backwards parachute (figure 4.10b), however; her sideways parachute is present. The French angles show increasing flexibility of hips and knees.

Kate has now acquired a crawl with alternating use of her legs and flexion of the knees. But she still keeps her abdomen on or close to the floor (figure 4.10c). In standing position, she looks little different than she did three months ago. Kate learned to walk at 17 months corrected gestational age. She is shown at three years of age when she is still receiving physical and occupational therapies largely administered by her foster mother (figure 4.10d). She is an old hand at the large physical therapy ball. Here she munches cold cereal casually. Her vestibular system functions well; she is equally at home in many other positions on the ball. She runs and plays freely, limited only by her oxygen requirements.

Kate is an excellent example of a prematurely born child with transient neurologic abnormalities of infancy. She is at risk for problems in the early school years. She clearly does not have cerebral palsy, nor is she mentally retarded. She does well in language skills. The risk is that of learning disabilities.

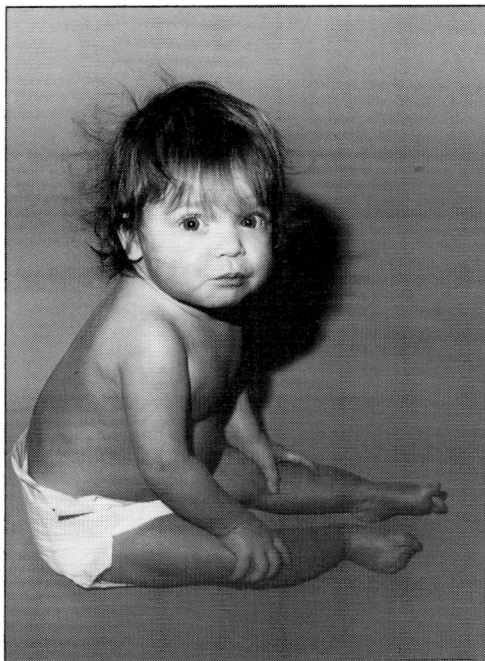

Figure 4.10a. Kate, at age 10-12 months, sits comfortably.

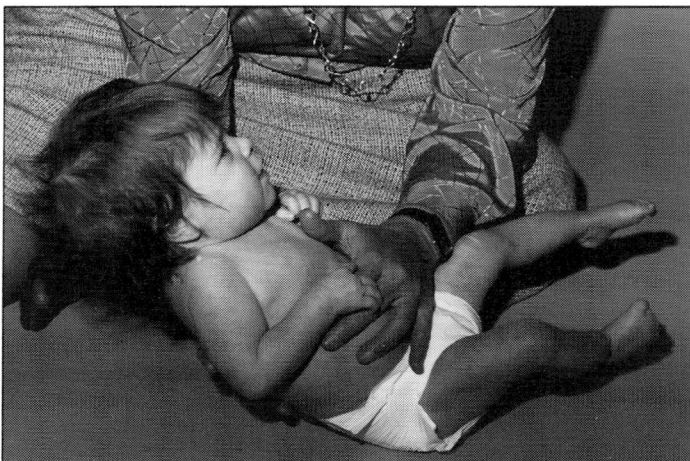

Figure 4.10b. Kate is still uncomfortable performing the backwards parachute, age 10-12 months.

Figure 4.10c. Kate crawling, age 10-12 months.

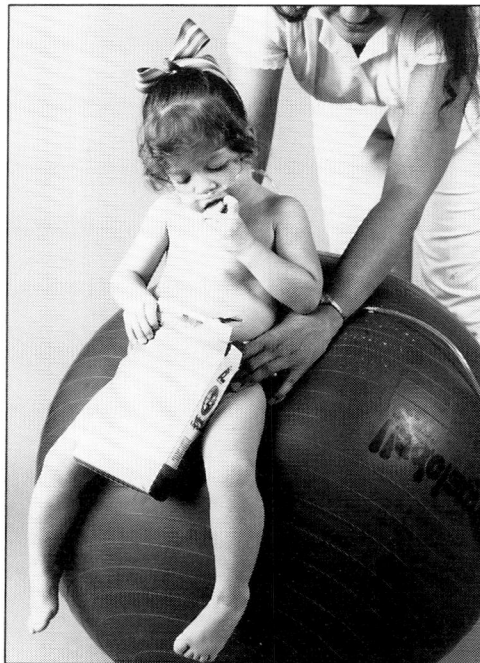

Figure 4.10d. Kate at 3 years old.

Another Example of Transient Neurologic Abnormality of Infancy

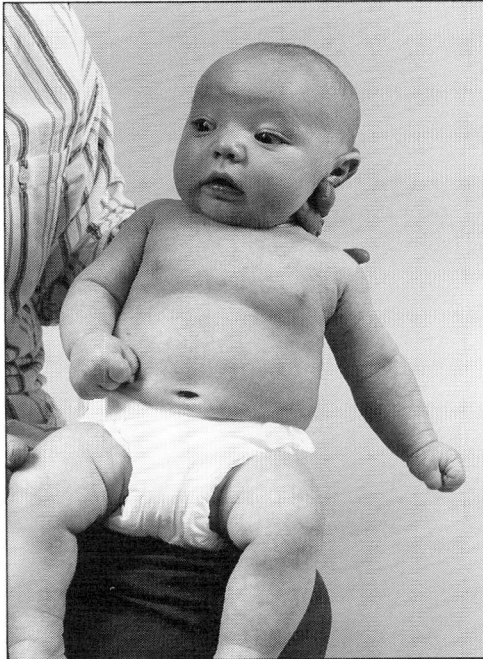

Figure 4.11a. Andrew during his first evaluation.

2. Andrew

Andrew was presumably delivered at home and found wrapped in a plastic bag in the garbage. After he was discovered, he was attended by paramedics and immediately taken to a nearby neonatal intensive care unit. He was judged to be full term. His course there was complicated by neonatal seizures. Thus he experienced neonatal hypoxia and ischemia and had some markers: neonatal seizures during the hospitalization and abnormal tone and posture in the months after discharge.

0-3 Months

Andrew was remarkable when first evaluated for his dull affect and his increase in extensor tone. Figure 4.11a shows a dull appearance but cannot capture his failure to look at the examiner. It was very difficult to capture and maintain Andrew's attention. He held his hands closed and clenched them with stimulation, especially with maneuvers that increased the extensor tone. He had an exaggerated and persistent asymmetric tonic neck reflex (figure 4.11b), an exaggerated tonic labyrinthine supine (figure 4.11c), and an exaggerated tonic labyrinthine prone (figure 4.11d).

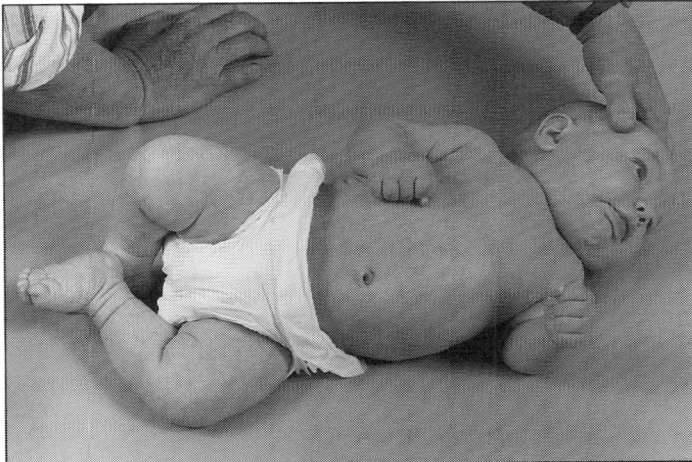

Figure 4.11b. Andrew with exaggerated asymmetric tonic neck reflex.

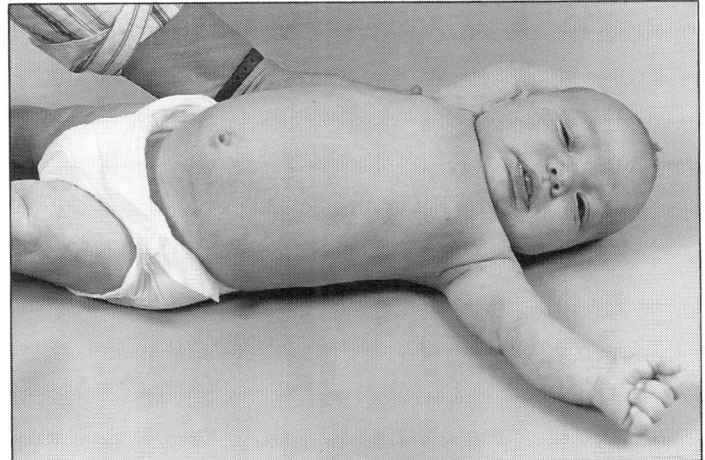

Figure 4.11c. Andrew exhibits exaggerated tonic labyrinthine supine characteristics during his first evaluation.

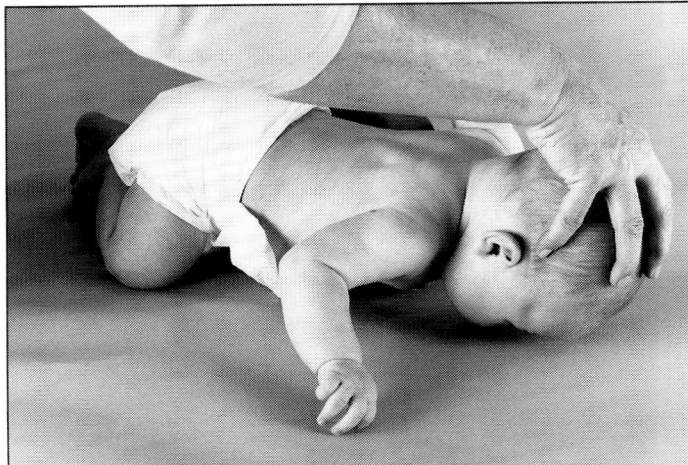

Figure 4.11d. Exaggerated tonic labyrinthine prone: Andrew at first evaluation.

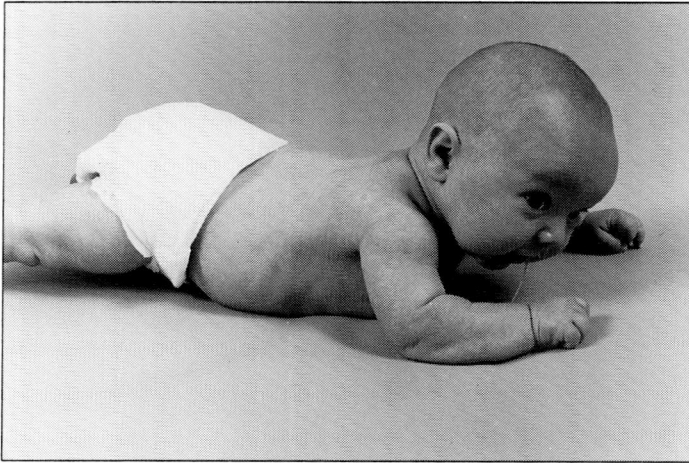

Figure 4.12a. Andrew in all-fours position.

Andrew's French angles were not abnormal because they are not expected to be flexible at this early time. The French angles are less useful for identifying spasticity at this age, whereas they show hypotonia very well. Two other items were also judged normal: all-fours (figure 4.12a) and pull-to-sit (fgure 4.12b).

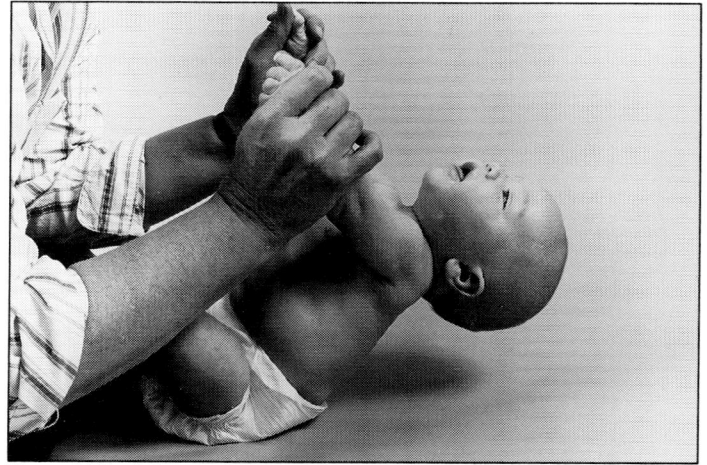

Figure 4.12b. Pull-to-sit: Andrew at first evaluation.

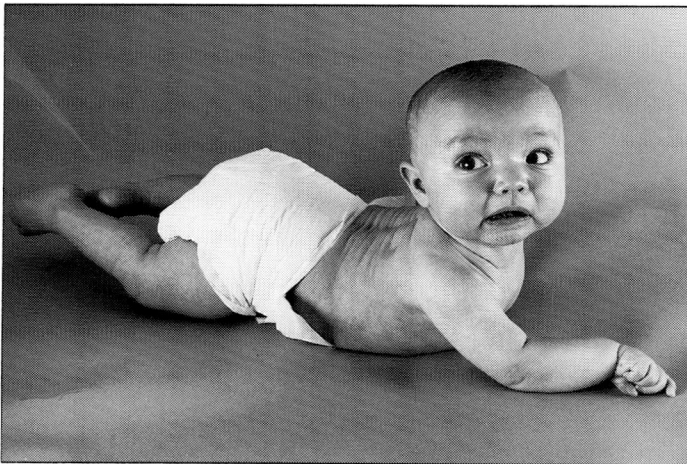

Figure 4.12c. Andrew exhibits extensor positioning of head and neck in the all-fours posture.

When next evaluated, Andrew's initially "good" head control had become "too good." In short, he had extensor positioning of head and neck. Whether placed on all fours (figure 4.12c), pull-to-sit (figure 4.12d), or placed in sitting position, he held his head, neck, and back in an arched position. This is not an example of precocious development; it is an example of excessive extension.

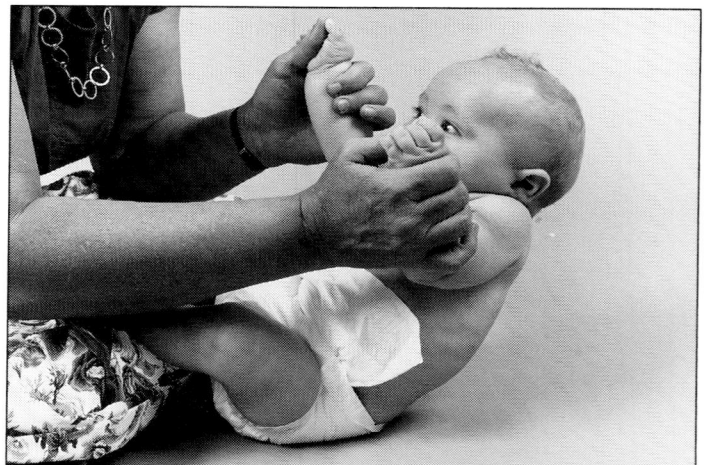

Figure 4.12d. Note Andrew's head and neck posture in the pull-to-sit maneuver.

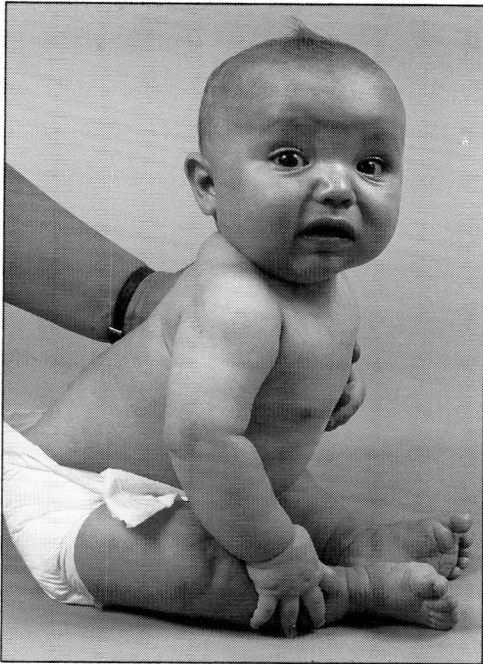

Figure 4.13a. Sitting with head extended, age 4-6 months.

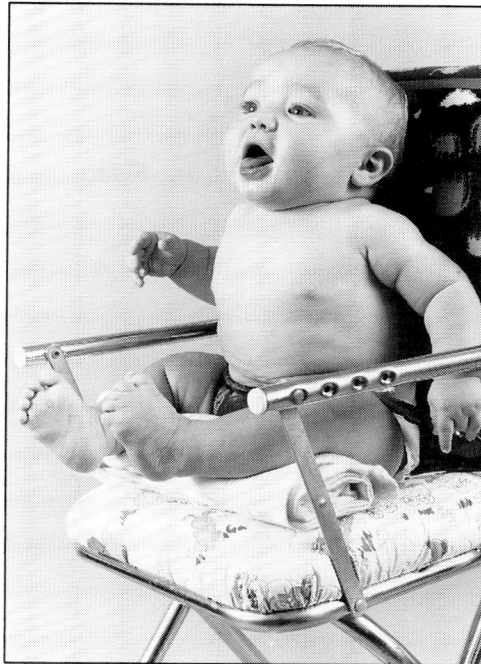

Figure 4.13b. Extension increased when Andrew was excited, age 4-6 months.

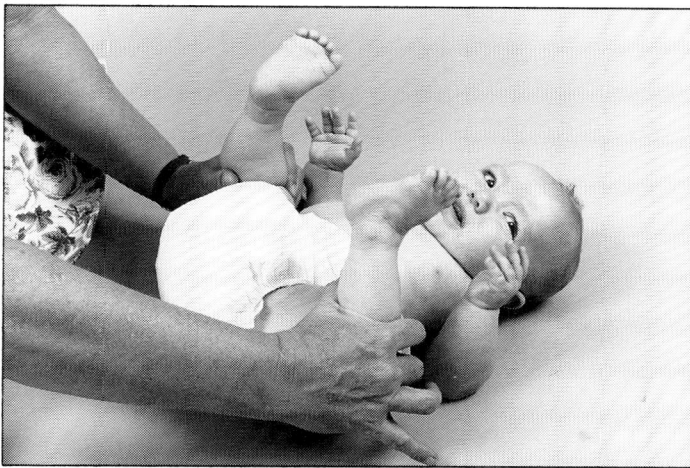

Figure 4.13c. Note the tightness of Andrew's popliteal angle at age 4-6 months.

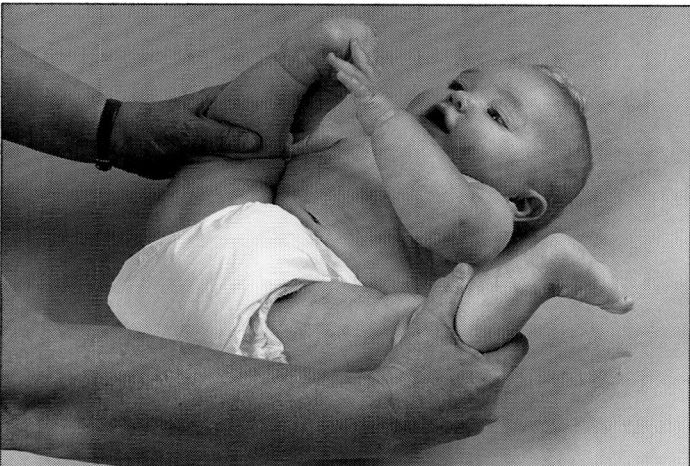

Figure 4.13d. Andrew's popliteal angle has improved significantly near the end of the 4-6-month quarter.

4-6 Months

In this quarter, Andrew improved neurologically. He still "helped" in pull-to-sit and he still sat too well for age, but less so (figure 4.13a). This became more obvious when he was excited (figure 4.13b). He was much more attentive to the examiner. His hands were open most of the time. In earlier evaluation, his popliteal angle was too tight (figure 4.13c), but by the end of the quarter, the popliteal angle (figure 4.13d) and heel-to-ear were more flexible.

His standing position was not normal (figure 4.13e); he refused to bear weight well. However, this is probably better than the extension of legs and early "too good" standing of spasticity.

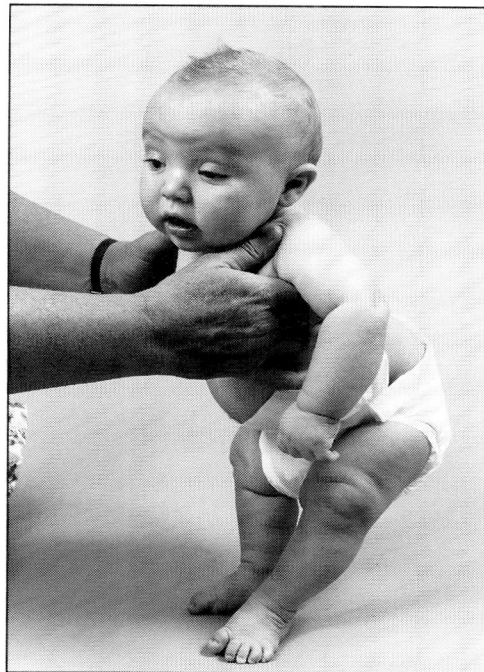

Figure 4.13e. Andrew still does not bear weight well in the standing position.

67

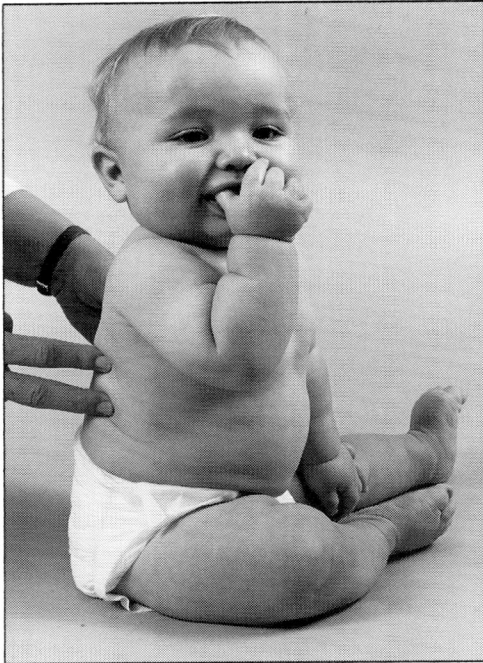

Figure 4.14a. While Andrew sits comfortably at 7-9 months, he has a tendency to push backwards.

7-9 Months

Andrew now sits comfortably, but he has a tendency to push backwards (figure 4.14a). He stands well with support (figure 4.14b). He is able to maintain an all-fours position with his abdomen off the floor (figure 4.14c). He has not yet developed a forward parachute (figure 4.14d).

Figure 4.14c. Andrew's abdomen remains off the floor in the all-fours position.

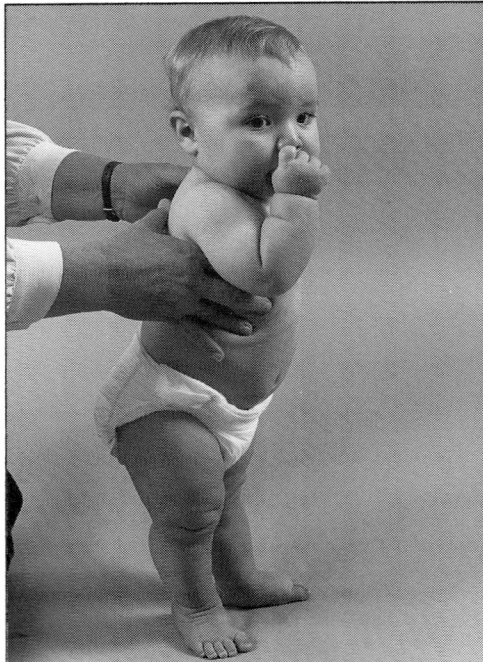

Figure 4.14d. Andrew has not acquired a forward parachute.

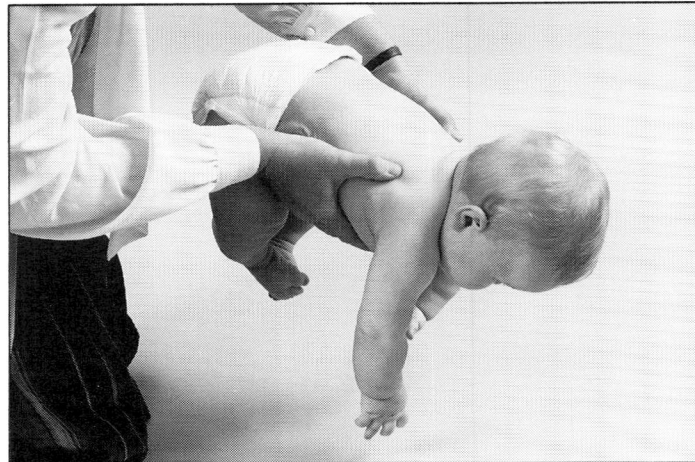

Figure 4.14b. Andrew stands well with support.

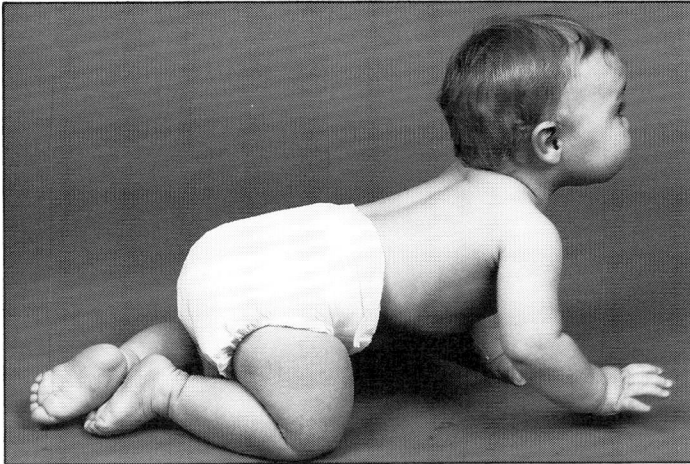
Figure 4.15a. By age 10-12 months, Andrew was an accomplished crawler.

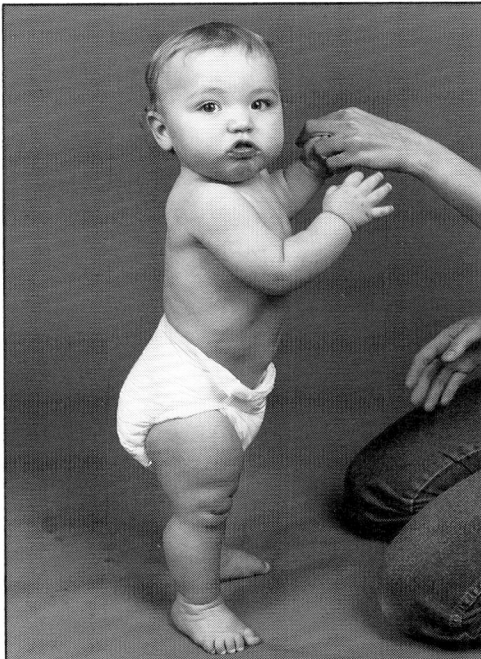
Figure 4.15b. Andrew needed little support to stand at age 10-12 months.

10-12 Months

When Andrew was next evaluated, he was an accomplished crawler (figure 4.15a). He needed just a little support for standing (figure 4.15b).

He had good forward parachute (figure 4.15c). His body rotative was like log-rolling; he moved his trunk as a unit. However, at age 13 months, after we had completed evaluations of his first year, Andrew walked (figure 4.15d).

Figure 4.15c. Andrew has developed a good forward parachute at age 10-12 months.

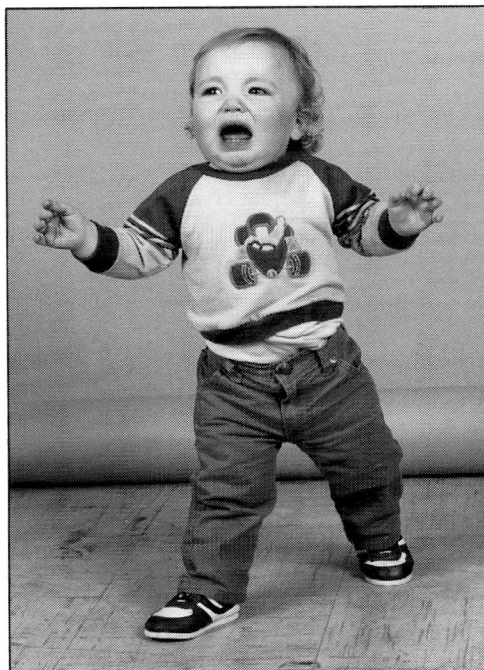
Figure 4.15d. At 13 months, Andrew walked.

An Example of Marked Abnormalities

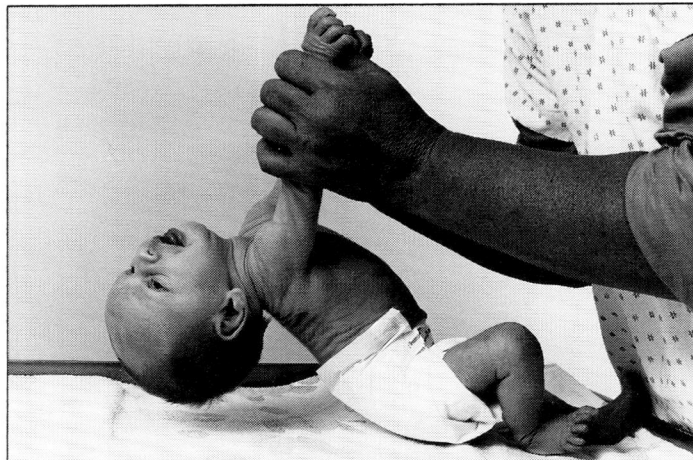

Figure 4.16a. Jeremy's pull-to-sit during his initial neonatal examination reveals a remarkable degree of hypotonia.

Figure 4.16b. Even with ventral support, the degree of hypotonia is extreme.

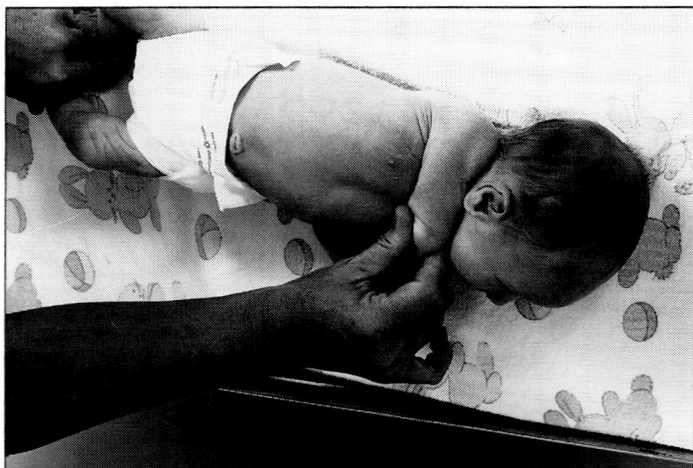

Figure 4.16c. Jeremy's scarf sign during the initial neonatal examination.

3. Jeremy

Jeremy had neonatal kernicterus with levels of total bilirubin above 30 mg/dl more than one occasion. He was treated with multiple exchange transfusions and phototherapy. He had neonatal seizures. On his neonatal neurologic examination he had moderate to severe hypotonia and downward-gazing eyes.

0-3 Months

Jeremy is the only child for whom we have photographs from the neonatal period. His initial examination was remarkable for the degree of hypotonia noted, shown well on pull-to-sit (figure 4.16a). With this amount of head lag, it is easier to support the infant at the shoulders (the head still lagged). The degree of his hypotonia is also remarkable with ventral support (figure 4.16b).

The French angles also showed hypotonia: in the scarf sign, his arm can be "wrapped" around his neck (figure 4.16c). His toes approach his nose on the heel-to-ear maneuver (figure 4.16d).

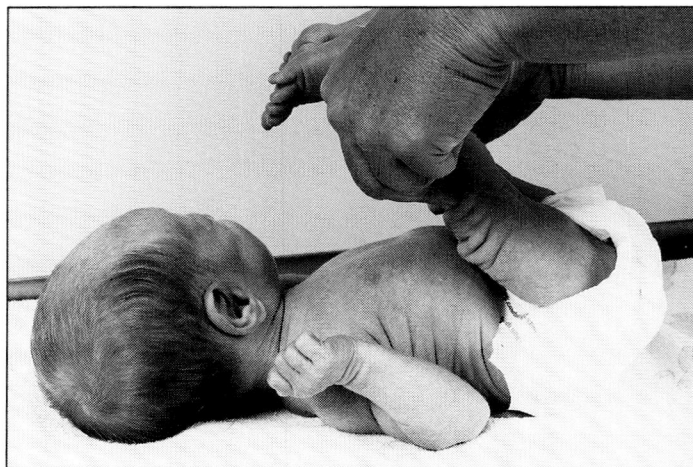

Figure 4.16d. The heel-to-ear maneuver during initial neonatal examination.

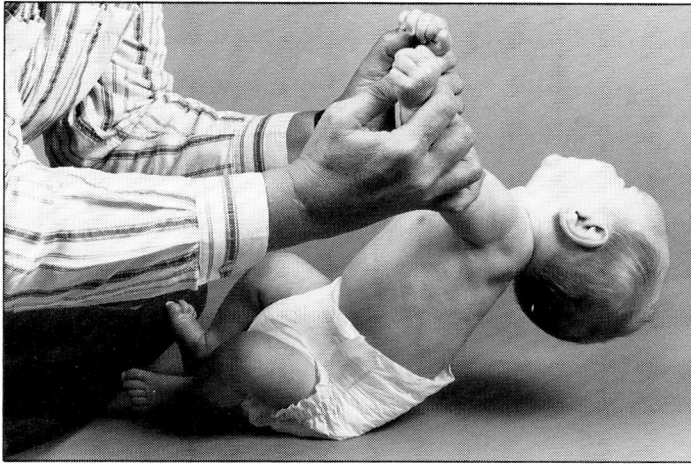

Figure 4.17a. Jeremy in pull-to-sit during a follow-up examination several weeks after delivery.

However, the primitive reflexes asymmetric tonic neck reflex, tonic labyrinthine prone, and tonic labyrinthine supine were present but not exaggerated.

When re-evaluated several weeks later, Jeremy continued to have poor head control. Now he clenched his fists with this maneuver although his hands were open at other times (figure 4.17a).

The French angles showed change. His scarf sign was still hypotonic but his arm did not "wrap" around his neck as easily as before (figure 4.17b).

But his heel-to-ear maneuver had decreased flexibility (figure 4.17c). Thus it identified his early proximal spasticity in the hips. The primitive reflexes now showed prompt, prolonged, and exaggerated responses (see figures 4.17d and 4.17e).

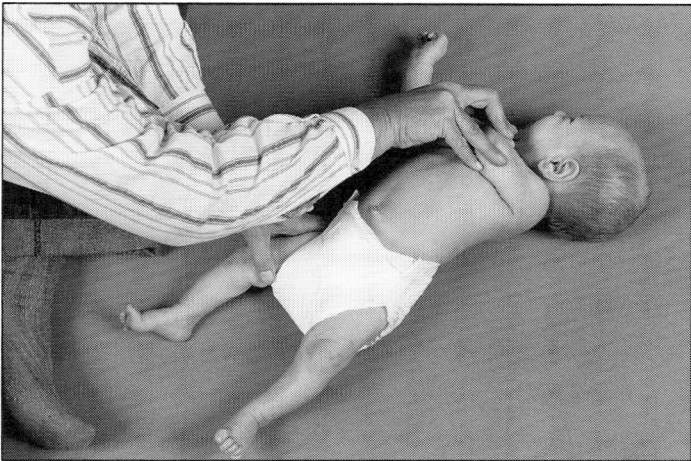

Figure 4.17b. Jeremy's scarf sign, while still hypotonic, does not wrap so readily around his neck.

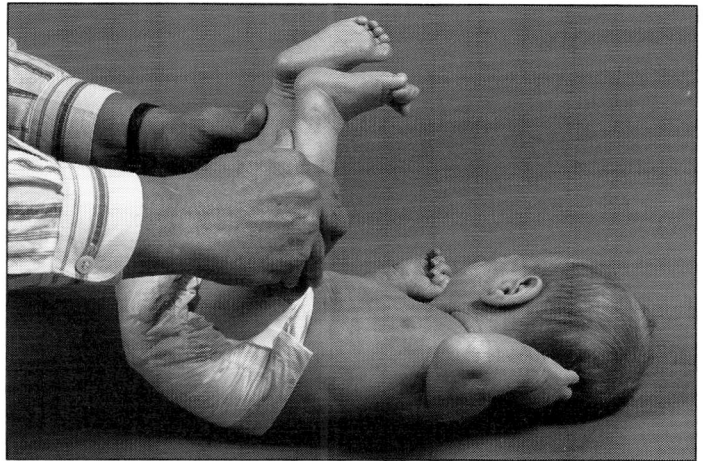

Figure 4.17c. The heel-to-ear maneuver reveals lessened flexibility.

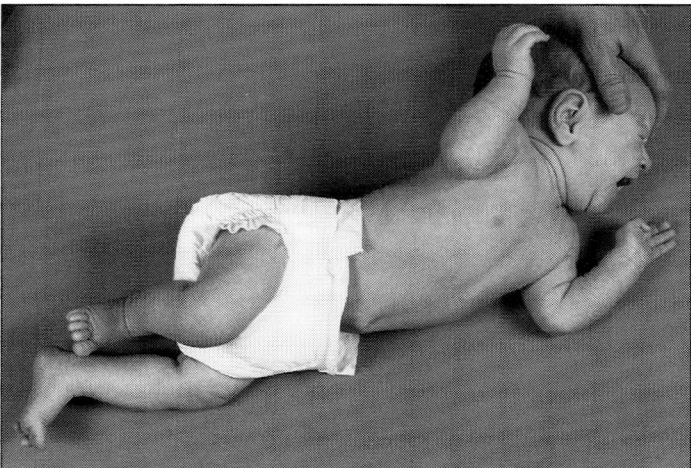

Figure 4.17d. Asymmetric tonic neck reflex in Jeremy's follow-up exam.

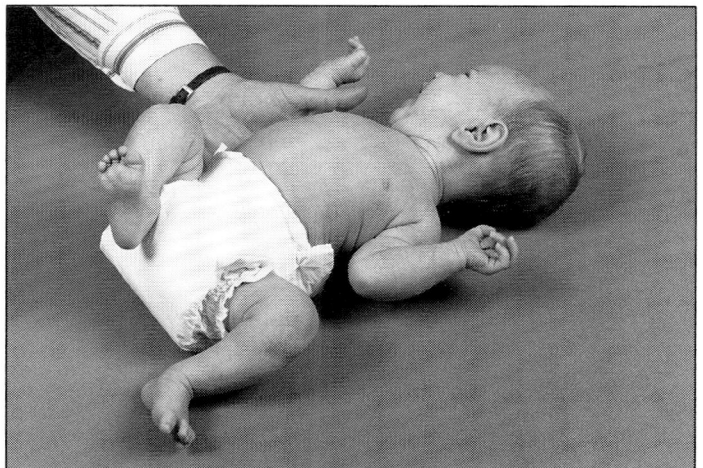

Figure 4.17e. Jeremy in tonic labyrinthine supine.

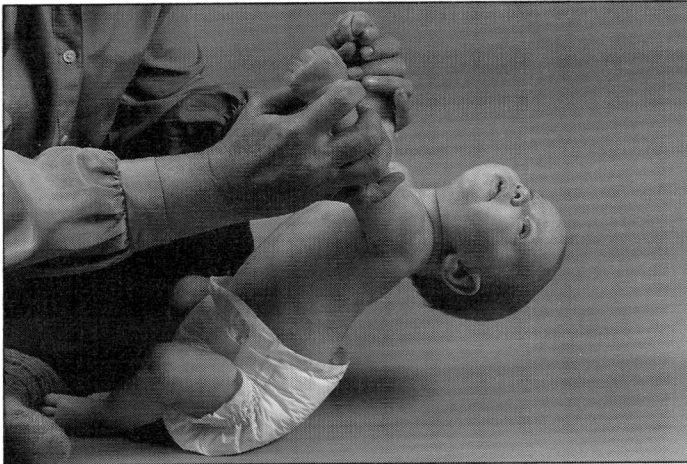

Figure 4.17f. Pull-to-sit at age 3 months.

Jeremy was evaluated again near the end of his first three months. His pull-to-sit continued to show severe head lag and fisting (figure 4.17f). In prone he could do little (figure 4.17g).

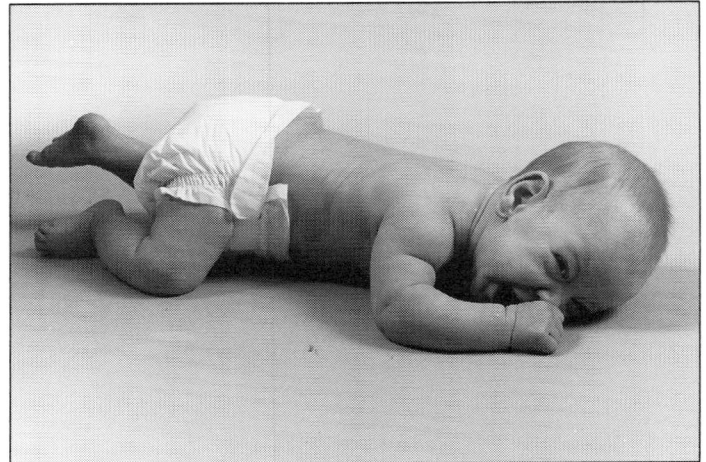

Figure 4.17g. Jeremy is still virtually helpless in the prone position at age 3 months.

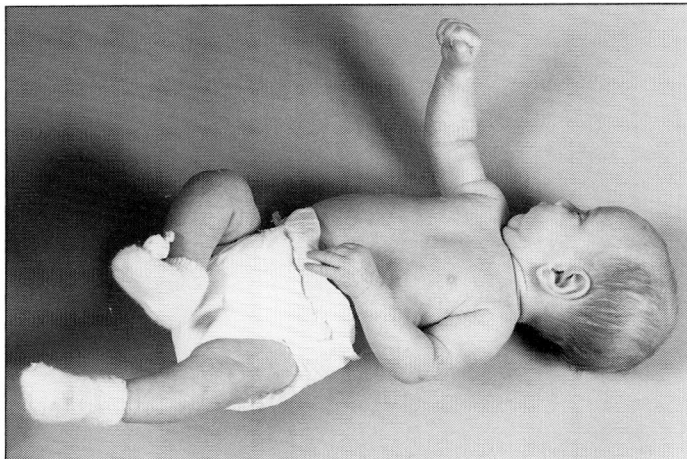

Figure 4.18a. Note Jeremy's asymmetric tonic neck reflex.

Almost any positioning on the firm surface used for the photographs elicited an asymmetric tonic neck reflex (figure 4.18a). Even maneuvers such as popliteal angle resulted in his turning his head to one side, clenching his fist, and assuming an upper body fencing position (figure 4.18b). Although this scores normal for age, it is worrisome because Jeremy was hypotonic, now has extensor postures, and has the pattern of development from which spasticity emerges.

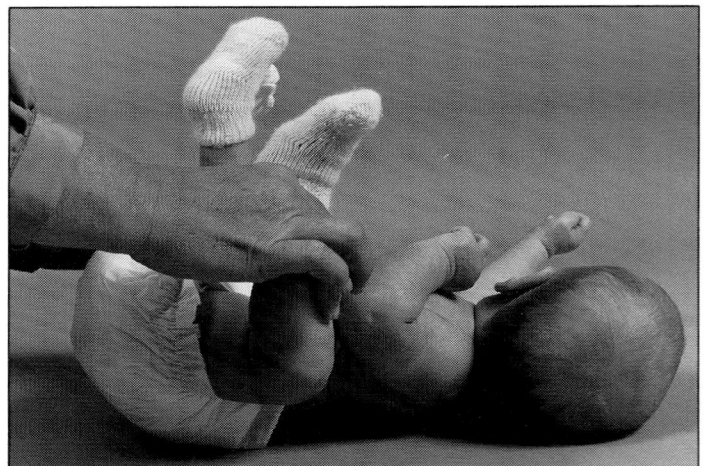

Figure 4.18b. Even the popliteal angle elicits a "fencing" position.

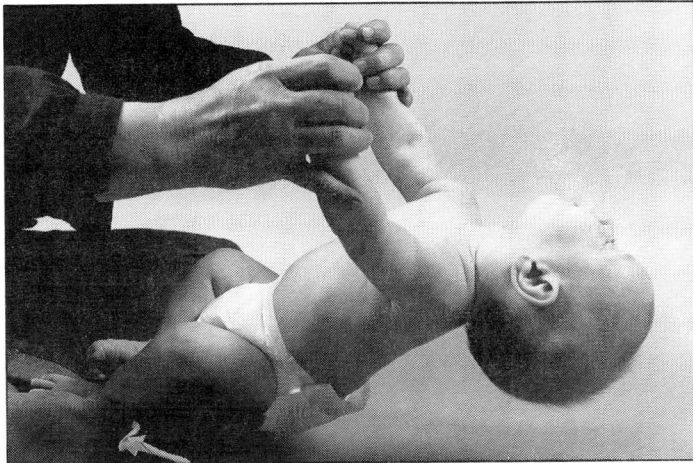

Figure 4.19a. At first evaluation at age 4-6 months, Jeremy's pull-to-sit showed no improvement.

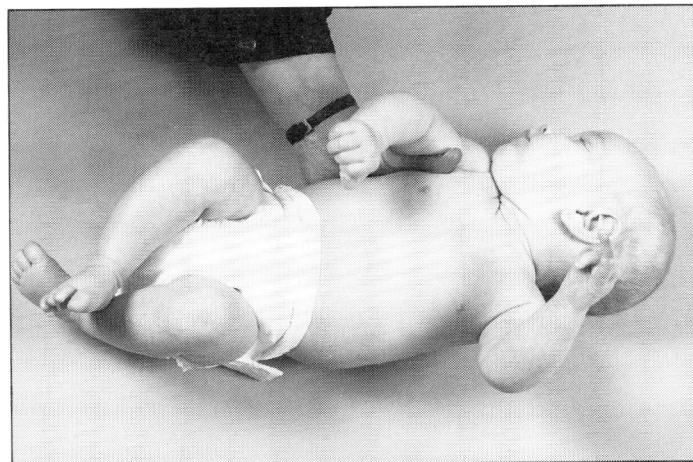

Figure 4.19b. Tonic labyrinthine supine maneuver at age 4-6 months.

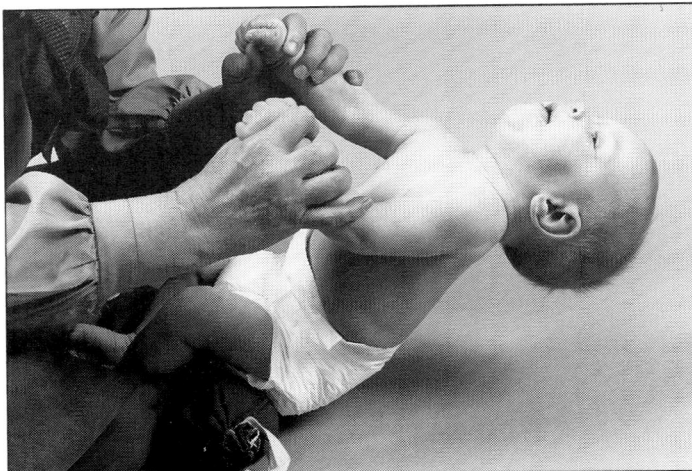

Figure 4.19c. In the latter part of the 4-6 month quarter, Jeremy's pull-to-sit still has not improved.

4-6 Months

When next evaluated, Jeremy showed no improvement on pull-to-sit (figure 4.19a). When placed in sitting position, he had poor trunk control. However, he now had open hands with this and some other maneuvers. In prone positions, he could do little with his head but managed to flex his knee and hip. Asymmetric tonic neck reflex positionings continued to occur spontaneously and with other maneuvers such as tonic labyrinthine supine (figure 4.19b).

In the latter part of his first six months, Jeremy showed no improvement in pull-to-sit (figure 4.19c). When placed in prone, he made small leg and hip flexion movements. When placed in a standing position, his legs buckled and his upper body slid through the examiner's hands (figure 4.19d).

With French angles, his scarf sign was now hypertonic. His heel-to-ear remained the same as on the previous evaluation. His popliteal angle remained flexible.

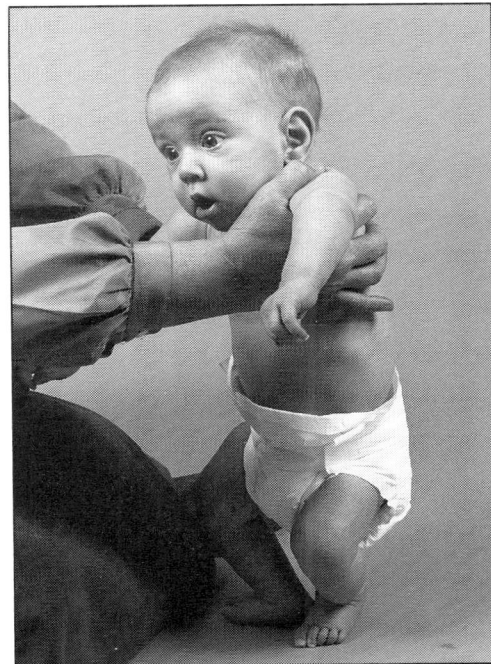

Figure 4.19d. Jeremy exhibits leg buckling in the standing position near the end of 6 months.

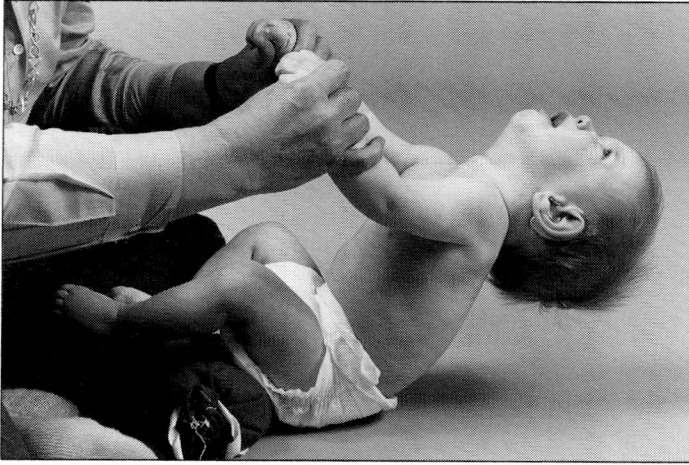

Figure 4.20a. Poor head control at age 7-9 months.

Figure 4.20b. Jeremy exhibits poor trunk control in the sitting position.

7-9 Months

Jeremy's head control remained poor (figure 4.20a). His sitting position continued to show poor trunk control (figure 4.20b).

His French angles again showed change. His scarf sign was hypertonic (figure 4.20c), and his popliteal angle, which had been flexible, *decreased*. The heel-to-ear maneuver remained about the same. Thus the increased tone or spasticity that was first identified in his hips was now present at his knees.

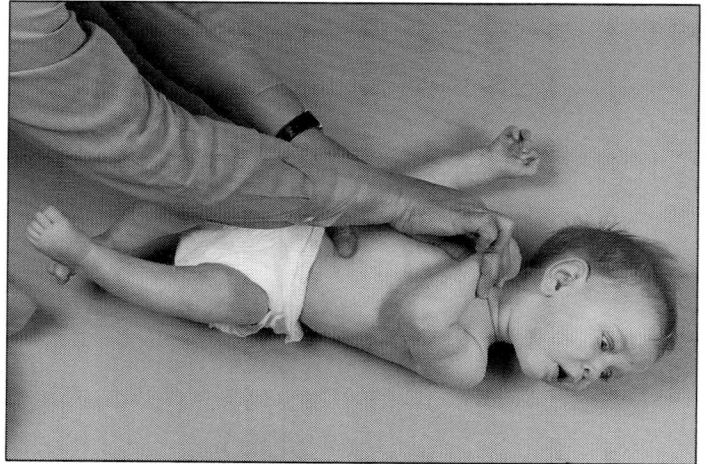

Figure 4.20c. Jeremy has a hypertonic scarf sign at age 7-9 months.

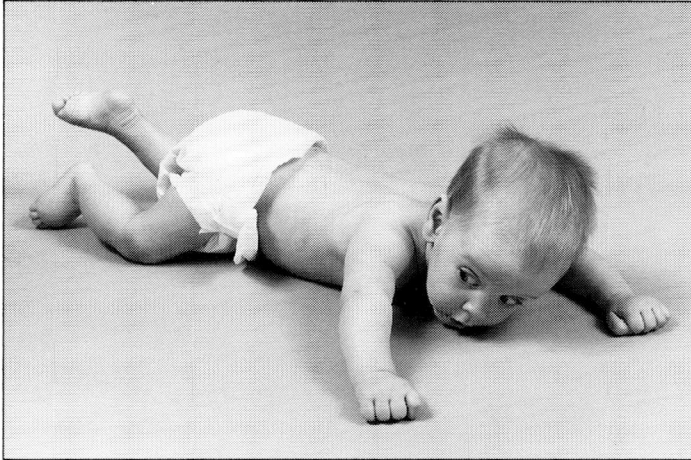

Figure 4.21a. Some progress is seen in head position in all fours at the end of the third quarter.

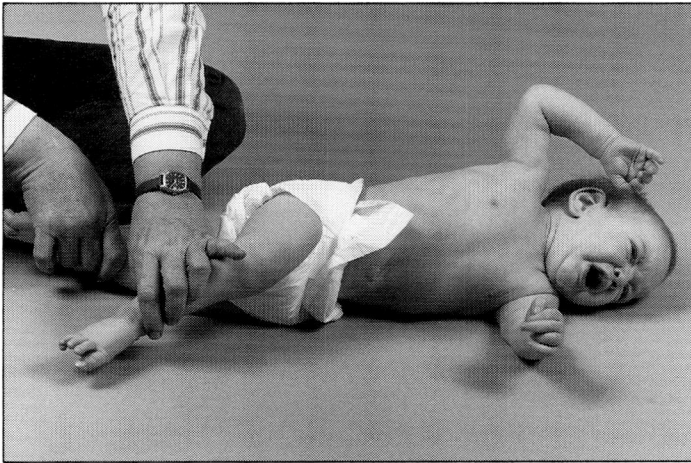

Figure 4.21b. Body rotative at the end of the third quarter. Note the arm extension.

Jeremy was evaluated again near the end of his third quarter of the first year. His head control remained as before. However, he has made some progress in head control in prone position (figure 4.21a). Unfortunately he continued to demonstrate an exaggerated tonic neck reflex. This occurred even with maneuvers such as body rotative. The extension of his arm effectively prevented him from rolling over (figure 4.21b). In standing position, he failed to bear weight or participate in support of his body (figure 4.21c).

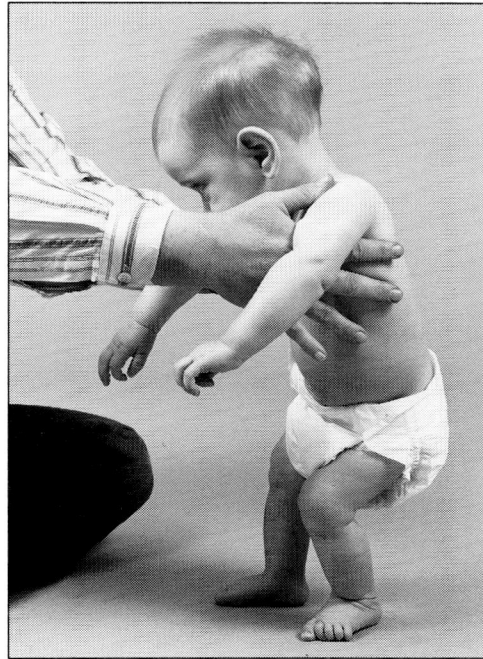

Figure 4.21c. Jeremy still cannot bear weight in the standing position at the end of the third quarter.

Figure 4.22a. Jeremy's pull-to-sit has not improved appreciably at age 10-12 months.

10-12 Months

One last picture is shown of pull-to-sit, partly to emphasize that extensive physical therapy did not change Jeremy's response to this maneuver (figure 4.22a). Similarly his sitting position remained hypotonic, although he now extended an arm for support. However, he could not extend his arm quickly (figure 4.22b). When testing for sideways parachute, he made no extension of his arms for support (figure 4.22c).

On the forwards parachute maneuver, he made no response (figure 4.22d). He did assume weight-bearing in standing position, but the stance was abnormal, head thrust back, positioned on his toes, his legs and arms extended (figure 4.22e).

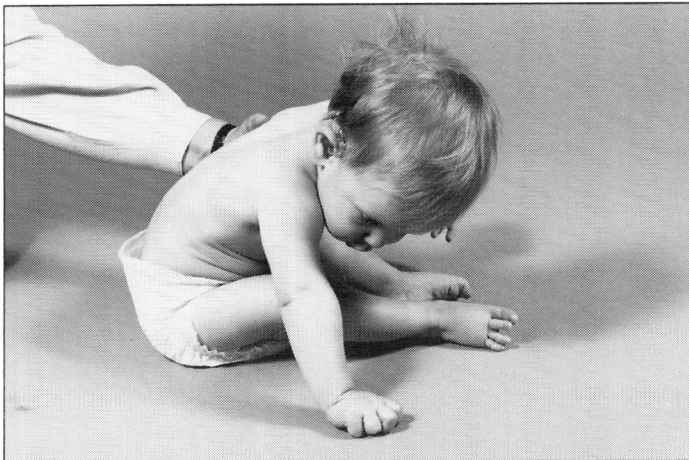

Figure 4.22b. At age 10-12 months the sitting position remains hypotonic.

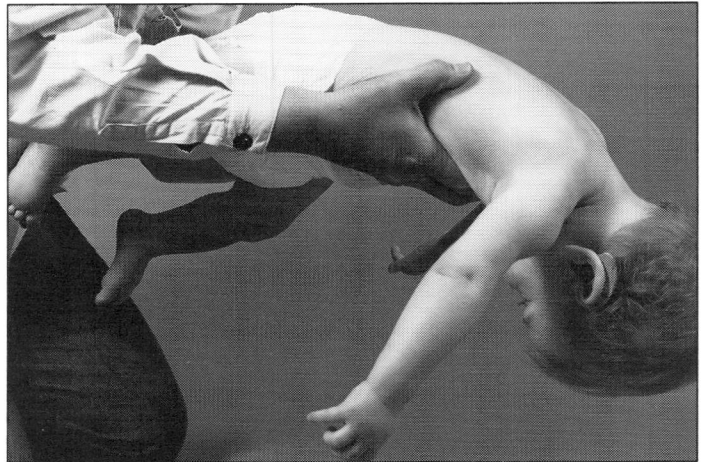

Figure 4.22d. Jeremy is unresponsive during the forwards parachute maneuver.

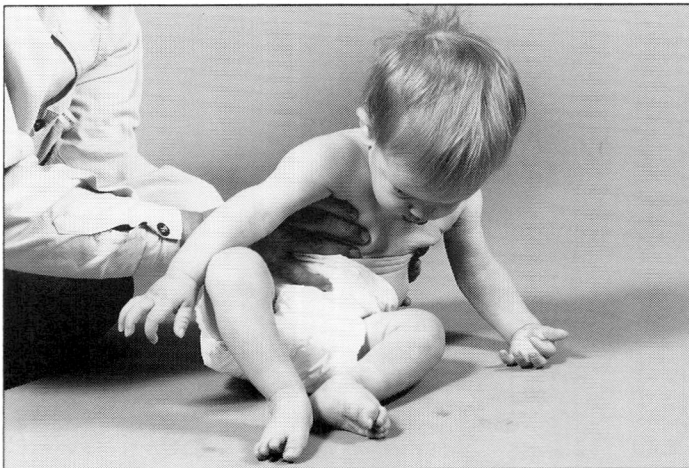

Figure 4.22c. Sideways parachute at age 10-12 months lacks arm extension for support.

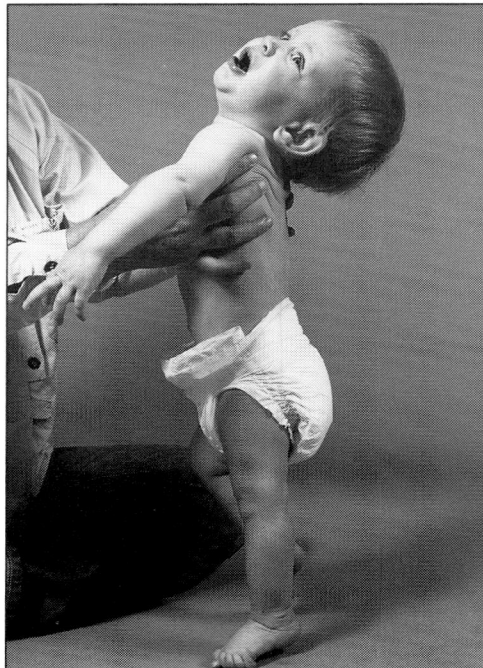

Figure 4.22e. In the standing position near age 12 months, Jeremy can bear weight, but his stance is abnormal.

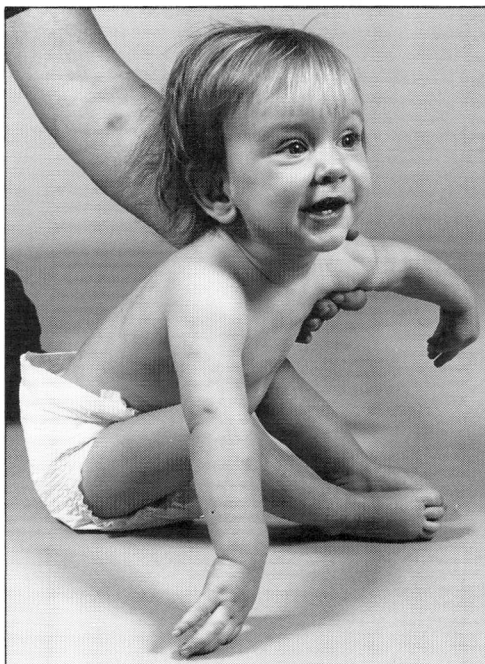

Figure 4.23a. While Jeremy can hold his head up in a sitting position near age 1 year, much hypotonia remained.

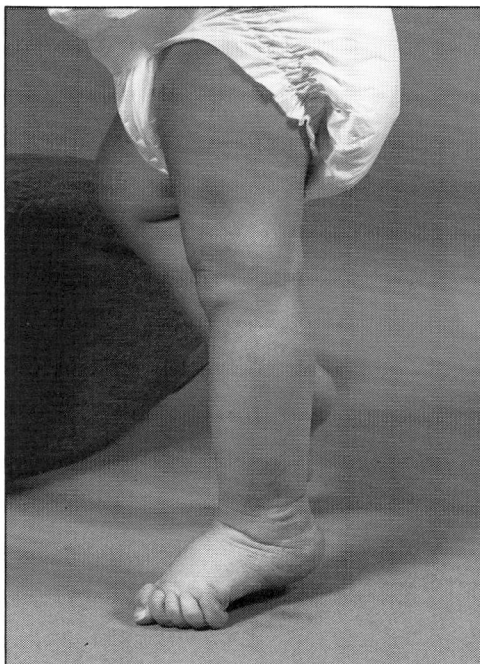

Figure 4.23b. Note Jeremy's curled toes in the standing position.

In the last set of evaluations and photographs near the end of his first year, Jeremy showed some improvement. He could hold his head up well in sitting position, although much truncal hypotonia remained (figure 4.23a). He had less posturing when placed in a standing position. His toes remained curled, an abnormal foot grasp (figure 4.23b). The abnormal foot grasp was also shown with that maneuver (figure 4.23c). His other primitive reflexes remained abnormal as in the tonic labyrinthine supine (figure 4.23d).

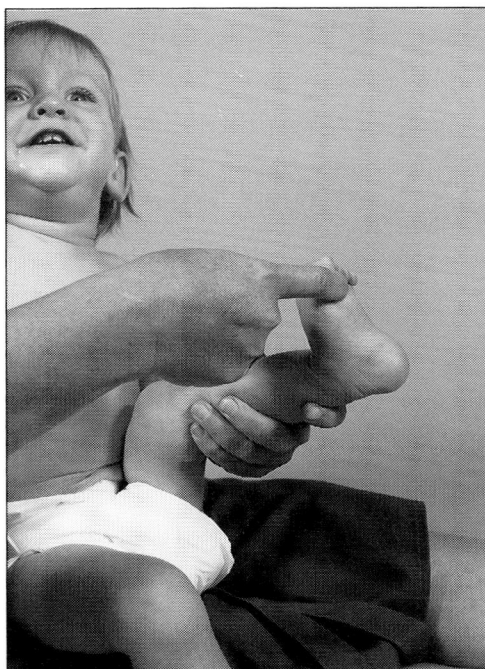

Figure 4.23c. Another example of abnormal foot grasp, near 1 year of age.

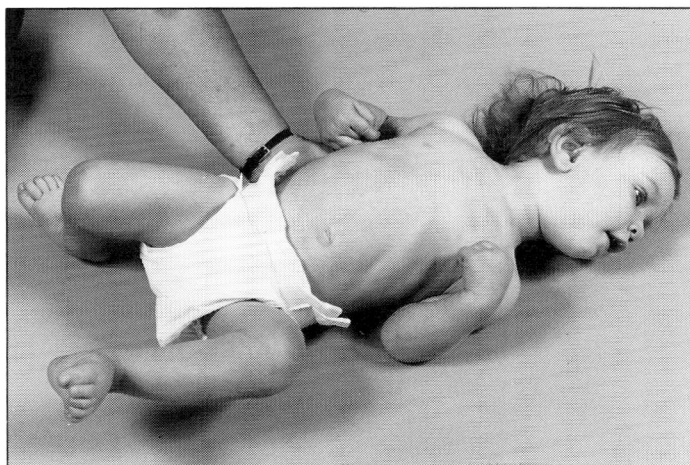

Figure 4.23d. Jeremy performs the tonic labyrinthine supine, near 1 year of age.

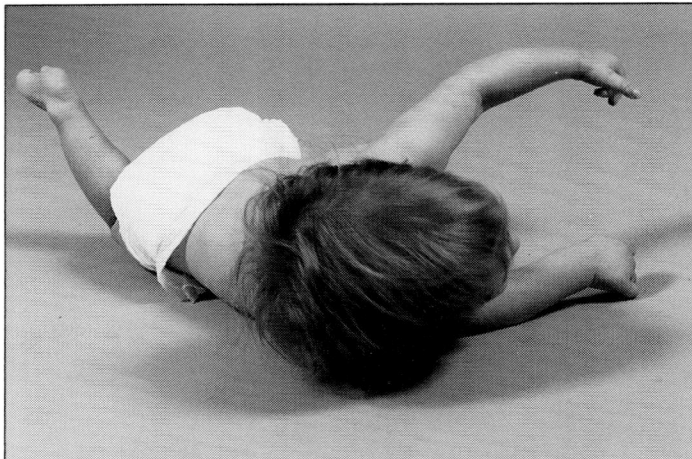

Figure 4.23e. Body rotative, near 1 year of age.

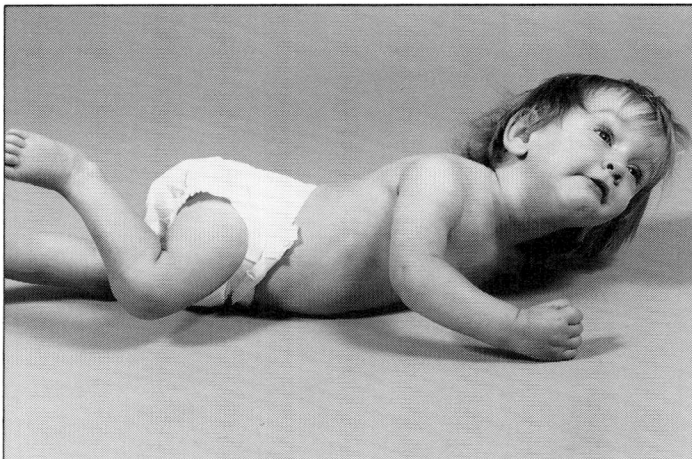

Figure 4.23f. While Jeremy can creep, he lacks coordination.

Jeremy had also some modest mobility on body rotative—he could roll from back to front if given a lot of assistance. See the top arm swinging over (figure 4.23e). He could creep although the coordination was very awkward (figure 4.23f).

We have used the term spastic tetraparesis/dyskinesia to describe children like Jeremy with four-limbed involvement and combinations of spasticity and dyskinesia. That term grew out of collaborative work in which one clinician always emphasized the dyskinesia while the other emphasized the spasticity—when actually both are seen in most such infants. Some infants have more of one quality than the other. Most have more spasticity when excited or irritated and more dyskinesia when relaxed.

Jeremy was very slow in the acquisition of motor skills. When last seen at age two, he still could not stand alone and certainly could not walk. However, he was very attentive to his environment and understood several signs. He also used a limited repertoire of gestures, such as sniffing when he spied some dried flowers.

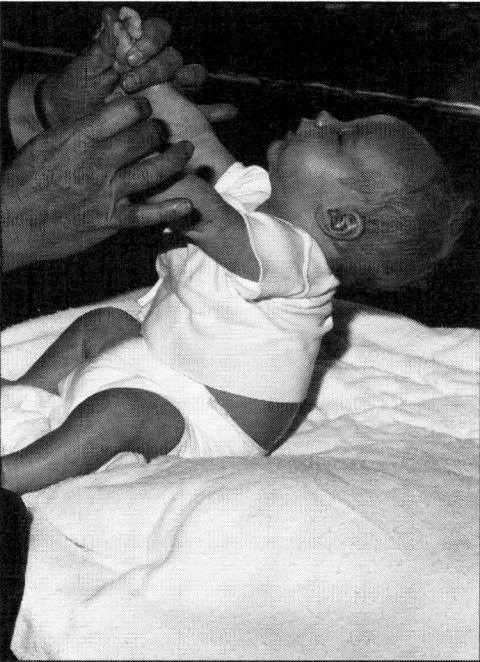
Figure 4.24a. Sammy performs pull-to-sit at age 1 month.

An Example of a Normal Infant

4. Sammy

Sammy was born at term with good Apgar scores, his birth weight over 2500 grams, and without evidence of congenital abnormality. He had no neonatal sicknesses. These are criteria that we have used in our research to select a "control" group of children in longitudinal studies from the neonatal intensive care units. Furthermore (for the purposes of this book), Sammy's father is a photographer. Sammy became the normal infant study in this series.

0-3 Months

At age one month, Sammy had a little head lag on pull-to-sit (figure 4.24a). This deviation from normal was not enough to place his total score at less than normal. His response to the asymmetric tonic neck reflex was brief, partial, and he overcame even that (figure 4.24b). His French angles were normal as shown in the heel-to-ear-maneuver (figure 4.24c). When placed in standing position, his legs briefly supported him but he offered no support of his upper body (figure 4.24d).

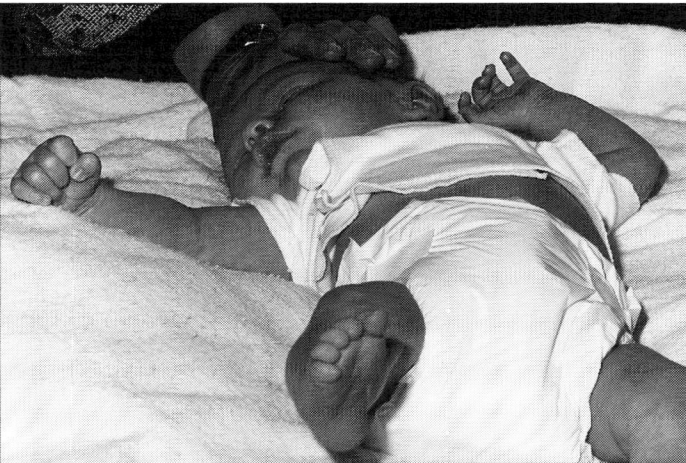
Figure 4.24b. The asymmetric tonic neck reflex—Sammy at age 1 month.

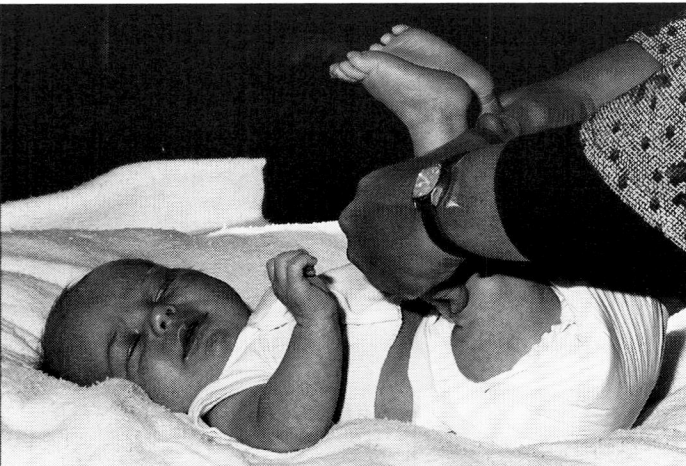
Figure 4.24c. Sammy exhibits normal response in the heel-to-ear maneuver.

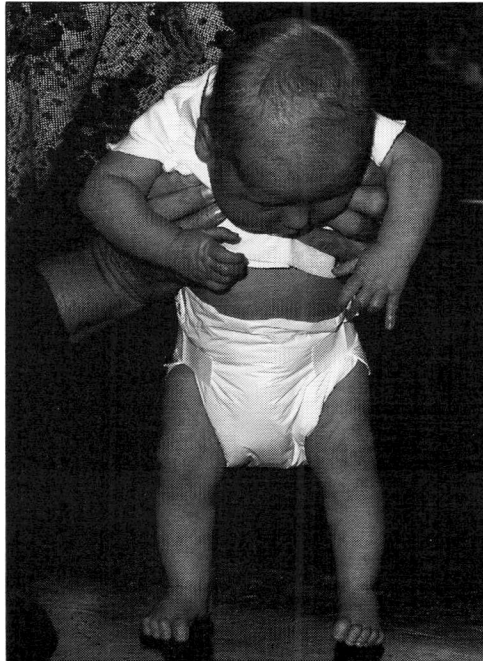
Figure 4.24d. Sammy in the standing position at age 1 month.

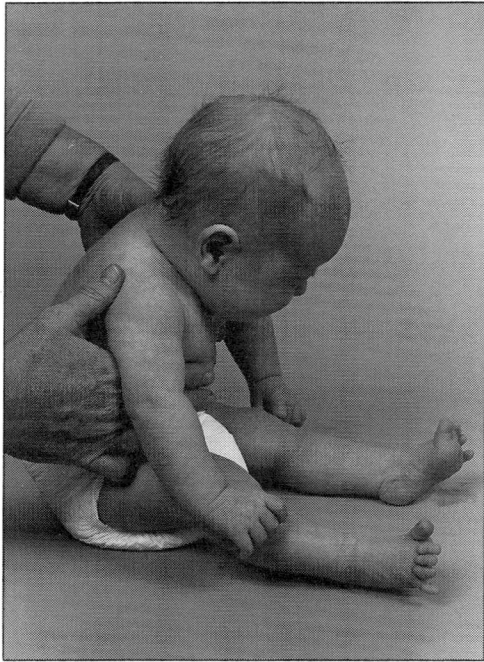
Figure 4.25a. Sammy exhibits normal sitting response at age 2 months.

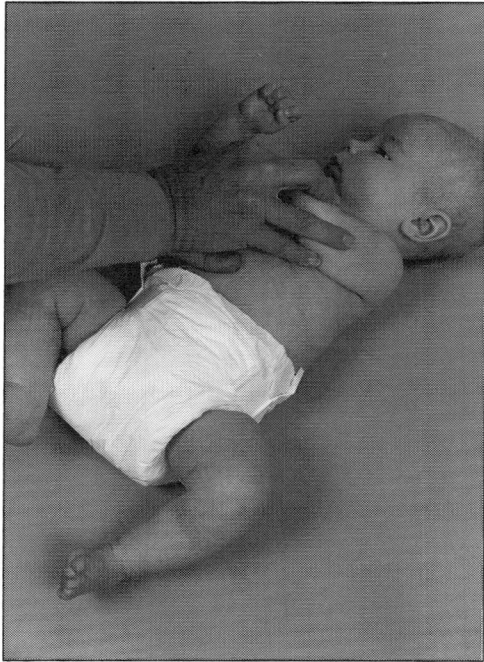
Figure 4.25b. Scarf sign—Sammy at 2 months.

At age two months, Sammy bends at L3 for sitting (figure 4.25a). His French angles remain normal: scarf sign (figure 4.25b), popliteal angle (figure 4.25c), and leg abduction (figure 4.25d).

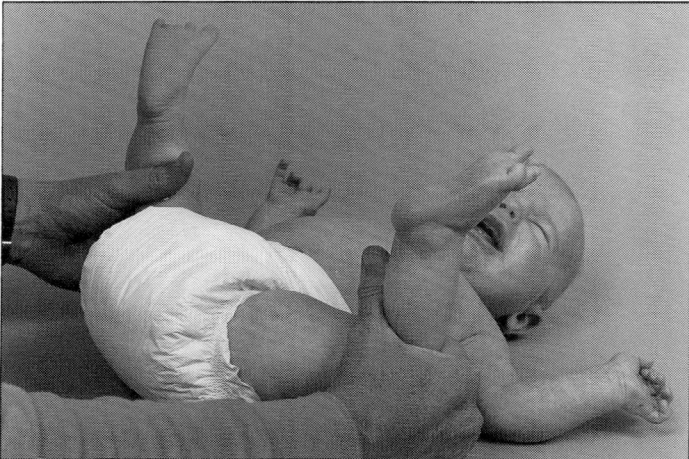
Figure 4.25c. Popliteal angle—Sammy at 2 months.

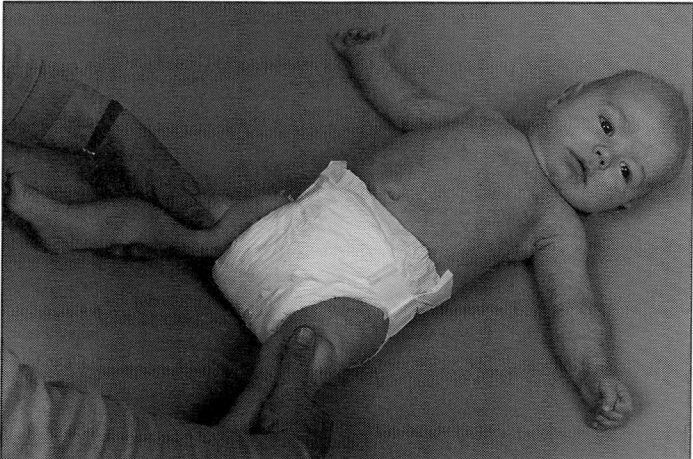
Figure 4.25d. Leg abduction—Sammy at 2 months.

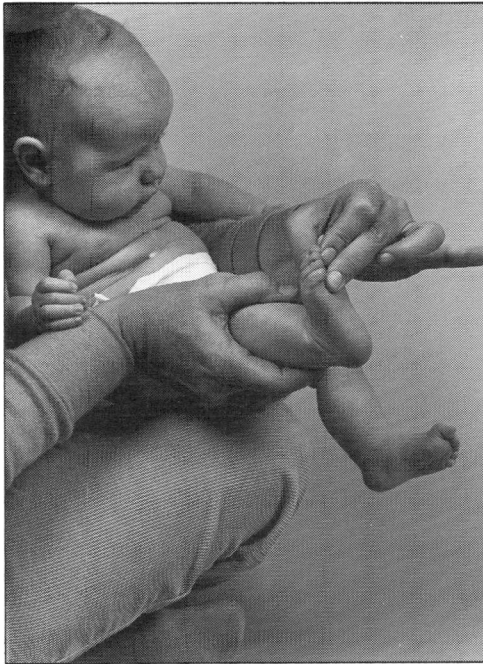

Figure 4.26a. Normal foot-to-leg response at 2 months.

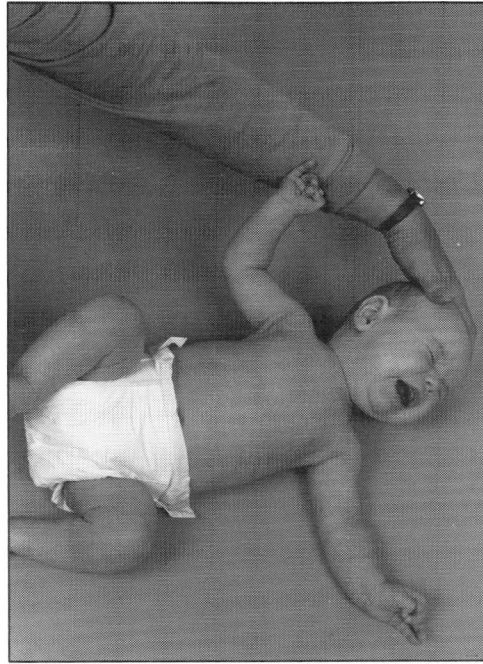

Figure 4.26b. Sammy shows no asymmetric tonic neck reflex at 2 months of age.

His foot-to-leg is normal (figure 4.26a). He has no asymmetric tonic neck reflex when the examiner turns his head, but he protests strongly (figure 4.26b).

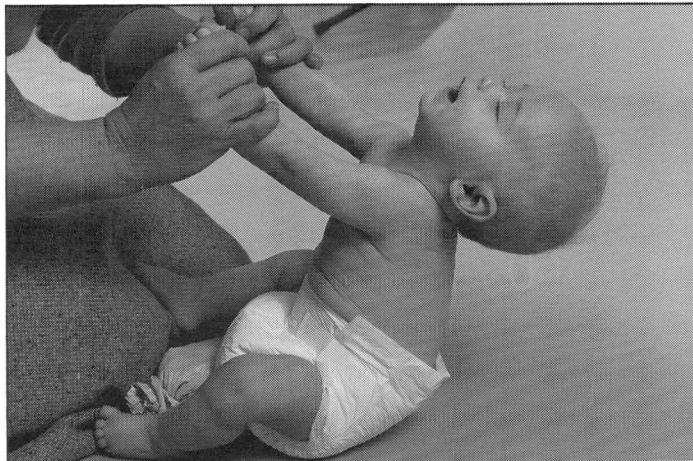

Figure 4.27a. Sammy performs pull-to-sit at age 3 months.

At age three months, Sammy still has some head lag in pull-to-sit (figure 4.27a). In sitting position he still bends at L3 but he needs less support from the examiner (figure 4.27b). His French angles are normal; he has no abnormal primitive reflexes. He stands briefly with support from the examiner before buckling his knees (figure 4.27c).

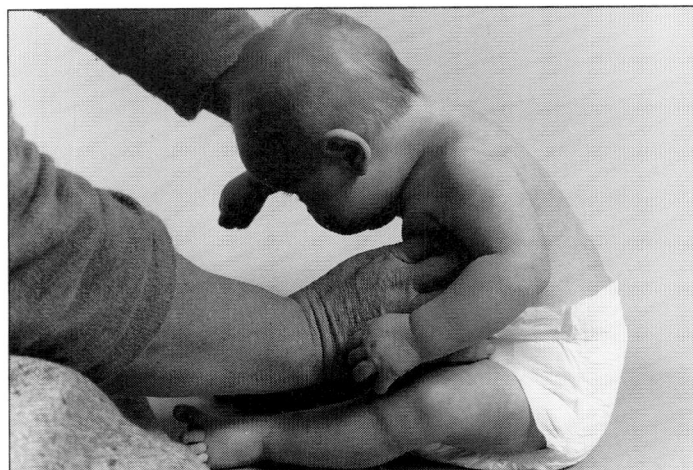

Figure 4.27c. Standing position, age 3 months.

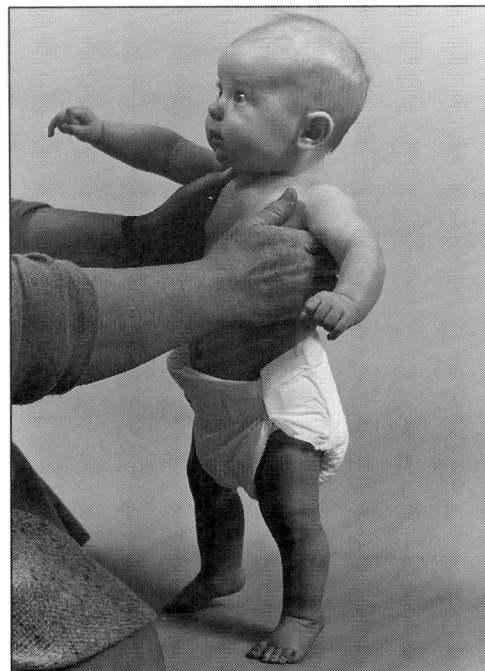

Figure 4.27b. Sitting position, age 3 months.

4-6 Months

At four months, Sammy assists on pull-to-sit, pulling his head forward and flexing his arms (figure 4.28a). He still needs some support with sitting position but he bends from L5 (figure 4.28b). In prone position, he holds his head up well and extends at least one arm (figure 4.28c). On body denotative, Sammy assists with his upper arm and completes the roll (figure 4.28d). In standing position, his legs are steadier and he straightens his trunk himself (figure 4.28e).

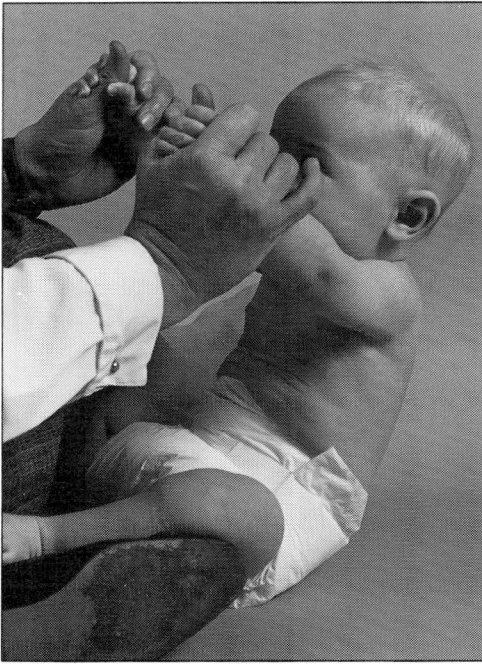

Figure 4.28a. Pull-to-sit at age 4 months.

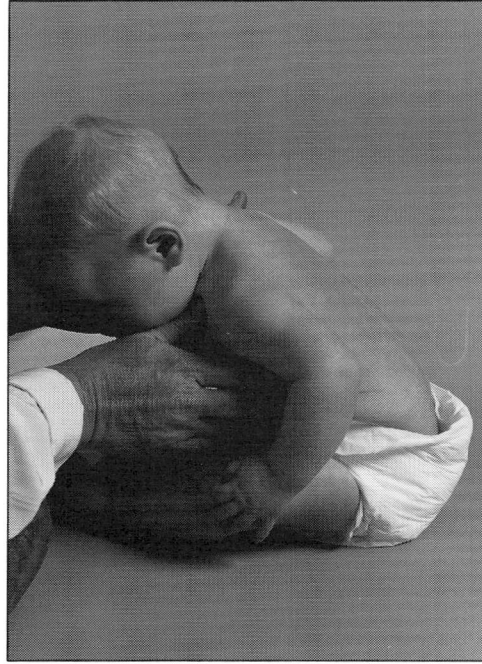

Figure 4.28b. Sitting position at age 4 months.

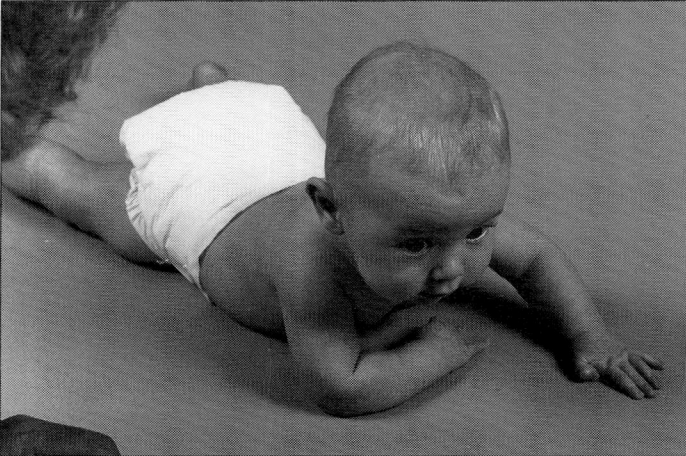

Figure 4.28c. Prone position with head held up well and one arm extended.

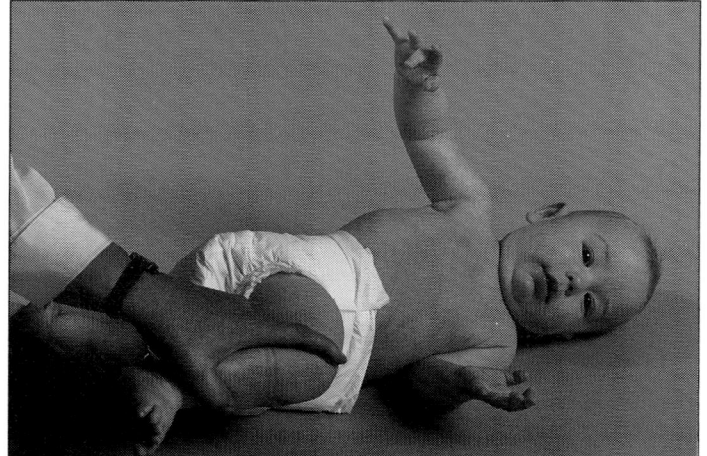

Figure 4.28d. Body denotative at age 4 months.

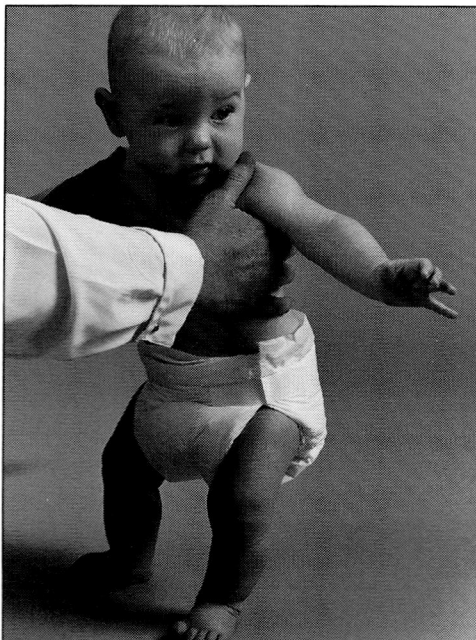

Figure 4.28e. Sammy straightens his trunk himself in the standing position.

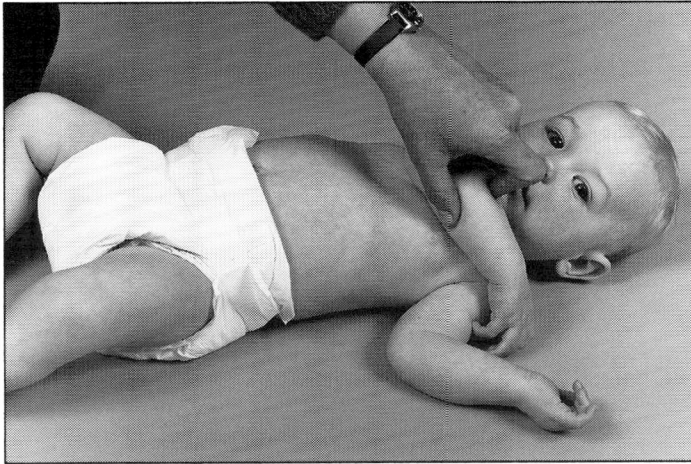

Figure 4.29a. Normal scarf sign at 6 months.

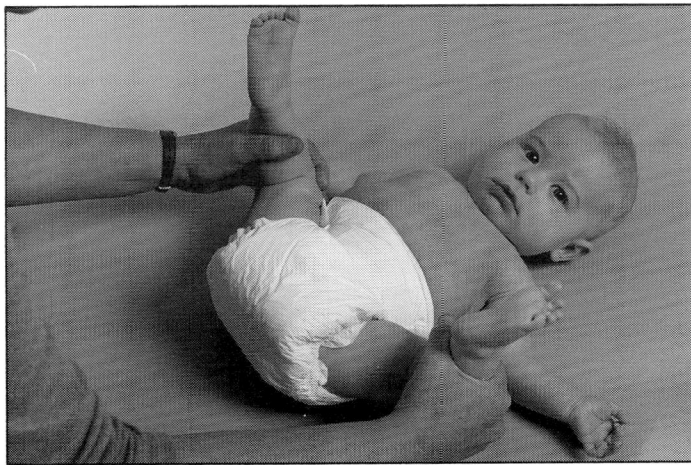

Figure 4.29b. Normal popliteal angle at 6 months.

At six months, his French angles are normal: Scarf sign (figure 4.29a), popliteal angle (figure 4.29b), heel-to-ear (figure 4.29c) and leg abduction (figure 4.29d).

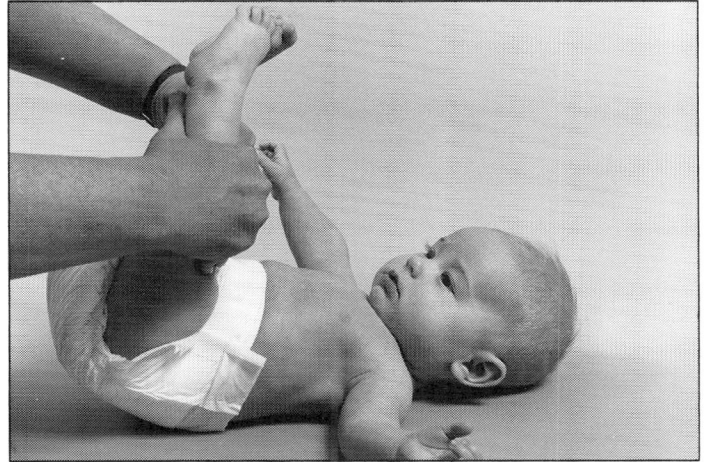

Figure 4.29c. Normal heel-to ear at 6 months.

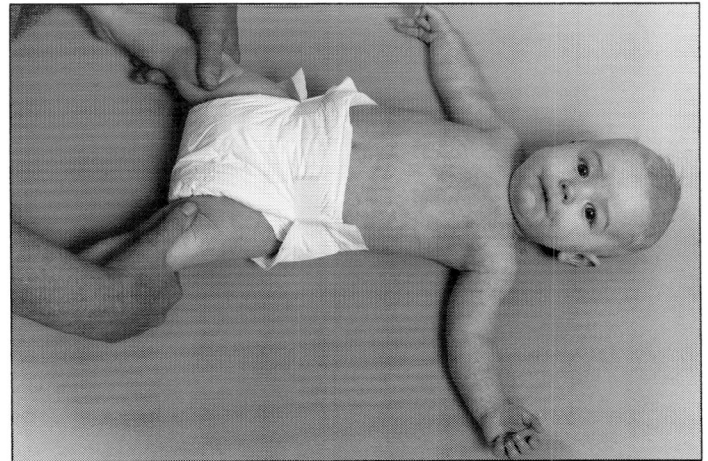

Figure 4.29d. Normal leg abduction at 6 months.

7-9 Months

In this quarter, Sammy has an independent sit (figure 4.30a). He has a sideways parachute (figure 4.30b). He is competent on all fours (figure 4.30c). He stands with buttocks tucked under and spine erect, requiring little support from the examiner (figure 4.30d).

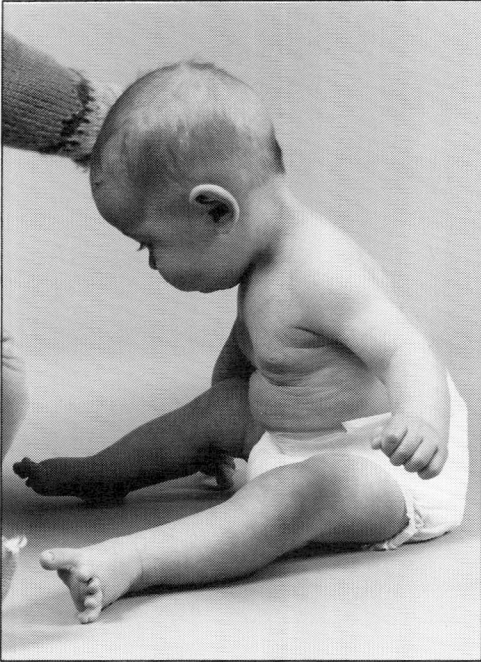

Figure 4.30a. In the third quarter Sammy sits independently.

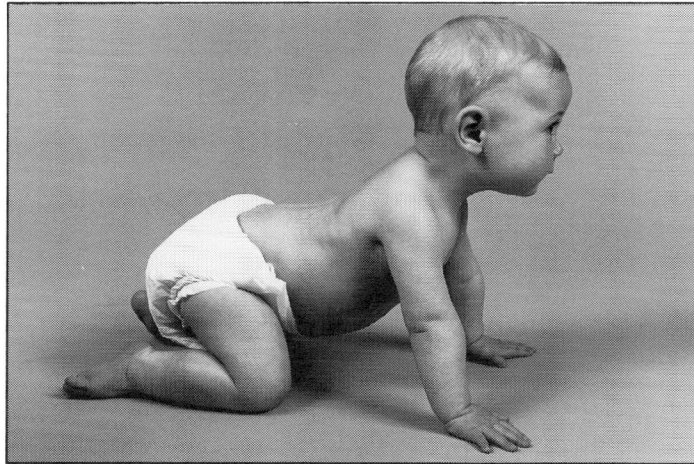

Figure 4.30c. Sammy on all fours, age 7-9 months.

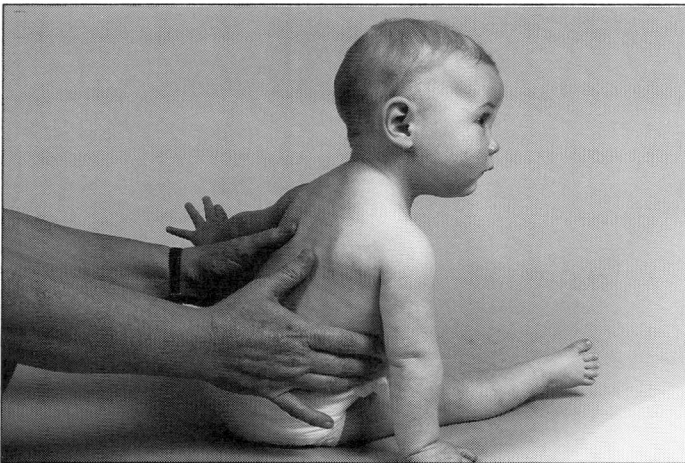

Figure 4.30b. Sideways parachute, age 7-9 months.

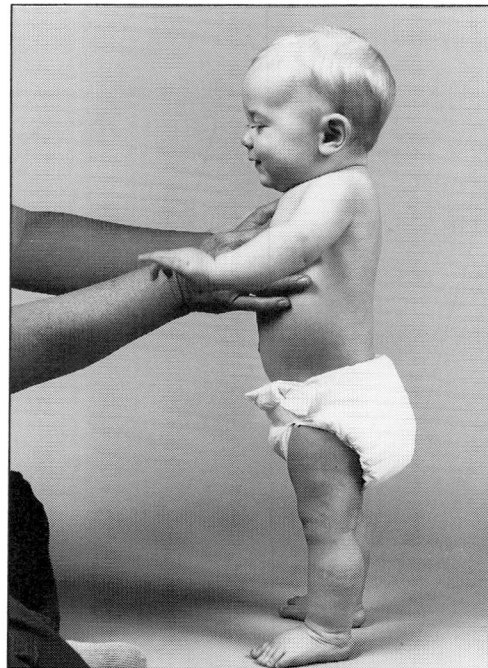

Figure 4.30d. Standing position, age 7-9 months.

Late in this quarter, Sammy has acquired his other parachutes: forwards (figure 4.31a) and backwards (figure 4.31b).

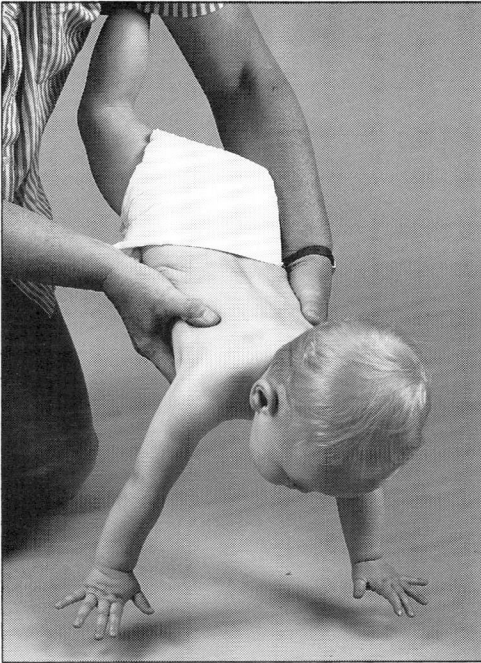

Figure 4.31b. Backwards parachute, late in third quarter.

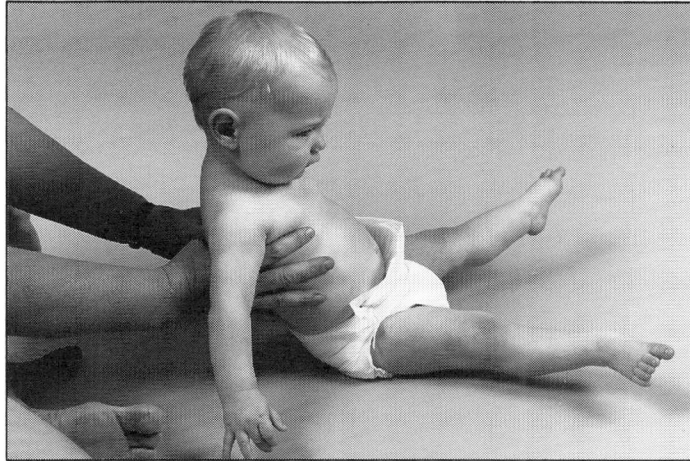

Figure 4.31a. Forward parachute, late in third quarter.

His French angles are normal: Popliteal angle (figure 4.31c), heel-to-ear (figure 4.31d), and leg abduction (figure 4.31e).

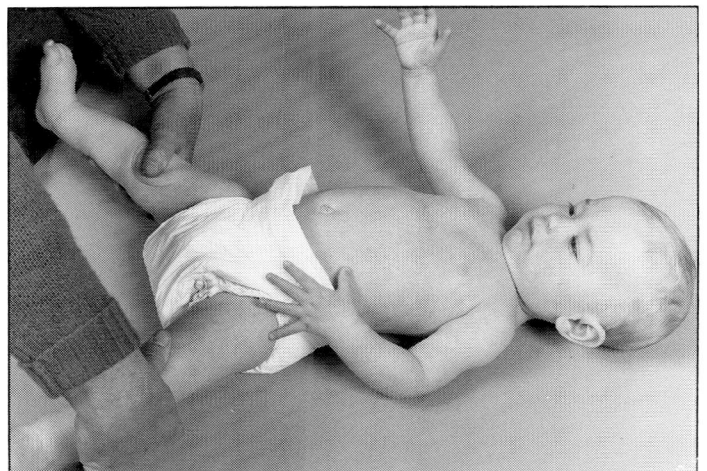

Figure 4.31d. Normal heel-to-ear in third quarter.

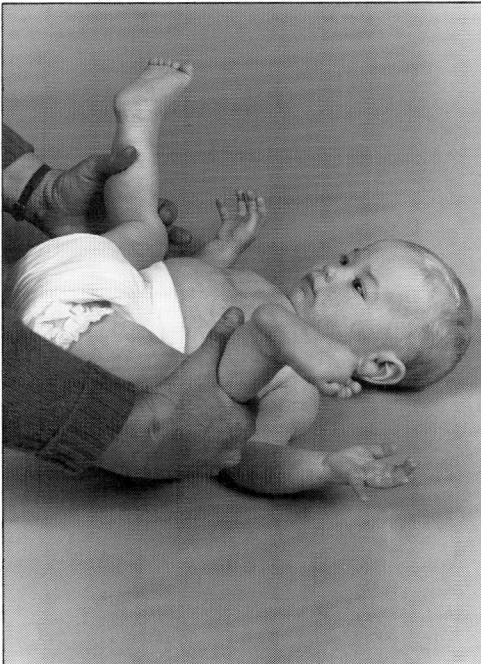

Figure 4.31c. Normal popliteal angle in third quarter.

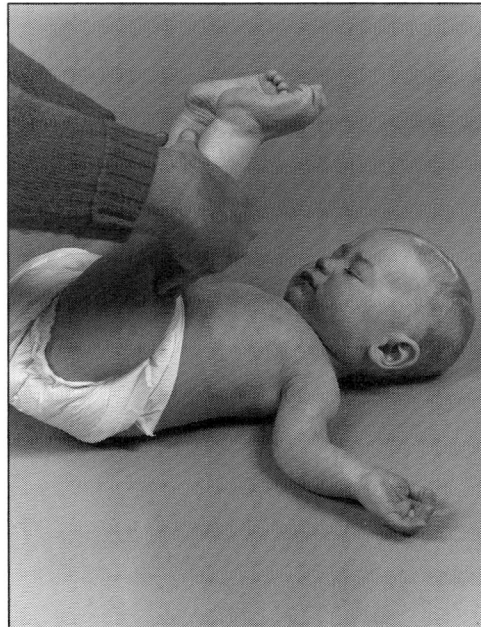

Figure 4.31e. Normal leg abduction in third quarter.

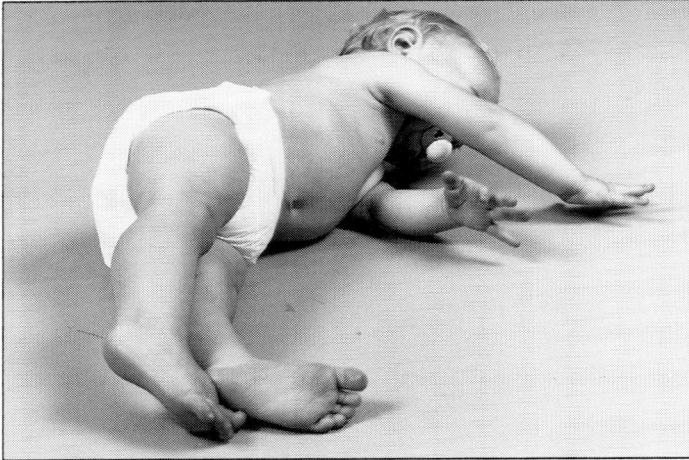

Figure 4.32a. Sammy rolls with ease in the last quarter of his first year.

10-12 Months

Sammy learned to walk in the last quarter of his first year, following our last set of photographs. When last evaluated, early in the fourth quarter, he rolled with ease and pulled to a standing position (figures 4.32a to 4.32c).

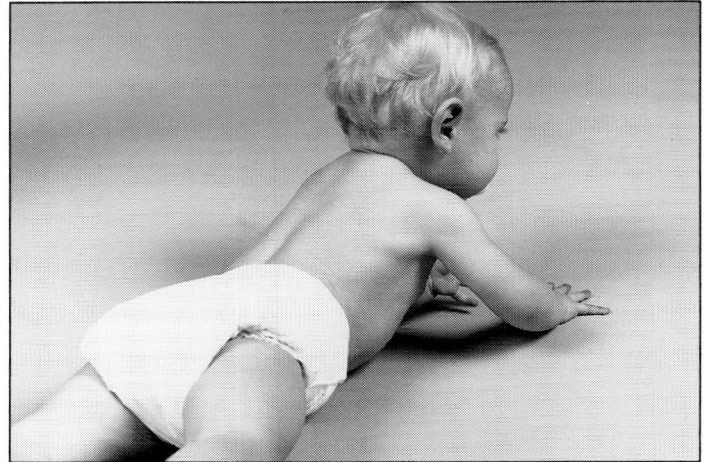

Figure 4.32b. Sammy after rolling over in the last quarter of his first year.

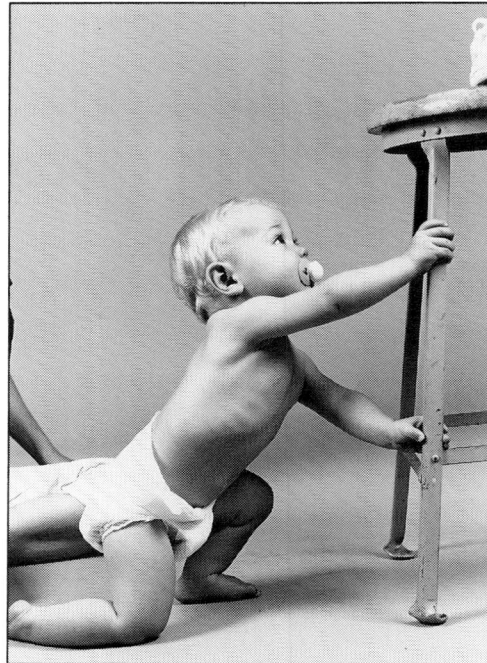

Figure 4.32c. Sammy pulls himself into a standing position in the last quarter of his first year.

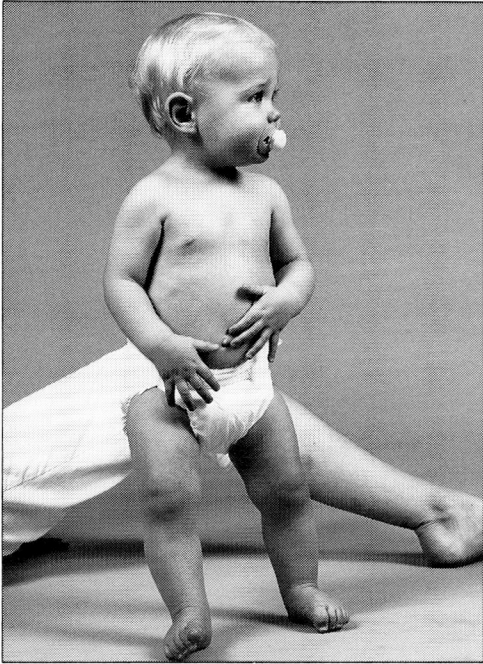

Figure 4.33a. Sammy stands alone near the end of his first year.

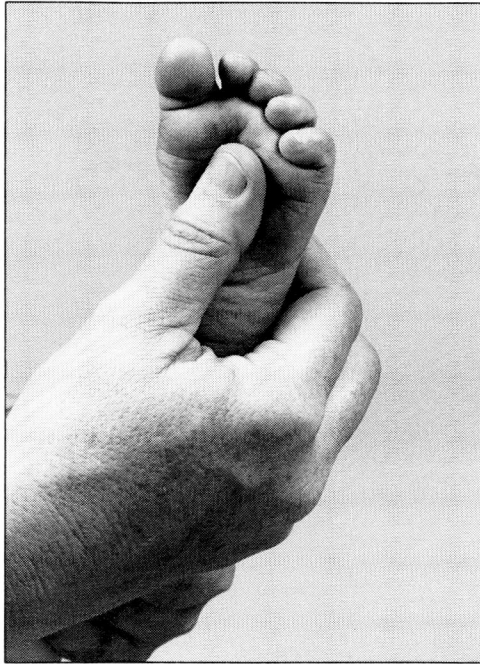

Figure 4.33b. Normal foot grasp near 1 year of age.

Sammy stood alone for a short time when placed in standing position (figure 4.33a). His normal foot grasp response is shown in figure 4.33b). His scarf sign (figure 4.33c), popliteal angle (figure 4.33d), heel-to-ear (figure 4.33e), and leg abduction (figure 4.33f) were normal.

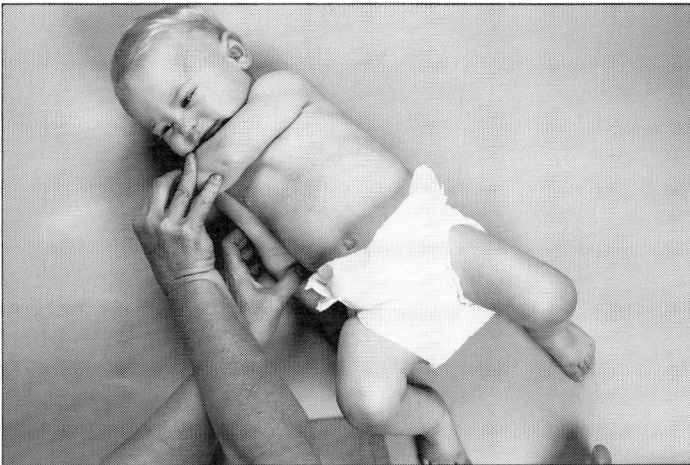

Figure 4.33c. Normal scarf sign, near 1 year of age.

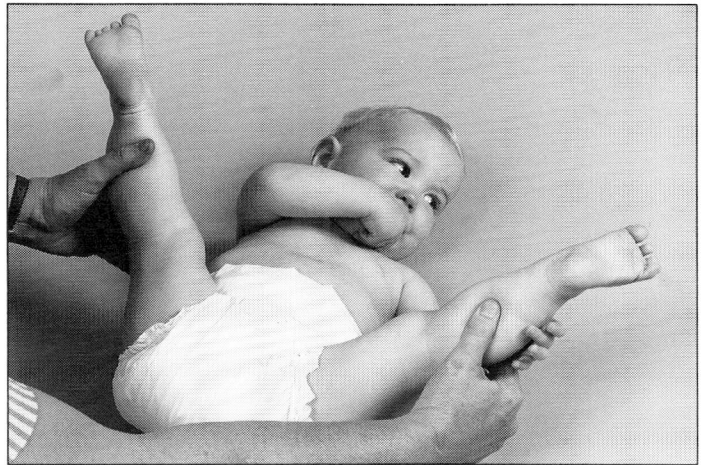

Figure 4.33d. Normal popliteal angle, near 1 year of age.

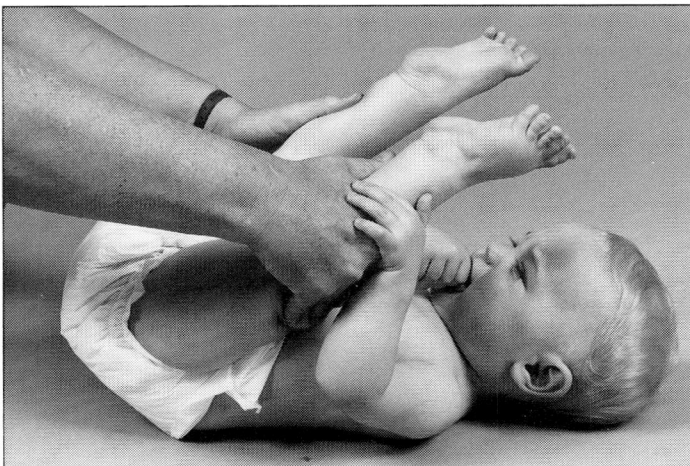

Figure 4.33e. Normal heel-to-ear, near 1 year of age.

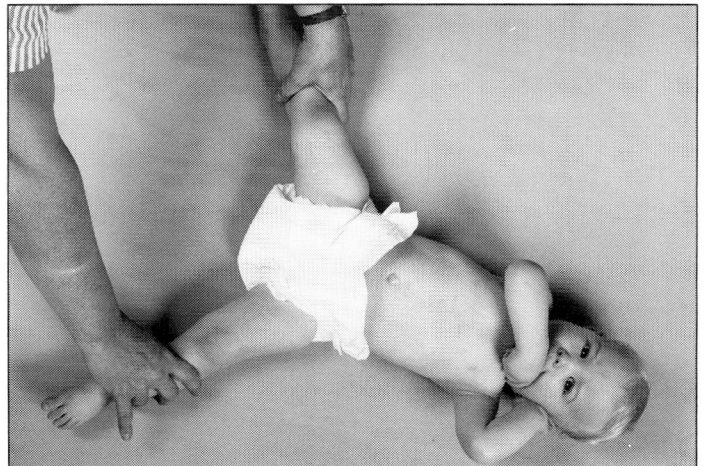

Figure 4.33f. Normal leg abduction, near 1 year of age.

5
Helpful Hints In Other Important Diagnoses

Many clinicians who examine infants can, and often do, gather extensive information about the infants. Theoretically, we have been taught to consider "the whole child." In this section, information is provided about some conditions that are often associated with delay in diagnosis or misdiagnosis, or which may present problems in regard to making good decisions about referral for additional diagnostic tests or additional consultation. In some situations, the achievement of the correct diagnosis might influence a family about further child-bearing (for example, the identification of certain hereditary conditions, particularly those with degenerative or terminating courses). In other situations, treatment might be initiated earlier.

Ataxia

Ataxia is not included in the *Infanib* assessment. Genuine ataxia is infrequent. In early infancy it is often difficult to identify well and it can be very difficult to separate from dyskinesia. As more eye-hand coordination develops, one can test for ataxia. A good item is that of reaching for an object, which appears on many developmental scales. Early reaching is often not precise and the infant's hand may waiver before grasping the object. One would not want to confuse this with ataxia. At 20 weeks the infant should be able to grasp an object held near the palm. The *Gesell Screening Inventory* defines the distance of the object from the palm as one inch. That is a very short distance in which to assess ataxia. At age 24 weeks the infant should be able to reach for and secure a toy. Thus the examiner can present an object from the front and observe any hand and arm movement that is a sweeping from side to side—or an inability to reach directly. Unfortunately, infants with dyskinesia may make quite similar movements. In general, one is not checking to see whether an infant with spastic tetraparesis/dyskinesia has some ataxia. The ataxias of interest here are more usually associated with hypotonia.

In the early stages of standing and walking, it should be easier to distinguish between ataxia and dyskinesia. The infants with dyskinesia generally have unusual posturing with standing. Those with ataxia tend to be delayed in walking, tend to put their feet farther apart (a phenomenon known as a wide-based gait), and keep that wide-based gait rather than decreasing it as most infants do in the progression of walking skills. Those with ataxia also lose balance more easily.

Since most early walkers do a lot of falling, the early stages of walking are not an easy time in which to judge ataxia. However, an ataxic grasping movement should warn one to look for ataxic walking movements. The infants may also do more leaning to either side or forward or backward. In short, they have difficulty maintaining balance in standing position.

Ataxia is rarely a form of cerebral palsy. Children with ataxia-telangiectasia are often identified in infancy as having cerebral palsy because of their delay in walking and their awkward gait. This is a genetic condition with progressive ataxia. Children with some of the rare metabolic disorders such as Hartnup's disease or methylmalonic acidemia may have intermittent ataxia. These are diagnosed by blood and urine samples that are tested for elevations of certain amino acids. Brain tumor may present with ataxias, although the infants are usually 18 months or older. The diagnosis is made by brain imaging—either computed tomography or magnetic resonance imaging.

Myoclonic Seizures

Often there is an information gap between the caretaker and the doctor in the identification of myoclonic seizures. The parents generally notice the repetitive, brief flexion or extension movements of the infant's head or limbs or trunk. Sometimes the infant has been taken to the family physician and nothing abnormal was observed. That is not surprising since the seizures do not occur all day every day. They tend to occur in flurries. Initially these may be modest in number, perhaps ten a day. It is important to note that an occasional myoclonic jerk, especially when dropping off to sleep is not abnormal. Repetitive myoclonic jerks are abnormal. The clinician who spends more time with the infant or who provides therapies may well be the first professional person to see them and to make the correct diagnosis.

Such an infant needs an electroencephalogram (EEG) because it usually registers abnormal and usually shows repetitive spike-wave (seizure) activity.

Many studies suggest that early diagnosis and treatment with the appropriate medication yields better outcomes. Please note that early diagnosis does *not guarantee* a good outcome. Myoclonic seizures can be a devastating form of seizure disorder associated with loss of skills even with early identification and treatment. The medicines used most frequently are: ACTH (by injection), prednisone, Clonopin, and Depakote. Any of these may be given along with phenobarbital.

Myoclonic seizures are more likely to occur in infants with other neurological problems such as abnormal tone and posture or developmental delay, but they can occur in otherwise normal infants. Early diagnosis and treatment is especially valuable in these normal infants. In addition to an EEG, an infant with myoclonic seizures needs an evaluation by a pediatric neurologist.

Persistent Hypotonia

Good judgment is needed in deciding to obtain further diagnostic evaluation for persistent hypotonia. Many infants who were initially treated in the neonatal intensive care units will be hypotonic. Some will progress to spasticity. The majority will improve—those with abnormal mental development more slowly than those with normal mental development. Which infants require more tests?

Those with worsening hypotonia who do not have a diagnosis such as Down syndrome. The chief concern here is Werdnig-Hoffman disease, a condition that affects the anterior horn cell. This condition is hereditary and it requires special attention to upper respiratory illnesses, which can cause rapid decompensation. Most of these infants will have absent reflexes—another clue.

Those who do not improve somewhat by 10 to 15 months and who do not have a diagnosis such as Down syndrome. Children with hypotonia are generally delayed in their gross motor milestones: rolling over, sitting and walking. They may walk between 15 and 18 months, but they still have some improvement in body tone. When there is no such improvement, a pediatric neurologist may choose to obtain more tests—a limited electromyographic study, muscle enzymes from the blood such as CPK, and eventually a muscle biopsy. Most of these conditions are not treatable (such as the congenital myopathies), and they may be genetic. In the past, I was more vigorous in doing some of this testing for hypotonic infants initially treated in the neonatal units; I found that it yielded little and became more conservative.

Those with absent reflexes. Pediatric neurologists have used this as a clue to underlying anterior horn cell, peripheral nerve, neuromuscle junction, and muscle disease. Absent reflexes provide good clues, but some children with these conditions do have reflexes. Again, good judgment will help avoid excessive testing.

Worsening Hemiparesis

The majority of infants with spastic hemiparesis continue to have hemiparesis even with appropriate therapies. They usually become more skillful in the use of the involved arm and leg. In fact, to the more casual observer, some children may seem without handicap.

Generally, the imaging studies of the brain in infants with hemiparesis show only modest abnormalities, such as a mild asymmetry of the ventricles. In some children, a larger area of abnormality is seen. In a very small number of children, the brain lesion is a cyst which is filled with fluid. In some cases, that cyst enlarges and increases the severity of the hemiparesis.

Thus the important identification is the infant with worsening hemiparesis or the infant who fails to make any progress with therapies across months. The latter judgment can also be complicated. Infants who are identified late—that is, after one year of age—tend to improve more slowly with therapies.

An infant with a worsening hemiparesis may need more studies, especially a brain imaging test, either computed tomography or magnetic resonance imaging.

Deafness

Since the advent of the brainstem auditory evoked response for newborns and infants, the late discovery of a deaf child, at age three or so, is most unusual. The more common undiagnosed deafness is partial and associated with ear infections and chronic serous otitis (fluid in the ears). Unfortunately, this often occurs in late infancy when language development is so important.

Other circumstances at risk for deafness include: meningitis, cytomegalovirus infection, ear malformations, cleft palate, Pierre Robin syndrome, and familial deafness.

Decreasing Visual Acuity

Recognizing this process in an infant is a matter of keen observation. It would be unusual to find this simply on the basis of a plateauing or very slow development in the use of eyes or eye-hand coordination skills. Rather the concern is *loss* of skills. This occurs in certain degenerative brain disease (such as neuronal ceroid-lipofuscinosis) and in certain tumors (optic glioma, hypothalamic glioma, or pituitary tumor). The mother may provide the clues. For example, one mother described that the infant no longer picked up tiny balls of lint from the rug. It is good rule of thumb to make these observations on two or more occasions. While we would all like to discover unusual disease processes, these conditions are infrequent and some are very rare. There should be a balance between enthusiasm for diagnosis and the risk of further alarming parents who may already be out of balance from previous medical testing.

6

What to Say When

To Parents

What we say to a parent ought to be based on the reliability of our assessment and the validity of that assessment for prediction to specific outcomes, knowledge of the impact of such statements on parents, and the experience to estimate the impact of such statements on particular parents. In short, we need the wisdom of Solomon.

Initial Comments After Identifying Abnormalities

With infants who have moderate to severe neuromotor abnormalities or developmental delay, the parents are often already aware that there may be a problem. Indeed that may already have been suggested by a grandparent, a friend, the doctor, or the parents themselves, especially with the easy availability of books and scales of child development. It is very helpful to find out the basis of the parents' concern. Perhaps it is most difficult to convey information about abnormalities when the parent does not suspect such.

Whether the parents suspect abnormality or are unaware of abnormality—and we are certain that there is abnormality—our statements need to be tempered with compassion, yet honest. Sometimes one can identify the abnormalities by description, rather than by diagnosis, and set the time for a second evaluation to test for significant change. However, parents may not tolerate the waiting period. A more constructive approach may be that of providing specific instructions for the parent to help the infant. That may work out very well when the professional who identifies the abnormalities is knowledgeable about positioning, carrying, stimulation, and even some basic stretch or therapeutic maneuvers for infants.

When an infant scores in the abnormal range on the *Infanib,* a more formal approach may be recommended by the clinicians involved. Therapies may be more formalized either through a home-based program or through a center-based program. Diagnosis may be formalized through various testing procedures under the supervision of medical specialists. It is important that testing information be discussed sufficiently enough that the parent attains a reasonable level of understanding.

Parents may convey such understanding at the time of discussion but later seem less able to articulate information about either the process or its level of abnormality. Some of this may be secondary to *denial,* a defense mechanism that protects all of us from information we cannot handle.

A second change in focus may occur within the program. When infants are moderately to severely impaired, professionals and parents tend to set different timetables for developmental milestones. The most modest gain is praised lavishly. Few people can function in a sea of despair. Thus the hope of progress fuels the daily routine. Glowing reports may accompany this: for example, _____ has made excellent progress in the last six months (even though _____ only learned to roll from back to front at age 15 months). But we must be careful not to confuse parents so that they think healing is occurring that will ultimately yield "a normal child" (and many parents do use this sort of language).

The Dilemma: Labeling vs. Not Labeling

In all the years of my work with the developmentally disabled, some parents have asked us as professionals not to label their children. Thus we provided new names: "mental retardation" became "developmental delay;" "epilepsy" became "seizure disorder;" "cerebral palsy" became lack of expected normal "physiologic development."

Yet insurance companies require the identification of certain abnormalities or various bills are not paid. Similarly, funding for services requires certain labels in many programs. There may be a tendency to provide a somewhat more serious label in order to qualify the child for services. Since most of us, whether physical therapists, occupational therapists, or speech therapists, believe in our remedial work at the most basic level (or how else could we spend the hours in it?), we often refer children with mild deficits for fairly intensive programs. Yet many studies show that mild deficits often correct themselves or that they require only a modest amount of intervention. For example, with mild speech delay secondary to otitis media, or chronic serous otitis, fairly infrequent speech therapy plus some education of parents and placement in groups of normal children may be sufficient to increase the language development to a normal level. The issues about labeling have not been resolved entirely and it may be impossible to do so.

Critical Times in Testing

Testing before adoption still requires the best of skills. This is an issue of pure predictive validity, without the complications of prenatal feelings, insurance company pigeonholes, or allegiances to our various disciplines—**unless the prospective adoptee is already in the home and under the care of the adopting parents.**

We need to be very careful in describing the child's weaknesses, particularly in adoptive homes in which the child has been resident for some time. Many adoptive parents in these circumstances will assume the responsibility for any weaknesses, and the guilt.

My recommendation is that the best available assessment methods—that is, those with high reliability and validity—be used to assess current function. Otherwise, predictive validity may be poor. Normal neuromotor function predicts very well to later normal neuromotor function. Thus the newborn or the infant assessed as normal with highly reliable and valid neuromotor assessment instruments has a high probability of remaining normal, barring unforeseen and unpredictable circumstances such as meningitis or head injury.

For those infants identified with transient neuromotor abnormalities, we must accept and describe the limits of our ability to predict and the limits of our ability to assess certain problems at certain ages. In this situation, the probability is that the infant will not develop learning disabilities, at a level of 51% or more. However, the infant is within a group at increased risk for learning disabilities. We cannot assess well for learning disabilities until the early school years.

The Comprehensive Assessment

The multidisciplinary full assessment in which the infant or child is evaluated by a group of professionals must be an awesome first experience for parents. The professionals bear an extra responsibility because they are often defined as *super* experts. Even *super* experts are limited by their experience and the reliability and validity of the assessment instruments that they use.

To Colleagues

Although education in developmental testing has been offered to prospective pediatricians and family practitioners for years, clinicians vary in their comfort with these tools in both developmental and neurologic assessment of young infants. From time to time, infants are still evaluated and described as "abnormal" by the follow-up team, yet were not so described by their physicians. This can be awkward.

The physicians who care for infants must be considered colleagues. Some are highly dependent on your knowledge for assessment. Others may prefer a role in which "bad news" is conveyed by someone else—such as the follow-up team, who should be expert in conveying bad news. Others really prefer to convey such information themselves. A call to the physician may yield considerable information about the preferred approach.

Differences of opinion may also arise over recommended therapies. These days some families have to pay part or all of the bill. Families with HMO health coverage may be very limited in the number and type of treatments, and the selection of therapists. Sometimes recommendations will need to be based on other information besides a description of the infant's abnormalities. Often the physician may have information about family resources, needs and numbers of other children, and the restrictions of the health insurance.

The follow-up team may advise a more limited therapeutic program based on such information. They may spend more time instructing the parent(s) so that therapies can continue at home in situations with restrictions.

To Lawyers

Lawyers need numbers and accurate descriptions. Reports that describe abnormalities in the language that has been developed in order to protect parents and perhaps to protect children serves no purpose here. Thus instruments that provide scores, including instruments that provide neuromotor or intelligence scores, may be very helpful.

Lawyers are also in need of information about predictive validity, although they would never ask the question that way. The lawyers are usually interested in the permanency of abnormalities. By this time, you would know that is a predictive validity question.

Lawyers do not, in general, want information about causation from therapists. They will use other experts for that.

Some clinicians will participate in the legal process by giving depositions or serving as expert witnesses in a trial. It has been my experience repeatedly that at legal trials for malpractice, when the child's problems must be explained to a jury in simple, clear language for lay people, the parent(s) then tells the lawyer: "This is the first time I ever understood what is wrong with my child." It is likely that many previous explanations were given, but a trial is a time of judgment in many different ways. For some parents, this aspect of a trial has been devastating. It may be wiser for some parents that they not attend all parts of a trial. Other parents have been waiting or perhaps even longing for clear explanations. Then the trial serves a different purpose, and those parents probably will wish to be present.

7

The Construction of the Infanib

The series of steps for the construction of an assessment instrument varies little whether that assessment concerns attitudes, neuromotor skills, behavior, or development (Canegelosi 1984). The steps are outlined here so that the reader becomes knowledgeable about them and can examine descriptions of the development of other assessment instruments as a basis for choosing an instrument with good reason.

1. The first step in constructing an assessment instrument is that of making a list of possible items. The original list for the construction of the *Infanib* included the five items from the French angles method that were considered very helpful: scarf sign, heel-to-ear, popliteal angle, leg abduction, and dorsiflexion of the foot. The items were retained from the method of Milani-Comparetti and Gidoni on the basis of analysis of a large set of data (Ellison et al. 1983). The primitive reflex items came from Capute et al. (Capute et al. 1978). A few items were added from the forms used for infants in the National Collaborative Perinatal Project.

2. The list was pruned. Infants will only endure so much. The list was pruned on the basis of experience and previous studies. This list was still longer than the final recommended method of evaluation. There is a tendency when clinicians initially form methods of evaluation to recommend extensive lists of items, perhaps under the consideration that nothing should be without description. As will be discussed later, many of these items are redundant. A clinician who develops a method of evaluation is thinking along certain lines and the chosen items reflect this.

3. The items were *scored.* Data analysis is built upon variance—a range in scores and subjects that represent that range. The first rule is: All scoring must go in one direction. Such scoring is called *monotonic*—normality is always scored at one end of the scale and abnormality at the other. Others have tried scoring neurological items. In some of these attempts, the score goes from abnormal to normal to abnormal again. This is *not* monotonic. It is very difficult to use in data analyses. The scores have to be re-done, which not only takes time but increases the chance of error.

Theoretically, each point in the score should be equidistant from the other. Achieving this with clinical data could be the focus of an entire research project. Each step of this type takes time and money. This step of *scaling* has not been well-studied. In general, clinical judgment and experience were used to estimate distances between scoring points.

4. Competent, compulsive examiners were requested to examine a large sample of infants who were initially treated in the neonatal intensive care unit. Examiners who are asked to obtain

hundreds of examinations must have certain qualities: perseverance, patience, and willingness to fill in every data entry point for every child. It is less important from which discipline they come (medicine, physical or occupational therapy, nursing) and more important that the project be done well. It is very discouraging to find sections of the test that were not filled in *after* the project is completed.

5. The examiner was asked to score each infant on a five-point "gestalt" rating after the evaluation and before examining the results of the evaluation. Most experienced clinicians probably use a mental "gestalt" process to form an opinion. The examiners in this study, who were physical therapists experienced in the examination of infants, were asked to rank each infant as normal, minimally abnormal, mildly abnormal, moderately abnormal, or severely abnormal. Any infant who was ranked as abnormal was also given a diagnosis by the examiner from one of the following: spastic tetraparesis/dyskinesia, spastic diplegia, spastic hemiparesis, or hypotonia.

6. These data were taken to the Department of Psychology, University of Denver, for my two-year National Institute of Health Senior Scientist Fellowship to study with Dr. John Horn, an expert in statistics and data analysis. Dr. Horn never examined data in a cursory or simplistic fashion. The fellowship granted the luxury of time. Course work in statistics—from the bottom basic undergraduate course, then working through the graduate student series—helped. But working with data was the biggest help. If the first steps—selection of items; pruning and scoring of items, and data collection—are done well, then data analysis is challenging and fun. Otherwise it is just challenging, and often somewhat disappointing because it is impossible to replace deficiencies. A good set of data has a certain beauty and intrigue to the data analyst.

   a. We examined the descriptive statistics for each item: means, standard deviations, kurtoses, skews.

   b. We obtained a correlation matrix. This is the heart of the matter—a description of the relations among variables. The correlations between the 20 items on the *Infanib* are shown in table 7.1.

   c. We used factor analysis to group the items mathematically— using different numbers of factors and different types of factor analysis (Horn 1965). The use of factor analysis is a long discussion. It should be used by those with considerable experience. There probably is no better method for grouping items. It is a far superior method to the a priori grouping of items by clinicians.

   d. We used the guidelines developed for factor analysis to choose a data analytic solution that described the data well: each factor had to be adequately identified (it had three or four items that loaded it with sufficient weight), the number of factors was appropriate, and the solution appeared to represent the data well.

   e. We pruned the items. Initially the four top-loading items for each of five factors were selected, resulting in a 20-item battery.

Table 7.1. Correlation Matrix of items in the *Infanib*

	ATNR	Pull-to-sitting	Sitting	Sideways parachute	Backwards parachute	Standing	Foot grasp	Forward parachute	All-fours	Body derotative	Body rotative	Scarf sign	Heel-to-ear	Popliteal angle	Leg abduction	Dorsiflexion of foot	Positive support reflex	Tonic labyrinthine supine	Tonic labyrinthine prone	Hands closed/open
ATNR	1.00																			
Pull-to-sitting	.50	1.00																		
Sitting	.45	.64	1.00																	
Sideways parachute	.51	.67	.81	1.00																
Backwards parachute	.03	.21	.23	.11	1.00															
Standing	.31	.50	.64	.60	.23	1.00														
Foot grasp	.30	.30	.40	.35	.35	.55	1.00													
Forward parachute	.36	.47	.43	.54	.30	.36	.29	1.00												
All-fours	.32	.53	.53	.60	.28	.54	.39	.29	1.00											
Body derotative	.51	.70	.70	.67	.15	.62	.43	.38	.61	1.00										
Body rotative	.10	.23	.25	.14	.80	.32	.41	.34	.40	.27	1.00									
Scarf sign	.53	.31	.34	.34	.18	.32	.37	.31	.22	.32	.23	1.00								
Heel-to-ear	.54	.40	.47	.45	.25	.42	.51	.41	.41	.49	.34	.58	1.00							
Popliteal angle	.56	.46	.48	.46	.24	.46	.48	.39	.40	.55	.33	.60	.81	1.00						
Leg abduction	.45	.34	.30	.28	.30	.31	.41	.27	.26	.32	.32	.59	.66	.77	1.00					
Dorsiflexion of foot	.20	.26	.28	.30	.14	.43	.56	.23	.28	.32	.19	.27	.46	.41	.36	1.00				
Positive support reflex	.33	.25	.25	.31	.13	.45	.49	.19	.23	.27	.19	.38	.43	.45	.38	.41	1.00			
Tonic labyrinthine supine	.76	.59	.59	.58	.12	.44	.38	.36	.39	.61	.19	.54	.57	.58	.47	.29	.36	1.00		
Tonic labyrinthine prone	.64	.54	.53	.53	.08	.41	.39	.31	.33	.55	.13	.43	.47	.47	.38	.35	.30	.80	1.00	
Hands closed/open	.69	.52	.54	.58	.17	.45	.52	.40	.39	.56	.20	.50	.58	.61	.48	.30	.43	.74	.60	1.00

f. We obtained values for internal consistency (reliability) for the factors and for the total scores for two different ages—above and below eight months. Internal consistency is a mathematical calculation based on the correlation coefficients (strength of association among items) and the number of items in the assessment (Nunnally 1978). Adding more and more items may seem a logical way to increase the internal consistency. To a certain extent that is true. At a point, more items decrease the internal consistency. Usually, one simply runs out of items with high correlations to the other items. A high internal consistency indicates that the items will measure a similar quality. This mathematical calculation does not indicate just what the quality is; the researcher must name the quality. This calculation is a key indicator of reliability. For the *Infanib,* the alpha coefficient or internal consistency was .88 for infants seven months of age or less, .93 for infants eight months or more, and .91 for all subjects. This is more than high enough for research purposes and it is high enough to discriminate well among infants for clinical work. If all the previous work had not been done well, these values would be low. They could be low for other reasons—that the items were not strongly associated with each other, for example.

Any worthy assessment method must meet certain reliability criteria. Unfortunately for most methods of assessment now in use, aside from the psychological methods such as the Bayley, the calculations for internal consistency have not been published. They may never have been calculated.

7. A scoring sheet was created for the 20 items, using a five-point scale. All items were scored monotonically; abnormality received fewer points and normality the maximum numbers of points (five). The assessment method was then taken to the clinic for use by a group of physicians and physical therapists who knew nothing about the instrument. They were very helpful in suggesting improvements for the scoring sheet and in commenting about the items. As a result, two items were discarded; substitutes were selected from the next highest loading item on that particular factor. In addition, the five-point scale was changed to three-point scale (one, three, and five points) because the physicians had difficulty making decisions on a five-point scale.

8. Cut points were made after reviewing the scores of the different levels of abnormality and the different types of abnormality described by the physical therapists in the initial evaluation and on the basis of clinical experience. In intelligence testing, different levels have been defined by standard deviations from the mean. I do not consider this a good approach for neuromotor assessment. Since we know that most infants with transient abnormality recover motorically, I thought that this category should be quite broad. It had comprised about 21 percent of the infants from the neonatal unit in two previous studies. In this study, 46 percent of the infants were described as normal, 37 percent as transiently abnormal, and 17 percent as abnormal.

The results of assessment for infants, especially infants from the neonatal unit, must be described with care because most infants with neuromotor abnormality are not going to remain motorically abnormal. They are going to improve at least until age seven years, the oldest age at which we have studied them.

Thus phrases such as "abnormality" or "cerebral palsy" should be used with great care. This is especially applicable when parents seem to have only one picture of cerebral palsy: a child in a wheelchair. On the other hand, it is awkward to send an infant for physical therapy without a diagnosis. These days all billing requires a code. Billing codes often find their way to parents. It would be better to be straightforward from the beginning. Some infants with "transient neurological abnormalities of infancy" will receive physical therapy. Very few of them would be expected to retain their abnormalities into early childhood. A larger percent of infants with designated neurological abnormalities of a degree more severe than "transient" will receive physical therapy. Many of them will also recover but it usually takes longer and often some clumsiness remains.

8

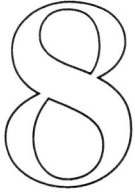

Methodological Issues

Why should a clinician be interested in methodology? Is that not the turf of the researcher? *A clinician needs to know enough to check up on the assessment methods knowledgeably and to choose well.* A clinician needs a *higher* level of reliability for his/her work than the researcher. The researcher deals with groups (or samples) of children. The data analysis will never single out only one child. The clinician has to make statements and often decisions about one child (or at least one child at a time). The clinician carries an even heavier burden because he/she usually makes statements of authority to others: parents, other caregivers, social service agencies, lawyers. The assessment methods chosen by the clinician must be *reliable* and *valid*.

Very few clinicians have formal training in methodology and research unless they have achieved a doctoral degree in a discipline other than medicine. Some M.D.s take statistical courses through the Schools of Public Health, often at the level of the master's degree. These courses are usually not the type, sequence, or amount required for doctoral degrees. Yet most clinicians want to do good clinical work.

Solid methodology is the foundation upon which good assessment instruments are based. Specifically, high reliability and validity are the foundations of good assessment methods. Solid methodology must be coupled with good judgment and extensive clinical experience.

Observation in Early Years

In the early years of a discipline or the development of core ideas, most methods of assessment will be descriptive. This period has spanned almost 30 years in the infancy neurological examination. It is clear from the early writings that clinicians knew that they could not simply adapt the adult neurological examinations to infants. They began to make lists of items that were considered neurologic and that seemed to distinguish normal from abnormal babies. Initially a lot of these distinctions were between the most abnormal and absolutely normal babies. In early separations, the distinctions tend to be polar. The descriptions that came from physicians were generally directed toward making a diagnosis.

Probably the majority of those diagnoses had no known medical treatment—and most still do not. Therapies developed through other disciplines—physical, occupational, and speech therapies. For infants, these therapies were largely directed toward the facilitation of acquisition of motor skills: rolling over, sitting and walking, or feeding. As time passed, observations became more finely tuned, especially for the *quality* of movement. Furthermore, physical and occupational therapists were not "permitted" to make diagnoses although many are quite capable of doing so. It is awkward at best to become skillful in description—and not be permitted to apply the umbrella descriptor.

The present scenario is surely ironic. The physician who is theoretically able to make diagnoses may be less observant than the physical therapist, occupational therapist, or nurse. Indeed, in many situations, such as the neonatal intensive care units or the follow-up programs, the detailed neurological description is often done by the physical or occupational therapist. In my experience, physical and occupational therapists have worried for years about the delays by physicians in referral and delays in recognition of infants with neurological deviations.

Does Recognition of Abnormality Require Doing Something About It?

Physical, occupational, and speech therapies surely do not hurt infants. Do they help them? This is a complex research question sadly in need of more work. Certainly many aspects of therapy help: teaching the parent(s) how to handle the baby, providing support for the parent(s), placing the baby in key positions so that other appropriate skills for age are encouraged (such as observations of the environment and development of eye-hand coordination).

These days the practitioners of no discipline have the financial resources to do what they would like to do for neurologically impaired children. In most situations, we must make good allocations of resources—time and money. The issue of which infants should receive therapies for how often and how long are critical research questions. These basic questions should not be confused with *hope*—from the parents, the therapists, and the physician—that the child will improve and that some new development will help the child.

These questions direct us right back to the bottom rung of the ladder—*good methodology*. How will we identify those infants who will benefit most from therapy?

Enter the Computer

Computers sneak into many people's lives unnoticed. But they serve a critical role because they permit the acquisition of data about large numbers of children. Whether we like it or not, computers are forcing us to change our ways.

1. Computers permit us to follow large samples. So much work in the infancy field is based on very small sample sizes. Researchers have to be especially careful about drawing conclusions from small samples—25 or 50 infants are not enough.

   One of the reasons that large samples (over 100, even better over 250, or over 500) are needed in this work is that abnormality is low in frequency (for which we are surely grateful). Even when we start with very large samples we may find that only a handful of children actually had the condition we were interested in. With small samples, we risk the danger of *capitalizing on chance.* That means that what we show or do not show simply reflects our data set, not the condition under study. We even risk capitalizing on chance with large samples sizes, especially if the condition of interest is no longer as serious as it once was (asphyxia in well managed urban and suburban hospitals is an excellent example of this). For many issues in developmental work, concepts evolve through *replication* (always a firm basis for seeking scientific truth). However, clinical work is not like the laboratory. Our replications are never exactly the same—or they are not real replications since each researcher wants to be innovative and perform creative work. We end up evolving our concepts by a process that one of my colleagues calls "bootlegging." The results or a part of the results of one study are used in combination with the results or part of the results of another study. Then one says, "I think this process works about this way because. . . ." And that is the *most* we should say. And it may be the most we will ever be able to say.

2. Computers and the subsequent data analyses point out our shortcomings. In every study we have done, *missing data* are a problem—sometimes more, sometimes less. There is nothing like a list of data with holes in it, scattered here and there to demonstrate our lack of thoroughness in evaluation and data collection. There are ways of working with missing data but they can never equal the accuracy of the actual data.

3. Computers force us to change our descriptions. For years physical and occupational therapists have written long paragraphs of descriptions about children. No one can criticize their care in observation or recording. However, that approach does not translate readily into computer use or subsequent data analysis. The acquisition of data, even the original collections form, can influence the amount of missing data, can be done in ways that describe conditions well (or poorly), can be directed at the key questions (or can approach them sideways).

4. Computers permit data analysis. If we see 25 infants with 25 characteristics each (625 data points) and we simply want to count how many of those characteristics each had, we generally do not need a computer. We might use a hand calculator. We are *only counting* and we will *not* learn much. If the study includes 100 children with 50 data points (5,000 data points), some researchers might use chi square or t-tests, both tests of statistical significance. Others will switch to statistics based on the correlation matrix—a table of correlations between all possible pairs of data points (50 x 50 in the previous data set). From the correlation matrix, one can progress to multivariate analyses, which examines more than two variables. This important step is the only way that we will begin to tease apart the really tough research questions.

5. Computers can help us to improve our assessment methods. They enable us to store and analyze large amounts of data. We can construct better assessment instruments and we can obtain the mathematical calculations through which we can increase their reliability and validity.

Reliability

The word "reliable" is bounced about quite freely in discussion among clinicians. In previous writings, I defined reliability as "an index of the consistency of a measure, which may refer to the agreement of different items with each other, the agreement of different examiners, or of the same test on different occasions with itself" (Ellison 1990). Most clinicians want to use highly reliable assessment instruments. Indeed, the reliability of our conclusions can only be as reliable as that of the assessment instruments. As the corollary, the less reliable the assessment instruments, the less likely we are to be correct in our assessment of a child; the less reliable the assessment instruments, the less likely we are to find scientific truths in our research.

The key to reliability is *internal consistency,* which is a measure of the strength of the associations between items on a test and the number of items in the test. A well recognized index of this is coefficient alpha (Nunnally 1978). A high coefficient alpha indicates that the test items are sufficiently strongly related to each other and that there are enough items that whatever is being measured should be adequately measured by the assessment instrument. Of course, the numbers do not tell you what is being measured. The clinician judges and names that.

Inter-rater Reliability

What increases the chance that two examiners will come to the same conclusions after using the same assessment instrument? Surely motivation to do so and acquiescence to the requirements of the evaluation are the most important. Clinicians who do neuromotor examinations often are not experienced in giving a certain test. For physicians, the neuromotor examination was usually learned from the tutelage of another physician who was higher in the hierarchy. The evaluation was usually used as a tool to help in making a diagnosis. If you got the diagnosis right, it did not matter whether you did the examination precisely the same way. The exception was missing a key finding noted by one's chief. In that case, one probably also missed the diagnosis. The eye of the physical therapist had to be trained differently—to judge quality. Now quality of movement and recognition of abnormal movement for diagnostic purposes may overlap (as in notation of extensor posturing) or they may be separate. *All clinicians must follow the format and scoring method of a test such as the Infanib—especially in research studies.* Privately, they may add additional items, but these should not be part of the scoring. Physicians in different parts of the world have told me that they always add a certain item or even two to the *Infanib* because they consider the additional items important. Thus far, these additional items have never been the same.

Inter-rater reliability will also be higher if the items are well-anchored, that is, by written descriptions or photographs that explain clearly how to perform the item. Scoring choices must also be clearcut. Increasing the range of scores per item decreases the chance that two evaluators will select the same score. Specifically, if there is a choice among nine points for an item, it is less likely that two evaluators will make the same choice than if there are only three choices. However, scores with a fairly wide range of points can be taught to evaluators in closely controlled programs (for example, the Boston-based training sessions for the Brazelton method of neonatal evaluations). The fact that inter-rater reliability is high does not necessarily mean that the test is a good one. It simply means that some combination of duplicating the assessment and scoring choice and "motivation" has yielded very similar results.

In a study of 65 infants with seven evaluators using the *Infanib* with each infant independently examined by two testers on each occasion and each infant tested on two occasions (a total of 234 assessments), the inter-rater reliability for total scores on the *Infanib* was very high ($r = .97$) (Castro et al. 1985).

Test-retest Reliability

Does the infant have the same score on subsequent examinations? If the time period between evaluations is short, a day or two or even a week or two, the test-retest score should be very similar on a good instrument with a good examiner. However, for longer time spans the reliability may be lower—for reasons that may not be secondary to the test itself. Most particularly, infants with abnormalities are subject to change. There is a general decrease in neurological abnormalities throughout infancy for many infants treated in the neonatal intensive care unit. On the other hand, the small number of moderately to severely abnormal infants with spasticity or dyskinesia may score at lower levels as they go from generalized hypotonia to spasticity/dyskinesia. Pediatric neurologists do not consider that something new (or more or worse) is happening to the child's brain. Cerebral palsy is considered a static encephalopathy—something happened to the brain early in development and no new brain result occurred. Clearly the clinical expression changes.

For neurologically normal infants, the test-retest is amazingly similar. In our largest data set (nearly 1,000 infants) with examinations at 6 and 15 months, the correlations between scores for normal infants at 6 months and scores at the 15-month assessment were over .95, using the Milani-Comparetti and Gidoni method of assessment. This demonstrates again the concept that once the infant obtains a normal neuromotor status, he/she keeps it.

In the study cited previously for inter-rater reliability, the test-retest reliability for the *Infanib* was also very high ($r = .95$) (Castro et al. 1985).

Validity

This is a concept about the correctness of inferences from the results of the testing. The type of validity that most clinicians ask about is *predictive validity.* If the infant was described as neurologically abnormal, will the infant always be neurologically abnormal? If the infant at age 12 months is described as neurologically abnormal, was that infant described as neurologically abnormal at 6 months? Since a lot of neurologic abnormality disappears, one expects a smaller number of abnormal infants at 12 months than at 6 months, especially in a sample of infants who were treated in the neonatal intensive care units. We should not fault the assessment instrument for lesser predictive validity in infants who improve. With good assessment instruments with well identified sub-scales ("well identified" means a sufficient number of items with adequate mathematical "loading" on that subscale—see the factor loadings for the *Infanib*, table 8.1), we should be able to determine which subscales identify infants who will remain abnormal. On the other hand, we do not want to "miss" or fail to identify abnormalities at 6 months and then find them at 12 months.

Table 8.1. The 20 Items Selected for the *Infanib* Using Factor Analysis (Promax Rotation)

	Factor	Items	Factor Loading	Reliability*
I.	Spasticity	asymmetric tonic neck reflex	.71	
		tonic labyrinthine in prone	.78	
		tonic labyrinthine in supine	.77	
		hands held open or closed	.61	.86
II.	Head and trunk	sitting	.65	
		pulled to sitting	.71	
		all fours	.73	
		body derotative	.74	.86
III.	Vestibular function	backwards parachute	.88	
		forward parachute	.88	
		sideways parachute	.63	
		body rotative	.89	.89
IV.	Legs	standing	.56	
		foot grasp	.70	
		dorsiflexion of foot	.67	
		positive support reflex	.66	.72
V.	French angles	scarf sign	.67	
		heel-to-ear	.75	
		popliteal angle	.78	
		abductor's angle	.82	.89

*Total score reliabilities: All subjects .91, 7 months or less .88, 8 months or more .93

Stavrakas et al. did a study of 243 infants using the *Infanib* as the assessment instrument with evaluations at 6 and 12 months. The spasticity and head and trunk subscales (factors) at 6 months were highly predictive of cerebral palsy at 12 months—86.8% and 87.1% respectively with discriminant function analyses (Stavrakas et al. 1991).

Thus far, there are no data for the predictive validity of the *Infanib* from infancy to older ages. However, in the longitudinal study of children born in 1975-76 in Southeastern Wisconsin and treated in the neonatal intensive care units in Milwaukee, the path coefficient between the infancy neuromotor examination using the Milani-Comparetti and Gidoni method and neuromotor examination at six-seven years for 185 children was .64 for the items that grouped mathematically to form what we called the "hard" portion of the neuromotor evaluation (Ellison and Foster 1992). The path coefficient between the infancy neuromotor examination and the "soft" portion of the neuromotor examination was .42. These are very large path coefficients between variables from one age to another, especially in the long time span that elapsed between infancy and six-seven years. I think these large path coefficients indicate high predictive validity for the Milani-Comparetti and Gidoni methods of assessment.

Since the *Infanib* was constructed to increase the internal consistency of assessment, I would assume that predictive validity for the *Infanib* is higher, but I do not yet have data to test that.

Concurrent validity compares the results of one method of assessment with those of another method of assessment. In the neurologic examination of infancy, one could assess a sample of infants with the Milani-Comparetti and Gidoni method, and then with the method of Amiel-Tison, obtain scores for each and obtain correlations between the two methods. If the correlations were reasonably high and statistically significant, one could speak of concurrent validity and claim that each was measuring something similar. If the correlations were low, then the two methods measured different entities.

I have taken a slightly different approach to this. I have assumed that an experienced examiner who has extensive experience with both normal and abnormal infants forms a "gestalt" of that infant during the process of evaluation. One main reason to construct an instrument such as the the *Infanib* is to form a configuration or gestalt for examiners with less experience (as well as making certain that examinations are done similarly). Thus, examiners were asked in the original study to rate the infants as normal to abnormal on a five-point scale and to name the type of abnormality. The scores from the factors and total score were then correlated with the "gestalt" scores of the initial examinations. This is a form of concurrent validity.

Construct validity assumes that there is a theoretical framework for any test. For example, we could assume that some infants "ought" to be neurologically abnormal—such as prematurely born children who had certain sicknesses or full-term newborns who were severely asphyxiated. This type of thinking is very useful in the early descriptive stages. One excellent example of this type of thinking is Prechtl's optimality scale (Prechtl 1968). In many previous studies, Prechtl's scale was used to form two groups of newborns, one "normal" and the other "abnormal." Maternal characteristics, either before or during pregnancy, the type of variables that formed the bulk of the Prechtl scale, correlated poorly with outcomes in the National Collaborative Perinatal Project. The neonatal conditions on the Prechtl Scale were not sufficient to predict well to normal/abnormal outcomes, especially for premature children. The neonatal conditions should be better considered and provide better construct validity for neurologic abnormality on the scoring sheet (See table 1.5, page 20).

In summary, only *some* infants will have neurological abnormality from newborns presumed abnormal. Or, the corollary, a lot of neurological abnormality disappears from the neonatal to infancy periods.

Building Research into Follow-Up

Research in follow-up programs stems from several sources. Many clinicians who supervise or participate in follow-up programs need to do research and to write papers to achieve promotions, especially those with an academic affiliation. Indeed, this prompted some of my early attempts at research. As a new assistant professor who was keenly interested in follow-up, it was suggested that I start some research projects and write a grant. I learned by doing in the research and look back on the grant as just plain silly (a position I am able to state some 15 plus years later). Good clinical research requires training in statistics and research methods in the same way that good laboratory research requires training in laboratory methods.

There is also a huge temptation to store large amounts of data because of the computers. Surely one might do something with it. If you are serious about research in the academic setting, expand your horizons to course work at the local department of psychology, department of statistics, or the department of biostatistics. The type of statistics you eventually choose to enlarge upon would differ with the type of research you intend. At the beginning, they are all much alike. Follow the coursework in statistics with a course or two in research methods.

Then armed with knowledge about research design, statistics, and methodology, with access to a large sample of appropriate children and backed up by a good computer system, where could you start?

1. Bite off a chewable chunk. No study will answer all questions. We are lucky to gain some knowledge about one or two important questions in each study. Clinical research moves ahead slowly and builds on previous research.

2. Focus your study on questions that can probably be answered in your sample. Good sense can help you judge this. For example, many clinicians would like to study asphyxiated babies. These days there are fewer severely asphyxiated babies, especially in large university and community hospitals with good obstetrical departments. One could pose the question: What would I like to study? But one might better pose the question: What could I study in the samples available to me?

3. Focus the question. This reminds me of using the microscope or telescope, or camera. At first, the image is blurry. You want to make the image sharp. A clinical researcher cannot be muddling around in a slough of tentative possibilities. What do you want to learn? Can you express this in a series of statements, which you may eventually choose to call hypotheses.

4. It is unlikely that examination of very small parts will contribute much. For example, a study that focuses on one item in the neurological examination is meaningless to this researcher.

True, we all have favorite items. But in general, the neurologic exam is built on a configuration. Most useful concepts in clinical work are based on configurations and that means using more than two variables (for example, IVH and cerebral palsy). That leads us right back to multivariate analyses.

5. Allow time and money for data analyses. If you need three years to gather data, you need at least a year to do the data analyses, unless you are doing "starter" projects, hoping to get the pieces in order enough to proceed to a synthesis. Years ago, one of my pathology professors yelled at us daily: "Synthesize, synthesize!" And he was right. But it took a long time to learn that—and a long time to learn how to do it.

Providing Some Feedback to the Neonatologists

Perhaps the follow-up clinicians will eventually understand that most will not do major research. However, with the use of computers, the follow-up programs could provide some basic information about infants to the neonatologists with the use of some reliable and valid outcome measures. This would be frequency data based on counting. It will give feedback, but it will not lead to a good understanding of process, and should not be conceived as such.

Excellence in Service

Surely, there can be no more worthy goal than to achieve excellence in service. That is the reason that most of us became clinicians. Perhaps it seems strange that a chapter on methodology would end with an ode to service and those who perform it. My reasoning is thus: Excellence in clinical research is based on excellence in clinical work. On the other hand, the excellent clinician has to understand enough about research methods even to choose well among assessment methods in order to be an excellent clinician.

Appendixes

Appendix A

Neurologic Examination of Newborns and Infants

I. General Description

Head circumference
___ Centimeters
___ Percentile
___ Head configuration abnormalities

| | 1 = No | 2 = Yes |

If *yes*, then check all that apply:
- ☐ Unilateral coronal suture
- ☐ Brachycephaly
- ☐ Dolichocephaly
- ☐ Oxycephaly
- ☐ Trigonencephaly
- ☐ Associated hand anomalies
  Describe: _____
- ☐ *Other:* _____

___ Anterior fontanelle abnormalities   1 = No   2 = Yes
If *yes*, then check all that apply:
- ☐ Bulging
- ☐ Concave
- ☐ Too large
- ☐ Too small
- ___ Size of fontanelle (centimeters)
- ☐ *Other:* _____

___ Other fontanelle abnormalities   1 = No   2 = Yes
If *yes*, then check all that apply:
- ☐ Open posterior fontanelle
- ☐ Third fontanelle
- ☐ *Other:* _____

___ Other skull abnormalities   1 = No   2 = Yes
If *yes*, then check all that apply:
- ☐ Cephalohematoma
- ☐ Caput succudeum
- ☐ Molding
  ___ 1 = Mild   2 = Moderate   3 = Severe
  Overlapping sutures
  ___ 1 = Mild   2 = Moderate   3 = Severe
- ☐ *Other:* _____

___ Eye abnormalities   1 = No   2 = Yes
If *yes*, then check all that apply:
- ☐ "Setting sun"
- ☐ Wandering
- ☐ Conjugate deviation
- ☐ Nystagmus
- ☐ Strabismus
- ☐ Conjunctival hemorrhage
- ☐ *Other:* _____

___ Skin abnormalities   1 = No   2 = Yes
If *yes*, then check all that apply:
- ☐ Cafe au lait
- ☐ Depigmented spots
- ☐ Hemangiomas
- ☐ Nevi
- ☐ Ecchymoses
- ☐ *Other:* _____
and complete the following:
  Size: _____
  Location: _____

___ Dysmorphic features   1 = No   2 = Yes
If *yes*, then check all that apply:

☐ Eyes	☐ Arms
☐ Hypertelorism	☐ Legs
☐ Hypotelorism	☐ Palmar creases
☐ Skull	☐ Dermatoglyphics
☐ Neck	☐ Digits
☐ Palate	☐ Joints
☐ Chest	☐ Genitalia
☐ *Other:*	

and complete the following:
  Describe: _____
  _____

___ Organomegaly   1 = No   2 = Yes
If *yes*, then check all that apply:
- ☐ Liver
- ☐ Kidney
- ☐ Spleen
- ☐ Heart
- ☐ *Other:*
and complete the following:
  Describe: _____

___ Seizures   1 = No   2 = Infrequent
             3 = Repetitive   4 = Status epilepticus
If *yes*, then check all that apply:
- ☐ Subtle
- ☐ Focal clonic
- ☐ Myofocal clonic
- ☐ Multifocal
- ☐ Tonic
- ☐ Myoclonic
- ☐ *Other:* _____

___ Apnea   1 = No   2 = Infrequent   3 = Recurrent

___ Brachial plexus injury   1 = No   2 = Yes
  Describe: _____

continued

___ Hand preference   1 = No   2 = Yes
If *yes*, then check all that apply:
- ☐ Right
- ☐ Left

II. Cranial Nerves

A. Vision and Hearing

___ Funduscopic examination abnormalities
    1 = No   2 = Yes
If *yes*, then check all that apply:
- ☐ Retinal hemorrhage
- ☐ Chorioretinitis
- ☐ Optic nerve hypoplasia
- ☐ Cataract
- ☐ Cherry red spot
- ☐ *Other:* _____

___ Visual acuity abnormality   1 = No   2 = Yes
Describe: _____

___ Cranial nerve III, IV, or VI abnormalities
    1 = No   2 = Yes
If *yes*, then check all that apply:
- ☐ Paresis involving III
- ☐ Paresis involving IV
- ☐ Paresis involving VI
- ☐ Strabismus
- ☐ *Other:* _____

___ Pupillary abnormalities   1 = No   2 = Yes
- ☐ Not round
- ☐ Unequal
- ☐ Unreactive to light
Describe: _____

___ Hearing abnormalities   1 = No   2 = Yes
- ☐ Right
- ☐ Left
Indicate how this was determined:
- ☐ Clinical observation
- ☐ Brainstem auditory evoked response
- ☐ Behavioral audiometry
- ☐ *Other:* _____

B. Facial

___ Cranial nerve V abnormality   1 = No   2 = Yes
Describe finding: _____

___ Cranial nerve VII abnormality   1 = No   2 = Yes
If *yes*, then check all that apply:
- ☐ Central paresis
- ☐ Peripheral paresis
- ☐ *Other:* _____

C. Bulbar function

___ Cranial nerve IX, X, or XI abnormalities
    1 = No   2 = Yes
Describe finding: _____

___ Sucking abnormality   1 = No   2 = Yes
Describe finding: _____

___ Swallowing abnormality   1 = No   2 = Yes
Describe finding: _____

___ Cranial nerve XII abnormalities   1 = No   2 = Yes
Describe finding: _____

___ Tongue abnormality   1 = No   2 = Yes
If *yes*, then check all that apply:
- ☐ Large tongue
- ☐ Tongue atrophy
- ☐ Tongue fasciculation
- ☐ Tongue thrust
- ☐ *Other cranial nerve abnormalities:* _____

III. Special Situations

A. Altered Mental Status

___ Impaired level of consciousness   1 = No   2 = Yes
- ☐ Hyperexcitable
- ☐ Stuporous
- ☐ Comatose

___ Degree of coma   1 = Light   2 = Deep
If stupor or coma is present, then complete the following:
___ Abnormal pupillary response to light 1 = No   2 = Yes
If *yes*, then check all that apply:
- ☐ Dilated
- ☐ Responsive
- ☐ Fixed
- ☐ Midpoint
- ☐ *Other:* _____

___ Other cranial nerve abnormalities	1 = No	2 = Yes
___ Corneal reflex	1 = increased	2 = normal
___ Doll's eyes	1 = increased	2 = normal
___ Gag reflex	1 = increased	2 = normal
___ Respiration	1 = increased	2 = normal
___ Heart rate	1 = increased	2 = normal
	3 = decreased	4 = absent
	3 = decreased	4 = absent
	3 = decreased	4 = absent
	3 = decreased	4 = absent
	3 = decreased	4 = absent

- ☐ *Other:* _____

B. Spinal Cord

___ Spinal cord abnormality   1 = No   2 = Yes
If *yes*, then check all that apply:
- ☐ Abnormal pinprick response
- ☐ Abnormal sweating
- ☐ Abnormal urination stream
- ☐ Neurogenic bladder
- ☐ Absent anal wink
- ☐ Constipation
- ☐ *Other:*

and complete the following:
___Level of motor loss
___Level of sensory loss
Describe: _____
_____

___ Dysraphism   1 = No   2 = Yes
If *yes*, then check all that apply:
- ☐ Open
- ☐ Closed
- ☐ Leaking cerebrospinal fluid
- ☐ Meningocele
- ☐ Encephalocele
- ☐ Myelomeningocele
- ___Level of involvement

Describe: _____
_____

Appendix B

INFANIB

NAME Kate

CIRCLE ONE

Date of Exam _____

Corrected Gestational Age 7 months

ITEM	START SCORE	MAJOR CHANGE								Score columns
1	Birth		**SUPINE** Hands closed/open	Clenched	Clenched with stress maneuver	Closed	Sometimes closed	(Open)		5				
2	Birth		Scarf sign	Less Than #1	0° to 15° — 1	15° to 45° — 2	45° to 60° — 3	(60° to 85° — 4)	Past #4					3
3	Birth		Heel to ear	Over 100°	(90° to 100°)	60° to 90°	40° to 60°	10° to 40°	Under 10°					3
4	Birth		Popliteal angle	Under 80°	80° to 90°	90° to 110°	110° to 150°	150° to 170°	Over 170°					1
5	Birth		Leg abduction	Under 40°	40° to 70°	(70° to 100°)	100° to 130°	130° to 150°	Over 150°					3
6	Birth		Dorsiflexion of foot	0° to 10°	10° to 40°	(40° to 70°)	70° to 80°	80° to 90°					5	
7	Birth	9 mos.	Foot grasp	(No Grasp)	Barely Grasp	Average grasp	Excessive grasp or grasp with stress maneuver						5	
8	Birth	6 mos.	Tonic labyrinthine supine	(Absent)	Some shoulder retraction or some extension of trunk or legs	Shoulder retraction and full leg extension or flexed arms and legs				5				
9	Birth	6 mos.	Asymmetric tonic neck reflex	(Absent)	Postures in, can move out	Persistent or spontaneous				5				
10	Birth		Pull to sitting	Head extended Arms extended	(Head up Arms ext.)	Head flexed Arms ext.	Head flexed Arms flexed				1			
11	4 mos.		Body derotative	(Present to both sides)	Slow or mildly asymmetrical	Absent or markedly asymmetrical				5				
12	9 mos		Body rotative	Present to both sides	Slow or mildly asymmetrical	Absent or markedly asymmetrical					0			
13	Birth		**PRONE** All fours	Lifts Head	Head up 45°	Forearms only	Head up 90°	(Bears weight on extended arms)	Assumes all fours unsteadily	Assumes all fours well	Stands up through Plantigrade	3				
14	Birth	9 mos.	Tonic labyrinthine prone	(Absent)	Some shoulder protraction or some flexion of legs	With Head Flexion Shoulder protraction and arms, hips, or legs under trunk				5				
15	Birth		**SITTING** Sitting position		(L3 →)	L5 →					1			
16	6 mos.		Sideways parachute	Present in both arms	Slow or mildly asymmetrical	(Absent or markedly asymmetrical)					1			
17	9 mos.		Backwards parachute	Present in both arms	Slow or mildly asymmetrical	Absent or markedly asymmetrical					0			
18	Birth		**STANDING** Weight bearing	Primitive reflex	No weight bearing	(Poor weight bearing Breaks at knees)	Unequal weight bearing							1
19	3 mos.		Positive support reaction	(Feet flat)	5 to 30 sec. on toes then drop to feet flat	>30 sec. on toes							5	
20	7 mos.		**SUSPENDED** Forward parachute	Present	Slow or mildly asymmetrical	(Absent or markedly asymmetrical)					1			

FACTOR SCORES | 20 | 10 | 2 | 16 | 10

TOTAL SCORE 58

Overall: Normal = 5, Mildly abnormal = 3,
Markedly abnormal = 1

SCORING

Corrected gestational age

Comments

ITEM	0-.9	1-1.9	2-2.9	3-3.9	4-4.9	5-5.9	6-6.9	7-7.9	8-8.9	9-18 months	matches age = 5
1.	Closed		Some times closed	Open			At any age, clenched or clenched with stress maneuver = 1				One stage delay = 3 Two stage delay = 1 One closed, one open = 1
2.	0 - 15° (1)			15 - 45° (2)			45 - 60° (3)			60 - 85° (4)	5 = Picture matches age
3.	100 - 90°			90 - 60°			60 - 40°			40 - 10°	3 = One stage away ← or →
4.	80 - 90°			90 - 110°			110 - 150°			150 - 170°	1 = Two stages away ← or → As above except definite asymmetry = 1
5.	40 - 70°			70 - 100°			100 - 130°			130 - 150°	As for # 2 & 3
6.	0-10° = 1 40-80° = 5 10-40° = 3 80-90° = 3		0-10° = 1 10 - 40° = 3 40 - 70° = 5				70 - 80° = 3 80 - 90° = 1				Definite asymmetry = 1
7.	Excessive grasp or grasp with stress maneuver = 1 , Other = 5						Absent = 5 Barely Grasp = 3 Grasp = 1				Definite asymmetry = 1
8.	Shoulder retraction and full leg extension or flexed arms and legs = 1, Other = 5						Absent = 5 Some = 3 Full = 1				
9.	Persistent or spontaneous = 1, Other = 5					Absent = 5	Postures in Can move out = 3 Persistent = 1				
10.							Full = 5 Partial head lag or not using arms = 3 Complete head lag and not using arms = 1				Picture matches age = 5 One stage delay = 3 Two stage delay = 1 0-4 months head flexion and arm flexion = 1
11.					Present to both sides = 5		Slow or mildly asymmetrical = 3		Absent or markedly asymmetrical = 1		
12.							Present = 5 Slow or mildly asymmetrical = 3 Absent or markedly asymmetrical = 1				
13.	Lifts Head	Head up 45°	Forearms only	Head up 90°	Bears weight on extended forearms	All fours unsteadily	All fours well		Plantigrade		Picture matches age = 5 One stage delay = 3 Two stage delay = 1
14.	Shoulder protraction , arms, hips or legs under trunk = 1 other = 5						Absent = 5 Some = 3 Full = 1				
15.			L3 →		L5 →						Picture matches age = 5 One stage delay = 3 Two stage delay = 1 0-5 months L5 break and head extension = 1
16.						Present in both arms = 5	Slow or mildly asymmetrical = 3	Absent or markedly asymmetrical = 1			
17.							As Above				
18.	Primitive Reflex	No Weight-bearing	Poor weight bearing Breaks at knee			Unequal weight bearing					Picture matches age = 5 One stage delay = 3 Two stage delay = 1
											Persistent weight-bearing (> 60 sec) at 2.5 - 5 months = 1
19.				Maintains weight feet flat = 5		5 - 30 sec. on toes then drop to feet flat = 3			> 30 sec on toes = 1		
20.							Present = 5 Slow or mildly asymmetrical = 3 Absent or markedly asym. = 1				

Degree of normality/abnormality based on total score

Less than 4 months	4 to 8 months	8 months or more
Abnormal ≤ 48	Abnormal ≤ 54	Abnormal ≤ 68
Transient 49 - 65	Transient 55-71	Transient 69-82
Normal ≥ 66	Normal ≥ 72	Normal ≥ 83

Category of abnormality

If abnormal, choose a category

☐ Spastic Tetraparesis/Dyskinesia ☐ Spastic Hemiparesis ☐ Spastic Diplegia ☐ Hypotonia

References

Amiel-Tison, C., and A. Grenier. 1986. *Neurological assessment during the first year of life.* New York: Oxford University Press.

André-Thomas, Y. Chesni, and S. Saint-Anne Dargassies. 1960. The neurological examination of the infant. *Clinics in Developmental Medicine No. 1.* London: National Spastics Society.

Aylward, G. P., N. Gustafson, S. T. Verhurst, et al. 1987. Consistency in the diagnosis of cognitive, motor and neurologic function over the first three years. *Journal of Pediatric Psychology* 12:77-98.

Bloch Petersen, M., G. Greisen, R. Kovacs, H. Munck, and B. Friis-Hansen. 1990. Status at four years of age in 280 children weighing 2300 grams or less at birth. *Danish Medical Bulletin* 37:546-52.

Cangelosi, J. S. 1984. Another answer to the cut-off score question. *Educational Measurement: Issues and Practice.* Winter: 23-24.

Capute, A. J., F. B. Palmer, B. K. Shapiro, R. C. Wachtel, A. Ross, and P. J. Accardo. 1984. Primitive reflex profile: A quantitation of primitive reflexes in infancy. *Developmental Medicine and Child Neurology* 26:375-83.

Capute, A. J., P. J. Accardo, E. P. G. Vining, J. Rubenstein, and S. Harryman. 1978. *Primitive reflex profile.* Baltimore: University Park Press.

Castro, A. V., I. E. de Sanchez, and N. S. Landinez. 1985. Reliability of the infant neurological international battery (Infanib) for the assessment of neurological integrity in infancy to high risk Colombian infants. Unpublished thesis. Instituto Materno. Infantil of Bogota. Bogota, Colombia.

Drillien, C. M. 1972. Abnormal neurologic signs in the first year of life in low birthweight infants: Possible prognostic significance. *Developmental Medicine and Child Neurology* 14:575-84.

Drillien, C., A. Thomson, and K. Burgoyne. 1980. Low birthweight children at early school age: A longitudinal study. *Developmental Medicine and Child Neurology* 22:26-47.

Ellison, P. H. 1990. The infant neurological examination. *Advances in Developmental and Behavioral Pediatrics* 9:75-138.

_____. 1984. Neurologic development of the high-risk infant. *Clinics in Perinatology* 11:41-58.

Ellison, P. H., C. A. Browning, B. Larson, and J. Denny. 1983. Development of a scoring system for the Milani-Comparetti and Gidoni method of assessing neurologic abnormality in infancy. *Physical Therapy* 63:1414-23.

Ellison, P. H., C. Browning, and T. Trostmiller. 1982. Evaluation of neurologic status in infancy: Physical therapist versus pediatric neurologist. *Journal of the California Perinatal Association* 2:63-66.

Ellison, P. H., and M. Foster. 1992. Developmental pathways through childhood for children treated in the neonatal intensive care unit (NICU) *Acta Paediatrica Scandinavica Supplement* 380:1-14.

Ellison, P. H., M. Foster, M. Sheridan-Pereira, and D. MacDonald. 1989. Electronic fetal heart monitoring, auscultation, and neonatal outcome. *American Journal of Obstetrics and Gynecology* 164:1281-89.

Ellison, P. H., G. Greisen, M. Foster, M. Bloch Petersen, and B. Friis-Hansen. 1991. The relation between perinatal conditions and developmental outcome in low birthweight infants: Comparison of two cohorts. *Acta Paediatrica Scandinavica* 80:28-35.

Ellison, P., D. Prasse, J. Siewert, and C. Browning. 1985. The outcome of neurological abnormality in infancy. In *The at risk infant*, edited by S. Harel and N. T. Anastasio, 253-260. Baltimore: Paul H. Brookes Publishing Company.

Horn, J. L. 1965. A rationale and test for the number of factors in factor analysis. *Psychometrika* 30:179-85.

Knobloch, H., B. Pasamanick, and E. Sherard. 1966. A developmental screening inventory for infants. *Pediatrics* 38:1095-1108.

Knobloch, H., F. Stevens, A. Malone, P. Ellison, and H. Risemberg. 1979. The validity of parental reporting of infant development. *Pediatrics* 63:872-78.

McCarthy, D. 1972. *McCarthy scale of children's abilities.* New York: The Psychology Corporation.

Milani Comparetti, A., and E. A. Gidoni. 1967a. Pattern analysis of motor development and its disorders. *Developmental Medicine and Child Neurology* 9:625-30.

_____. 1967b. Routine developmental examination in normal and retarded children. *Developmental Medicine and Child Neurology* 9:631-38.

Paine, R. 1960. Neurologic examination of infants and children. *Pediatric Clinics of North America* 7:471-510.

Paine, R., and T. E. Oppé. 1966. Neurological examination of children. *Clinics in Developmental Medicine*, Nos. 20 and 21. London: William Heinemann Medical Books Ltd.

Prechtl, H. F. R. 1968. Neurological findings in newborn infants after pre- and paranatal complications. In *Aspects of Prematurity and Dysmaturity,* edited by J. H. P. Jonxis, H. K. A. Visser, and J. A. Toclstra. Leiden: HE Stenfert Kroese.

Stavrakas, P. A., G. E. Kemmer-Gacura, S. C. Engelke, and T. C. Chenier. 1991. Predictive validity of the infant neurological battery (Infanib). *Developmental Medicine and Child Neurology Supplement.*

Vojta, V. 1981. *Die zerebralen Bewegungstorungen im Säulingsalter.* Stuttgart, West Germany: Ferdinand Enke.

Additional Reading

Papers about data from the National Collaborative Perinatal Project:

Broman, S. H. 1979. Perinatal anoxia and cognitive development in childhood. In *Infants born at risk,* edited by T. Fields et al., 29-52. New York: Spectrum.

Nelson, K. B., and J. H. Ellenberg. 1986. Antecedents of cerebral palsy. Multivariate analysis of the risk. *New England Journal of Medicine* 315:81-86.

_____. 1985. Antecedents of cerebral palsy I. univariate analysis of risk. *American Journal of Diseases of Children* 139:1031-38.

_____. 1984. Obstetric complications as risk factors for cerebral palsy or seizure disorders. *Journal of the American Medical Association* 251:1843-48.

_____. 1982. Children who "outgrew" cerebral palsy. *Pediatrics* 69:529-36.

_____. 1979. Neonatal signs as predictors of cerebral palsy. *Pediatrics* 64:225-32.

Nelson, K. B., and S. H. Broman. 1977. Perinatal risk factors in children with serious motor and mental handicaps. *Annals of Neurology* 2:371-77.

For a critique of the data analyses in these papers see:

Ellison, P. H. 1986. Supplement to Chapter 24, Assessment of brain injury. (1990). In *Medical malpractice: Handling obstetric and neonatal cases,* edited by M. D. Volk and M. D. Morgan. Colorado Springs, CO: Shepard's/McGraw, Inc.

Further explorations in methodology:

Cook, T. D., and D. T. Campbell. 1979. *Quasi-experimentation.* Boston: Houghton Mifflin.

Dodge, Y. 1985. *Analysis of experiments with missing data.* New York: John Wiley.

James, L. R., S. A. Mulaik, and T. M. Brett. 1982. *Causal analysis: Assumptions, models, and data.* Beverly Hills: Sage Publications.

Nunnally, J. 1978. *Psychometric theory.* New York: McGraw-Hill Book Co. 225-55.

Put these normal development materials to use in your pediatric therapy program . . .

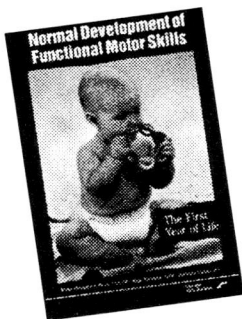

NORMAL DEVELOPMENT OF FUNCTIONAL MOTOR SKILLS
The First Year of Life
by Rona Alexander, Ph.D., CCC-SP, Regi Boehme, OTR, and Barbara Cupps, PT

Gauge the functional motor levels of children with this resource. Focus on normal development during the first year of life. You'll find this an effective tool in planning treatment of infants with neurological involvement. Each developmental stage includes a summary chart for quick record-keeping that outlines—postural control, gross and fine motor, vision, reach, respiration/phonation, and oral-motor/feeding.

0761641874-YTS

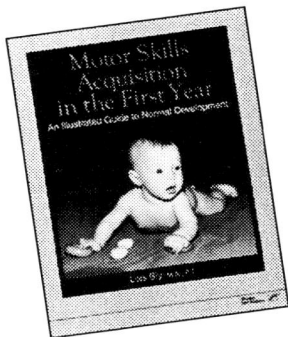

MOTOR SKILLS ACQUISITION IN THE FIRST YEAR
An Illustrated Guide to Normal Development
by Lois Bly, M.A., PT

Use this comprehensive resource to detect the development of different motor skills during the first year of life. Discover how specific motor components build the foundation for babies to achieve developmental milestones. Now, it's easy to understand how these turning points evolve into motor skills! **0761642285-YTS**

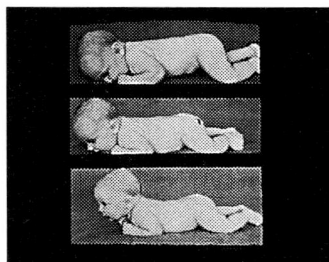

INFANT MOTOR DEVELOPMENT
A Look at the Phases
by Kerry Goudy, OTR, and Joan Fetzer, M.S., CCC-SLP

This 20-minute full-color VHS videotape provides you with a complete look at normal development from birth through 12 months. You'll be able to identify components of movement and specific skills that are acquired during the four phases of development—Infantile, Preparation, Modification, and Refinement. **0761641416-YTS**

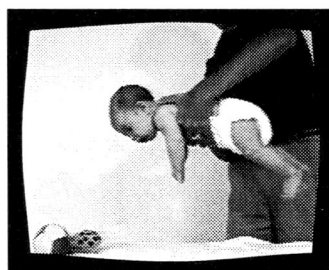

NORMAL INFANT REFLEXES AND DEVELOPMENT
by Sharon Friefeld, B.Sc.(OT), M.A., OT(C), and Laurie Snider, B.Sc.(OT), M.A., OT(C)

Use this 30-minute full-color VHS videotape to review normal infant development of primitive reflexes and reactions. This video reference includes a demonstration of how to elicit reflexes, an explanation of the role of reflexes, and the development of movement skills. You'll also have a Viewer's Guide that includes a script of the videotape for further reference. This video works well as an inservice training tool for paraprofessional and therapist education. **0761647147-YTS**

NORMAL DEVELOPMENT COPYBOOK
by Marsha Dunn Klein, M.Ed., OTR/L, Nancy Harris Ossman, B.S., OTR, and Barbara Tracy, B.S., PT

Completely reproducible, you'll find all your favorite pictures from the *Normal Development Poster Set.* Each page features a developmental age, skill illustration, and space for you to suggest "Helpful Hints." Individualize pages by writing at-home activities for reaching goals. As a special plus, 24 "Developmental Sequence" pages illustrate skill acquisition in a glance. On one convenient page you'll have pictures and steps showing a task through completion—a great overview for parents!

0761647325-.

NORMAL DEVELOPMENT POSTER SET

by Marsha Dunn Klein, M.Ed., OTR/L, Nancy Harris Ossman, B.S., OTR, Barbara Tracy, B.S., PT

Enhance your clinical environment with this set of four illustrated two-color posters. Based on an NDT approach to development, they'll give you a quick and easy reference to normal development from birth to 6 years. Posters cover fine motor development, gross motor development, self-feeding development, and dressing development. **076164217X-YTS**

APPROACH TO TREATMENT OF THE BABY (Revised)

by Regi Boehme, OTR

This easy-to-use manual gives you a detailed look at the baby with suspected or confirmed neuromotor dysfunction. Bobath and NDT approaches are included in the illustrated treatment rationale. Drawings and descriptions cover flexor control in supine, prone in play with arm support, head and trunk control for sitting, postural reactions in all positions, and more. **0761642188-YTS**

For current prices on these practical resources, please call 1-800-228-0752.

ORDER FORM

Ship to:

Institution: _____

Name: _____

Occupation/Dept: _____

Address: _____

City: _____ State: _____ Zip: _____

Please check here if this is a permanent address change. ☐

Telephone No. _____ ☐ work ☐ home

Payment Options:

☐ Bill me.   ☐ My check is enclosed.

☐ My purchase order is enclosed. P.O. # _____

☐ Charge to my credit card: ☐ VISA ☐ MasterCard ☐ American Express

Card No. ☐☐☐☐☐☐☐☐☐☐☐☐☐☐☐☐

Expiration Date: Month _____ Year _____

Signature _____

Qty.	Cat. #	Title	Amount

Prices are in U.S. dollars. Payment must be made in U.S. funds only.

- If your account is not currently listed as "tax exempt," applicable destination charges will be added to your invoice.
- Orders are shipped by United Parcel Service (UPS) unless otherwise requested. If another delivery service is required, please specify.
- For regular delivery service, your order will be charged 5% handling plus actual shipping charges.
- We occasionally backorder items temporarily out of stock. If you do not accept backorders, please tell us on your purchase order or on this form.

Money-Back Guarantee

You'll have up to 90 days of risk-free evaluation of the products your ordered. If you're not completely satisfied with any product, we'll pick it up within the 90 days and refund the full purchase price! **No questions asked!**

For Phone Orders

Call 1-800-228-0752. Please have your credit card and/or institutional purchase order information ready. Monday-Friday 7am-7pm Central Time. 1-800-723-1318 TDD / FAX 1-800-232-1223

Send your order to:

Therapy Skill Builders

a division of The Psychological Corporation
555 Academic Court / San Antonio, Texas 78204-2498